International Water Law and the Quest for Common Security

The world's freshwater supplies are increasingly threatened by rapidly increasing demand and the impacts of global climate change, but current approaches to transboundary water management are unsustainable and may threaten future global stability and international security. The absence of law in attempts to address this issue highlights the necessity for further understanding from the legal perspective.

This book provides a fresh conceptualisation of water security, developing an operational methodology for identifying the four core elements of water security which must be addressed by international law: availability, access, adaptability, and ambit. The analysis of the legal framework of transboundary freshwater management based on this contemporary understanding of water security reveals the challenges and shortcomings of the current legal regime. In order to address these shortcomings, the present mindset of prevailing rigidity and state-centrism is challenged by examining how international legal instruments could be crafted to advance a more flexible and equitable approach towards transboundary water interaction.

The concept of considering water security as a matter of 'regional common concern' is introduced to help international law play a more prominent role in addressing the challenges of global water insecurity. Ways for implementing such an approach are proposed and analysed by looking at international hydropolitics in Himalayan Asia. The book analyses transboundary water interaction as a 'case study' for advancing public international law in order to fulfil its responsibility of promoting international peace and security.

Bjørn-Oliver Magsig is a research fellow at the Helmholtz Centre for Environmental Research, Department of Environmental and Planning Law (Leipzig, Germany), focusing on international environmental law, water diplomacy, and the link between natural resources and international security. His research critically assesses the current legal regime of transboundary watercourses against the backdrop of regional security and instability and aims to contribute to the evolving body of public international law. Bjørn-Oliver has extensive project experience on law and transboundary river basins, serves on the Managing Board of the European Environmental Law Forum (EELF) and is a member of the IUCN World Commission on Environmental Law.

Earthscan Studies in Water Resource Management

Sustainable Water and Sanitation Services
The Life-cycle Approach to Planning and Management
By Livelihoods & Natural Resource Management Institute, International Water & Sanitation Centre, Centre for Economic and Social Studies, Watershed Support Services & Activities Network

Water for Food Security and Well-being in Latin America and the Caribbean
Social and Environmental Implications for a Globalized Economy
Edited by Bárbara A. Willaarts, Alberto Garrido and M. Ramón Llamas

Water Scarcity, Livelihoods and Food Security
Research and Innovation for Development
Edited by Larry W. Harrington, Myles J. Fisher

Adaptation to Climate Change through Water Resources Management
Capacity, Equity and Sustainability
Edited by Dominic Stucker and Elena Lopez-Gunn

Hydropower Development in the Mekong Region
Political, Socio-economic and Environmental Perspectives
Edited by Nathanial Matthews and Kim Geheb

Governing Transboundary Waters
Canada, the United States and Indigenous Communities
By Emma S. Norman

Transboundary Water Politics in the Developing World
By Naho Mirumachi

International Water Law and the Quest for Common Security
By Bjørn-Oliver Magsig

Water, Power and Identity
The Cultural Politics of Water in the Andes
By Rutgerd Boelens

Water and Cities in Latin America
Challenges for Sustainable Development
Edited by Ismael Aguilar-Barajas, Jürgen Mahlknecht, Jonathan Kaledin and Marianne Kjellén

For more information and to view forthcoming titles in this series, please visit the Routledge website: http://www.routledge.com/books/series/ECWRM/

International Water Law and the Quest for Common Security

Bjørn-Oliver Magsig

Routledge
Taylor & Francis Group
LONDON AND NEW YORK

earthscan
from Routledge

First published 2015
by Routledge

2 Park Square, Milton Park, Abingdon, Oxfordshire OX14 4RN
711 Third Avenue, New York, NY 10017

Routledge is an imprint of the Taylor & Francis Group, an informa business

First issued in paperback 2017

British Library Cataloguing-in-Publication Data
A catalogue record for this book is available from the British Library

Library of Congress Cataloging in Publication Data
Magsig, Bjørn-Oliver, author.
International water law and the quest for common security/Bjørn-Oliver Magsig.
pages cm. — (Earthscan studies in water resource management)
Based on author's thesis (doctoral) - University of Dundee, 2013.
Includes bibliographical references and index.
1. Water rights (International law) 2. Right to water. 3. Water security—International cooperation. I. Title.
K3496.M34 2015
346.04'691—dc23
2014040492

ISBN: 978-1-138-81690-9 (hbk)
ISBN: 978-0-8153-7892-1 (pbk)

Typeset in Bembo
by Swales & Willis Ltd, Exeter, Devon, UK

Contents

Figures

Acknowledgements

This book began as my thesis for my PhD at the UNESCO Centre for Water Law, Policy and Science; University of Dundee, and I have accumulated many debts during my doctoral work and since.

I would like to express my deep appreciation and gratitude to my supervisors, Professor Patricia Wouters and Dr Alistair Rieu-Clarke, for their patient guidance and mentorship. My gratitude also goes to Dr Sergei Vinogradov. It was through him that I discovered the incredibly exciting field of international water law and environmental security. I was also privileged to have had Dr Owen McIntyre and Professor Robin Churchill as examiners for the PhD, both of whom provided comments which have been of great value in undertaking revisions for this book.

It would not have been possible for me to undertake the PhD without the generous scholarship I received from the Scottish Government. I should, however, extend my gratitude to the whole of Bonnie Scotland, as its magical Highlands and wonderful people made Dundee feel like a home away from home.

I would also like to express my sincere thanks to Professor Wolfgang Köck and Moritz Reese for encouraging me to develop my ideas further and incorporate them into the integrated 'Water Scarcity' project at the Helmholtz Centre for Environmental Research in Leipzig. Also, from Routledge, I would like to thank Ashley Wright, Tim Hardwick and Edward Gibbons for their kind support.

At every stage of the project, I have been fortunate to be surrounded by inspiring friends and colleagues who all played their part in supporting me to finish this book – either through stimulating discussions about international law and the freshwater crisis, or by providing me with welcome distractions far away from my desk.

Above all, I would like to thank my family for their love and invaluable support throughout my life. Thank you for always believing in me. However, the person to whom I am most thankful for is Ruby – my infinite source of inspiration, serenity and encouragement. I could not have asked for more.

1 Introduction

1.1 Life in the Anthropocene – the disrespect for planetary boundaries

We live in times of rapid change where the vigorous, and at times abrupt, shifts in societal and environmental realities demand a change in how we define the challenges we are facing as a global community and pursue the quest for finding solutions. Yet the ability of the human race to react and understand the changes around us cannot keep up with the pace in which we alter it, leaving us confronted with a whole range of serious, intractable challenges of global importance. Recent trends, however, show no sign of a fundamental change in strategy. The current position of the dominant powers in global politics remains to preserve what they perceive as *international* security by securing their own *national* interests. With regards to the environment, this has led to the fact that the rapid and non-linear changes to life-supporting ecosystem services we currently observe are unprecedented in human history. The 'international community' has not succeeded in slowing down, let alone reversing, adverse environmental changes.[1] According to the United Nations Development Programme (UNDP), the development progress in the world's poorest states might even be reversed within the next decades unless bold steps are taken now to prevent further global environmental degradation and conquer the deep inequalities within and among nations.[2]

According to the International Commission on Stratigraphy, we live in the Holocene – the era which began around 12,000 years ago after the end of the last Ice Age.[3] The Holocene marks a period with unusually stable climatic conditions, which had (and still has) potent implications for the development of civilisations.[4] However, some scientists believe that since the late

1 United Nations Environment Programme, *Global Environment Outlook 5: Environment for the Future We Want* (UNEP 2012) at 4.

2 United Nations Development Programme, *Human Development Report 2011: Sustainability and Equity: A Better Future for All* (Palgrave Macmillan 2011).

3 See the most recent (September 2010) International Stratigraphic Chart at <http://www.stratigraphy.org/ics%20chart/09_2010/StratChart2010.pdf>.

4 JT Houghton, *Global Warming : The Complete Briefing* (Cambridge University Press 2009) at 88.

eighteenth century we have been living in a new geological epoch marked by unprecedented human influences on the planet – matching major geological processes in their effect – the 'Anthropocene'.[5] Ever since we started burning fossil fuels, we have been modifying the whole world's climate system. There is no denial that humans have changed planet earth on a global scale. This in turn, some scholars argue, should trigger a new way of perceiving our environment, as we live in 'human systems, with natural ecosystems embedded within them'.[6] The days of conquering nature are long gone. Today we, supposedly, decide 'what nature is and what it will be'.[7]

However, it seems that so far we have not played the role of the earth's stewards that well. This is mainly due to the popular (mis)conception that natural resources are endlessly abundant, the ecosystems perpetually resilient, and thus limitless economic growth a reasonable goal. Over the last decades, several reports and studies have been published to counter this argument and warned of 'limits to growth'.[8] The resulting – and still ongoing – debate between the two camps (pro-development vis-à-vis pro-environment) brought forth the idea that we need to follow the course of sustainable development, ensuring that we 'meet the needs of the present without compromising the ability of future generations to meet their own needs'.[9] While this noble aim found a high degree of attraction among scholars, policy makers and NGOs, it was not able to turn the boat around. Looking at the challenges we face from the local to the global level – e.g., famines,[10] dramatic loss of biodiversity,[11] widening gap between the rich and the 'bottom billion'[12] and global climate change[13] – the idea of the sustainable society still seems to be illusive.

Recently, scientists have developed a framework of 'planetary boundaries', trying to help humanity to navigate the Anthropocene. Transgressing only

5 PJ Crutzen and EF Stoermer, 'The Anthropocene' (2000) Global Change Newsletter, 41, 17 at 17.

6 EC Ellis and N Ramankutty, 'Putting People in the Map: Anthropogenic Biomes of the World' (2007) *Frontiers in Ecology and the Environment*, 6, 439 at 445.

7 PG Crutzen and C Schwägerl for Yale Environment 360, 'Living in the Anthropocene: Toward a New Global Ethos' (24 January 2011) <http://e360.yale.edu/feature/living_in_the_anthropocene_toward_a_new_global_ethos_/2363/>.

8 DH Meadows and others, *The Limits to Growth: A Report for the Club of Rome's Project on the Predicament of Mankind* (Universe Books 1972).

9 World Commission on Environment and Development, *Our Common Future* (Oxford University Press 1987) at 43.

10 HCJ Godfray and others, 'Food Security: The Challenge of Feeding 9 Billion People' (2010) *Science*, 327, 812.

11 Secretariat of the Convention on Biological Diversity, *Global Biodiversity Outlook 3* (Secretariat of the Convention on Biological Diversity 2010).

12 See P Collier, *The Bottom Billion: Why the Poorest Countries Are Failing and What Can Be Done About It* (Oxford University Press 2007).

13 See, e.g., the detailed analysis of the Intergovernmental Panel on Climate Change, Climate Change 2007: *Impacts, Adaptation and Vulnerability – Contribution of Working Group II to the Fourth Assessment Report of the IPCC* (Cambridge University Press 2007).

one of the identified nine interdependent planetary boundaries might already trigger abrupt environmental change.[14] The goal of the concept of 'planetary boundaries' is to ultimately shift the environmental management approach away from the current sectoral analyses of 'limits to growth', which attempt to minimise negative externalities, towards a more complex roadmap of the safe operating space for sustainable development, in order to avoid major anthropogenic global environmental change.[15] Since, according to the scientists, we have already transgressed three of the boundaries (nitrogen cycle, biodiversity loss and climate change),[16] the proposed reforms call for far-reaching constitutional changes of the global governance system.[17]

1.2 Water – the gossamer linking a whole web of securities

When looking at the challenges ahead and the planetary boundaries limiting our room for manoeuvre, it becomes clear that freshwater plays an integral part in the future of our development. Today, it is being widely acknowledged that water is not exclusively a local, national, or international issue which can be governed at any of those levels in isolation.[18] Global interdependencies are being woven by the cross-cutting nature of water which makes addressing the global freshwater crisis cumbersome, as water interaction often cannot be separated from global trends and drivers. The challenges of freshwater management at any governance level are expected to become more intense in the future, as accelerated change creates new threats and interconnected forces increase uncertainty and risk.[19]

Water scarcity, droughts and floods already affect many countries around the world, with some of these events triggering local armed conflicts.[20] The resulting adverse impacts concern developed and developing states alike.[21] Recent studies show the disquieting trend of increased overexploitation of

14 The nine identified boundaries are: climate change, ocean acidification, stratospheric ozone, biogeochemical nitrogen (N) cycle and phosphorus (P) cycle, global freshwater use, land system change, biodiversity loss, chemical pollution, and atmospheric aerosol loading. See J Rockström and others, 'A Safe Operating Space for Humanity' (2009) *Nature*, 461, 472 at 473.

15 J Rockström and others, 'Planetary Boundaries: Exploring the Safe Operating Space for Humanity' (2009) *Ecology and Society*, 14, 1 at 1.

16 Ibid. at 22.

17 F Biermann and others, 'Navigating the Anthropocene: Improving Earth System Governance' (2012) *Science*, 335, 1306 at 1306.

18 United Nations World Water Assessment Programme, *The United Nations World Water Development Report 4 : Managing Water under Uncertainty and Risk*, vol. 1 (UNESCO 2012) at 2.

19 Ibid. at 20.

20 Integrated Regional Information Networks, 'Kenya: Drought Exacerbating Conflict among Pastoralists' (2 February 2009) <http://www.irinnews.org/Report.aspx?ReportId=82683>.

21 Recently, England has been hit by the worst drought in thirty years; and the fear that the dry conditions might become the new norm has even revived the long written-off plans to transport bulk water from Scotland down south via a Grand Contour Canal. See R Alderson for BBC News, 'Scots Offer to Send Water to Aid Drought-hit England' (9 March 2012) <http://www.bbc.co.uk/news/uk-scotland-17314545>.

freshwater in various regions around the world.[22] There is no doubt that a shortage of safe water would impede the socio-economic development of any society.[23] Despite governments expressing political commitment, billions of people around the globe are denied access to clean drinking water and adequate sanitation.[24] Within a couple of decades, some two-thirds of the world's population will suffer directly from lack of freshwater,[25] and water scarcity could reduce the annual global crop yield significantly (some estimate this to be the equivalent of all of the grain crops of the United States and India combined), which could wreak havoc against the predicted 70–90 per cent increase in global food demand.[26] Furthermore, freshwater systems are both hotspots for biodiversity and species endangerment.[27] Due to our remarkable ability to alter inland waterways – over 60 per cent of the world's large river systems have become moderately or highly fragmented – we have dramatically changed the underlying ecosystems.[28] Not only does this loss of natural habitat accelerate species extinction further, it also affects vital ecosystem services such as purification of water, natural flood protection and provision of food.[29] Given that current trends in unsustainable development, climate change and water use show no sign of relenting, freshwater ecosystems will remain under threat well into the future.[30]

New challenges related to the use and distribution of the world's water resources abound around the globe, affecting local, regional and international dependent communities in a myriad of ways[31] – threatening basic social,

22 I van der Molen and A Hildering, 'Water: Cause for Conflict or Co-Operation?' (2005) *Journal on Science and World Affairs*, 1, at 133.

23 See E Kemp-Benedict and others, 'Connections between Poverty, Water and Agriculture: Evidence from 10 River Basins' (2011) *Water International*, 36, 125.

24 See United Nations Department of Economic and Social Affairs, *The Millennium Development Goals Report 2008* (United Nations Department of Economic and Social Affairs 2008) at 40.

25 United Nations World Water Assessment Programme, *The United Nations World Water Development Report 3: Water in a Changing World* (UNESCO 2009) at 36.

26 World Economic Forum Water Initiative, *Managing Our Future Water Needs for Agriculture, Industry, Human Health and the Environment: The Bubble Is Close to Bursting: A Forecast of the Main Economic and Geopolitical Water Issues Likely to Arise in the World During the Next Two Decades* (World Economic Forum 2009) at 10.

27 DL Strayer and D Dudgeon, 'Freshwater Biodiversity Conservation: Recent Progress and Future Challenges' (2010) *Journal of the North American Benthological Society*, 29, 344.

28 Today, more than 40 per cent of the global river discharge is being intercepted by large dams; blocking around one-third of sediments vital for the world's coastal zones. Secretariat of the Convention on Biological Diversity, *Global Biodiversity Outlook 3* at 43.

29 United Nations Environment Programme, *Water Security and Ecosystem Services: The Critical Connection* (United Nations Environment Programme, 2009) at 10.

30 CJ Vörösmarty and others, 'Global Threats to Human Water Security and River Biodiversity' (2010) *Nature*, 467, 555.

31 JF Warner and R Meissner, 'The Politics of Security in the Okavango River Basin: From Civil War to Saving Wetlands (1975–2002) : A Preliminary Security Impact Assessment' in Jansky L, Nakayama M and Pachova NI (eds), *International Water Security: Domestic Threats and Opportunities* (United Nations University Press 2008) at 260.

economic, political and environmental securities around the world. With the integral and finite nature of this particular resource, water must be considered the key component of 'ultimate security'.[32] Increased competition over increasingly scarce natural resources – with water being the most critical – is evoking a bleak outlook for the future where historical observations may be of little or no relevance. In some areas with high levels of water stress (including northern China, north-west India and parts of Pakistan), one can also witness high variability of freshwater supply from year to year.[33] It is obvious that the situation gets more precarious in places where the demand for water is already relatively high compared to availability; as well as in areas where low-water years are common. Rising demand and declining quality are being aggravated by climate change, population growth, urbanisation and, more recently, a global economy lacking financial resources. These combined forces could lead to what John Beddington, the former United Kingdom (UK) Government Chief Scientific Adviser, referred to as the 'perfect storm' of food, energy and water shortages.[34] How should we address this convergence of security concerns? The fact that the global water crisis is already reshaping foreign policy – and will do so even more extensively in the future – puts 'water security' high on the political agenda.[35]

While elevating the concept of water security into global agenda-setting political circles has certainly helped raise awareness of the water crisis, water security still remains a concept that has been underexplored from an academic standpoint. This is mainly due to the various opposing definitions of the concept, depending on the motives of the actor (e.g., state official, NGO, or industry), the realm it is being discussed in (e.g., international relations, development aid, or economics), or the discipline in which the concept is being advanced (e.g., law, economics, political science, or environmental sciences). This is why

32 See N Myers, *Ultimate Security: The Environmental Basis of Political Stability* (W.W. Norton 1993). See also E Burleson, 'Water Is Security' (2008) *Environs: Environmental Law and Policy Journal*, 31, 197.

33 See the Aqueduct Water Risk Atlas by the World Resources Institute, available at <http://aqueduct.wri.org/>.

34 According to John Beddington, the demand for energy and food will increase by 50 per cent by 2030, while the demand for freshwater will increase by 30 per cent; J Beddington, *Food, Energy, Water and the Climate : A Perfect Storm of Global Events?* (Government Office for Science 2009).

35 See M Aydin and F Ereker, 'Water Scarcity and Political Wrangling: Security in the Euphrates and Tigris Basin' in Brauch HG and others (eds), *Facing Global Environmental Change : Environmental, Human, Energy, Food, Health and Water Security Concepts* (Springer 2009), P Bagla, 'Along the Indus River, Saber Rattling over Water Security' (2010) *Science*, 328, 1226; AD Brouma, 'Water and Security in International Relations: A Co-Operative Debate' (Water Security in the 21st Century); KBS Rasheed, 'Water Security in Eastern Himalayan Region' (2008) *South Asian Journal*, 21, 42; J Selby, '"New Security Thinking" in Israel-Palestinian Water Relations' in Brauch HG and others (eds), *Facing Global Environmental Change : Environmental, Human, Energy, Food, Health and Water Security Concepts* (Springer 2009); M Smith and others, 'The Big Question: Will Global Conflict Flow from the Quest for Water Security?' (2009) *World Policy Journal*, 26, 5; M Zeitoun, 'The Global Web of National Water Security' (2011) *Global Policy*, 2, 286.

the academic debate around water security is in dire need of more deliberate and extensive examination, in order to address the vagueness that currently surrounds the concept, and ultimately deepen knowledge and understanding of the contribution that a 'water security paradigm' can play in addressing the aforementioned global challenges. Not only is water a vital resource whose management deserves particular attention; it is also the main link between several other crises we are facing. Thus, by tackling water insecurity, we not only alleviate the global water crisis; we automatically contribute to addressing various other pressing challenges – such as food, energy and the environment.

1.3 The relevance of international law in addressing water insecurity

Acknowledging that we live in rapidly changing times facing social and environmental challenges of significant magnitude is a first step. While several scholars claim that humanity will always be able to count on its ingenuity and will invent itself out of crisis, we still need a roadmap for navigating the rough times ahead. Even though the use of technology can turn nature into an asset, this asset only has a potential value to society. In order to actually become of real value, regulatory frameworks – laws – must be in place. Only then can we prevent a 'plundered planet'.[36] Furthermore, security as such is an important human value; and its provision is one of the main purposes of any legal system.[37] Law, then, must be regarded as a major instrument for the pursuit of security. Hence, our understanding of (water) security determines what we expect from the legal system in this respect – which kind of framework we want it to provide, and which goals we want it to advocate.[38]

The difficulty in designing an effective legal methodology for water security, however, becomes apparent when one realises that not only is water spilling into various other matters; it also touches all levels of governance – from the local to the international. Around one-fifth of the world's renewable freshwater resources are shared between countries, including 276 transboundary river basins – home to 40 per cent of the global population.[39] These basins cover more than 45 per cent of the earth's land surface, while accounting for around 60 per cent of global river flow.[40] Those figures hint at the high level

36 See P Collier, *The Plundered Planet : How to Reconcile Prosperity with Nature* (Allen Lane 2010) at 4. Collier has tried to illustrate this endeavour with the help of two simplified formulas: (1) Nature + Technology – Regulation = Plunder; (2) Nature + Technology + Regulation = Prosperity.

37 N Duxbury, 'Human Security and the Basic Norm' (1990) *Archiv für Rechts- und Sozialphilosophie*, 76, 184 at 184.

38 See B von Tigerstrom, *Human Security and International Law* (Hart Publishing 2007) at 3.

39 UN Water, 'Transboundary Waters' (2013) <http://www.unwater.org/fileadmin/user_upload/unwater_new/docs/transboundary_waters.pdf>.

40 AT Wolf and others, 'Managing Water Conflict and Cooperation' in Renner M, French H and Assadourian E (eds), *State of the World 2005 : Redefining Global Security* (W.W. Norton 2005) at 83.

of interdependence; making it easy to imagine the dilemmas faced by basins like the Danube or the Nile, which are shared by 17 and 11 states respectively. Yet, even countries which are not directly reliant on transboundary freshwater resources are affected by, and are affecting, the management of transboundary basins around the world – due to linkages which are rather hidden. For instance, a recently published report found that the UK relies heavily on 'virtual water' (imported in goods) from drought-prone countries; and thus, water should be put at the centre of its international development policy to avoid surging water insecurity at home – as well as abroad.[41]

International water law provides a framework for the cooperation of states regarding their rights to, and responsibilities for, transboundary freshwater resources. By establishing the rules of the game, it aims to avoid, manage and resolve water disputes.[42] However, this foundation upon which transboundary waters should be managed peacefully has not yet accomplished a truly level playing field between states sharing the vital resource. While the cornerstone of international water law – the principle of equitable and reasonable utilisation – has the concept of 'equity' at heart, it seems to fall short in converting it into transboundary freshwater cooperation which is based on solidarity. In analysing how effective international law is in addressing water security concerns, the main shortcoming of the current legal regime can be exposed and addressed: short-sighted state-centrism. Hence, in order to fulfil one of its key responsibilities – stabilising global peace and security – international law has to better address the complexities of water security.

During the period of research for this study, the amount of literature on the concept of water security has grown substantially.[43] Yet, despite the increasing depth of debate, the attempt to implement it into other disciplines (e.g., development studies) and the crucial role played by law, water security has received sparse attention from legal scholars.[44] The few legal scholars who have taken on the complex task of analysing the implications that the concept of water security has for international water law, have usually done so by applying a rather narrow (orthodox) definition of water security; which in turn only allows for

41 The Royal Academy of Engineering, *Global Water Security: An Engineering Perspective* (2010).

42 See S Vinogradov, P Wouters and P Jones, *Transforming Potential Conflict into Cooperation Potential: The Role of International Water Law* (UNESCO 2003); P Wouters and A Rieu-Clarke, 'The Role of International Water Law in Ensuring "Good Water Governance": A Call for Renewed Focus and Action' (2004) *Journal of Water Law*, 15, 89.

43 See, e.g., J Lautze and H Manthrithilake, 'Water Security' in Lautze J (ed.), *Key Concepts in Water Resource Management : A Review and Critical Evaluation* (Routledge 2014); B Lankford and others (eds), *Water Security : Principles, Perspectives and Practices* (Routledge 2013); D Waughray (ed.), *Water Security: The Water-Food-Energy-Climate Nexus* (Island Press 2011); NI Pachova, M Nakayama and L Jansky (eds), *International Water Security: Domestic Threats and Opportunities* (United Nations University Press 2008).

44 Notable exceptions include D Tarlock, 'Water Security, Fear Mitigation and International Water Law' (2008) *Hamline Law Review*, 31, 704; P Wouters, 'Water Security: What Role for International Water Law?' in Doddle F (ed.), *Human and Environmental Security: An Agenda for Change* (Earthscan 2005).

restricted analysis of the current legal framework and rather general proposals for the future development of international law.[45] Hence, there is recognition that we need a 'revolutionary re-think of the conceptual framework for water security, where the contribution of (water) law is more dynamically considered and integrated'.[46] Water security is the prime example of a key issue dominating the twenty-first century, which cannot be solved by any single country acting alone. The realisation that states need to cooperate more closely on transboundary water management comes at a time where several tools for global policy making have broken down.[47]

One hot spot where this dilemma is readily apparent is the region of Himalayan Asia. Here, the two hydro-hegemons (China and India) determine the rules of the game in order to secure their respective national (water) interests – without making huge efforts towards long-term stabilisation of regional security. In general, powerful riparians (such as India and China) are expected to be sensitive to relative gains by other states, since any gain might upset the status quo.[48] Thus, international law must work against this prevalent preference of powerful riparians to favour bilateral treaties over a multilateral approach which would include all basin riparians. For the case of Himalayan Asia, and in many other parts of the world, current international legal frameworks are struggling to meet contemporary challenges of the global water crisis and have often been seen as a hindrance rather than a part of the solution.[49] In order to prevent transboundary water cooperation from failing, legal scholarship requires a fresh approach able to analyse the complexities of the challenges revealed by the water security concept and develop international water law further.

1.4 Purpose, research question and outline of the book

This study examines the contemporary notion of security within the rapidly changing international context of extra-military threats and will employ water as the medium for critical discourse. The combined impact of increasing local,

45 See, e.g., Tarlock, 'Water Security, Fear Mitigation and International Water Law' at 716. Here, Tarlock defines water security to include 'the guarantee of sufficient water for a nation's sustainable food production'.

46 D Tarlock and P Wouters, 'Reframing the Water Security Dialogue' (2009) *Journal of Water Law*, 20, 53 at 60.

47 'The challenge of establishing a rules-based system for the production, consumption and trade of resources is immense, not least because it amounts to a comprehensive rewiring of the global economy. Despite the potential obstacles, it remains critical to seek pathways that will steer countries towards mutually advantageous models of cooperation, even though the appetite for enhanced global governance remains low.' B Lee and others, *Resources Futures* (Chatham House 2012) at 143.

48 NA Zawahri and SM Mitchell, 'Fragmented Governance of International Rivers: Negotiating Bilateral Versus Multilateral Treaties' (2011) *International Studies Quarterly*, 55, 835 at 843.

49 One often-quoted example is the Nile, where past treaties (from 1929 and 1959) made negotiations for a new basin-wide agreement difficult.

regional and global tensions over access to the world's diminishing natural resources – especially water – have created serious threats to global stability and have thus endangered the very foundation of modern legal order and international security.[50] Despite the commitments set forth in the Charter of the United Nations (UN Charter), which established the legal basis of the existing community of nations, serious problems challenge the UN Charter's principal objective 'to maintain international peace and security'.[51] While the notion of security in general, and water security in particular, may have different meanings and acquire various forms at the individual, local, national, regional and global levels, the primary focus of this study is on its international dimension and, more specifically, at the regional or international basin level. This is where the water security challenges have manifested themselves most visibly – yet the international legal response has been particularly weak.

This book addresses the question of whether a newly proposed conceptualisation of water security with a deeper connection to international water law opens up new pathways towards hydrosolidarity. The central hypothesis underlying the entire book is that an examination of international water law through a security lens brings forth an innovative legal architecture that can generate and strengthen transboundary water cooperation, which in turn will enhance the role of international law in general. In order to verify this, the study follows a three-step approach: (1) thoroughly examining how water security should be defined, (2) analysing the extent to which *lex lata* provides an enabling framework for achieving water security, and (3) giving impetus for *lex ferenda*, guided by the newly proposed understanding of water security (see Figure 1.1).

Structurally, the study is divided into seven chapters. Following this introduction, Chapter 2 conceptualises water security by reviewing existing perspectives and viewpoints from a range of disciplines on the concept. A definition

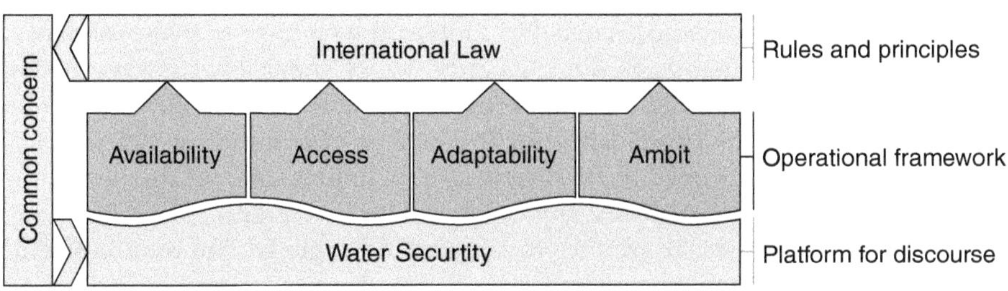

Figure 1.1 Research structure

50 For a detailed analysis of the evolving global security environmental problems, see IPPR Commission on National Security in the 21st Century, *Shared Destinies: Security in a Globalised World : The Interim Report of the IPPR Commission on National Security in the 21st Century* (Institute for Public Policy Research 2008).

51 Article 1(1) of the Charter of the United Nations (26 June 1945; entered into force 24 October 1945) 1 UNTS XVI [hereinafter UN Charter].

of water security enhances the accessibility of the concept within international legal scholarship. While the concept of water security has been the subject of vigorous debate among social scientists and international relations scholars, it has yet to be appropriately defined in order to influence legal discourse and practice. While this seems astonishing, given its relevance to central features of international law, the relatively little attention from international lawyers might be mainly due to the embryonic state of the concept in terms of its normative content, and the diverse interpretations in meaning across disciplines.

After carving out a workable definition of water security which can be applied within the context of international law, Chapter 3 develops an operational methodology for identifying the core elements of water security which have to be addressed by international law: availability, access, adaptability and ambit. Then, in analysing the current legal framework governing transboundary freshwater resources, the main strengths, gaps and weaknesses within the current architecture are revealed. The first challenge is the (legal) tension between the task to provide for security of expectations (status quo) and the innovation needed to meet fluctuating demands and supplies – i.e., the ability to respond to change. The second challenge is the (environmental/political) tension between the ecological unity of the water resource and the diverging sovereign interests of states. This in turn leads to friction between the aims of maximising the overall benefit of sustainable aquatic ecosystems and maximising the relative benefit of states.

Having established the degree to which the existing legal framework of transboundary freshwater resources governance addresses water security, Chapters 4 and 5 of this book adopt a forward-looking approach. Chapter 4 introduces the concept of hydrosolidarity and explores the reasons why it has not been useful in turning transboundary water interaction around to date. Chapter 5, then, challenges the present mindset of prevailing state-centrism vis-à-vis hydrosolidarity by examining how international legal instruments might be crafted in a way that advances the concept of hydrosolidarity. This section therefore elaborates on the legal foundation needed to support the concept of hydrosolidarity, since the conceptualisation of water security, which inevitably has a normative dimension, raises questions about international law in general. In order to be able to implement hydrosolidarity for the benefit of common water security, established paradigms need to be reviewed – including some of the most fundamental tenets of international law, such as state sovereignty. Here, the concept of considering water security as a matter of 'regional common concern' is introduced in order to help international law play a more prominent role in addressing the challenges of global water insecurity. The purpose of this notion is by no means to replace the acknowledged principle of international water law – i.e., equitable and reasonable utilisation. On the contrary, it aims to support it by providing a space for debate and further development.

Chapter 6 of this study examines how the novel understanding of water security and its legal underpinnings could exploit gaps and provide opportunities for advancing an international water law agenda which can bring about hydrosolidarity in the region of Himalayan Asia, and considers the current state of affairs. The region serves as a perfect area of study, since several of the global challenges that transboundary water management is facing can be found here, such as climate change, population growth and urbanisation. In addition, political tensions between several of the states depending on the run-off of the 'Third Pole' (Afghanistan, Bangladesh, Bhutan, Burma, Cambodia, China, India, Laos, Nepal, Pakistan, Thailand and Vietnam) hamper regional cooperation – like the conflicts in the volatile areas of Kashmir and Tibet. If it can be demonstrated that even within this highly pressurised region, looking at international water law through the lens of common security can help advancing international cooperation and lead towards hydrosolidarity, it may serve as an inspiring model for other regions.

Finally, Chapter 7 of this book draws an overall conclusion and develops generic recommendations for international legal scholarship. Furthermore, it points towards prospects for the future of international water law by proposing a research agenda for the epistemic community.

Civilisation simply cannot afford to ignore the increasingly sophisticated and interconnected social and environmental challenges, mainly driven by overexploitation, over-consumption and inequity. The growing complexity and interdependence between states and communities demands us to break with the prevalence of thinking in silos and within national borders. What is required instead is a renewed effort to foster international cooperation on all issues shaping our common future. This study is looking at transboundary freshwater resources – the fault line of international conflict in the twenty-first century – as a 'case study' for advancing public international law in order to fulfil its responsibility of promoting international peace and security. As a result, this book advances existing literature by analysing the implications that the concept of water security has for international law, and vice versa.

While one cannot overvalue the recent entry into force of the UN Convention on the Law of the Non-Navigational Uses of International Watercourses,[52] it is no panacea for resolving all transboundary freshwater conflicts.[53] The newly gained legal weight of the UN Watercourses Convention should be utilised as an impetus for thinking about new ways of cooperation over transboundary water resources, rather than believing the job is done. It is hoped that this study will provide a direction for reviving the international legal discourse, where water security has remained largely uncharted territory, and demonstrate how the water crisis can be utilised as a change agent for international law.[54]

52 United Nations Convention on the Law of the Non-Navigational Uses of International Watercourses, UN Doc A/51/869 (21 May 1997; in force 17 August 2014) reprinted in 36 ILM 700 (1997) [hereinafter UN Watercourses Convention].

53 For a detailed discussion, see FR Loures and A Rieu-Clarke (eds), *The UN Watercourses Convention in Force: Strengthening International Law for Transboundary Water Management* (Earthscan 2013).

54 See W van Genugten and M Bulterman, 'Crises: Concern and Fuel for International Law and International Lawyers' (2014) *Netherlands Yearbook of International Law*, 44, 3; T Broude, 'Warming to Crisis: The Climate Change Law of Unintended Opportunity' (2014) *Netherlands Yearbook of International Law*, 44, 111.

2 Water security – conceptualising a buzzword

For many countries, water security is already one of the key factors determining foreign policy. One example is Kashmir, where the border between India and Pakistan, both nuclear-armed, has been continually contested – a situation which has led to a perpetual state of instability in the region. Fears by Pakistan that its powerful neighbour could use water control as a weapon have been exploited by extremists to make a bogeyman out of India by claiming it is stealing Pakistan's water.[1]

Not only volatile Kashmir, but the whole region of Himalayan Asia has to be considered a potential hot-spot of water insecurity. The glaciers of the Tibetan Plateau, also known as the 'Third Pole', feed the headwaters of the mighty rivers Yangtze, Yellow, Mekong, Salween, Brahmaputra, Indus, among others. More than 1.5 billion people downstream directly depend upon these waters – not to mention the implications stemming from current and predicted future 'virtual water' trade.[2] Since the outlook for this region is especially worrisome,[3] it seems reasonable to expect that governments will try to secure as much water resources as possible, which may force them to look beyond their borders – leading to even more geo-political tensions. How China, for example, manages and dams its waters, will not only have a major impact on the water quality and quantity downstream, but also on the political stability of the whole region; since most of the societies heavily depend on the seasonal river flows for their energy production, water and food security.[4] This renders the

1 N Amies for *Deutsche Welle*, 'Water Security the New Front in Kashmir Struggle Between India, Pakistan' (02/09/2010) available at <http://www.dw.de/dw/article/0,,5935413,00.html>.

2 X Jianchu, A Shrestha and M Eriksson, 'Climate Change and Its Impacts on Glaciers and Water Resource Management in the Himalayan Region' in Braun LN and others (eds), *Assessment of Snow, Glacier and Water Resources in Asia*, vol. 8 (International Hydrological Programme of UNESCO; German IHP/HWRP National Committee 2009) at 44.

3 2030 Water Resources Group, *Charting Our Water Future – Economic Frameworks to Inform Decision-Making* (2009) at 9.

4 See P Bosshard, 'China Dams the World' (2009) 26 *World Policy Journal* 43; PH Gleick, 'China and Water' in Gleick PH and others (eds), *The World's Water 2008–2009* (Island Press 2009); J Shaofeng, L Shijun and L Aifeng, 'Will China's Water Shortage Shake the World's Food Security?' (2010) *Water International*, 35, 6.

question about the future status of Tibet more sensitive, as its plateau stores an abundant wealth of freshwater – the vital resource which will only become more valuable. Acknowledging the fact that water is a key component of 'ultimate security', the securitisation of freshwater resources not only seems justified, but also inevitable.[5]

2.1 The changing perception of security

The origins of the term 'security' derive from the Latin *sine cura*, meaning a state of living without care and concern.[6] Wolfers suggests that 'Security . . . in an objective sense, measures the absence of threats to acquired values, [and] in a subjective sense, [refers to] the absence of fear that such values might be attacked.'[7] Thus, when taking a realist approach, objective security is achieved when the dangers posed by various risks, vulnerabilities and threats are being prevented or can be coped with; while from a social constructivist perspective, security is achieved once the perceptions of security risks, vulnerabilities and threats are overcome.[8] This implies that although objective factors are essential for the conceptualisation of security, they clearly are not sufficient, as the subjective factors have a big impact in the perception of security. The perception of security, in turn, depends on the certain 'value' given by society (*Wertidee*) and a universally applied 'normative concept'.[9] Within the discipline, traditional approaches to security studies have tended to focus primarily on military threats to the integrity of nation states.[10] This line of discourse changed with the end of the Cold War, when the distinction between internal and external security became increasingly blurred, and conceptual approaches needed to take into account the security-related issues arising out of new (or newly perceived) global threats – economic, social and environmental. Especially the framing of environmental issues in terms of security appears to have gained currency rather quickly. In 1989, Eduard Shevardnadze, in his role as Soviet Foreign Minister, called for the establishment of an Environmental Security

5 E Burleson, 'Water Is Security' (2008) *Environs: Environmental Law and Policy Journal*, 31, 197; B-O Magsig, 'Introducing an Analytical Framework for Water Security: A Platform for the Refinement of International Water Law' (2009) *Journal of Water Law*, 20, 61.

6 JF Warner and R Meissner, 'The Politics of Security in the Okavango River Basin: From Civil War to Saving Wetlands (1975–2002) : A Preliminary Security Impact Assessment' in Jansky L, Nakayama M and Pachova NI (eds), *International Water Security: Domestic Threats and Opportunities* (United Nations University Press 2008) at 254.

7 A Wolfers, *Discord and Collaboration: Essays on International Politics* (Johns Hopkins Press 1962) at 150.

8 HG Brauch, 'Concepts of Security Threats, Challenges, Vulnerabilities and Risks' in Brauch HG and others (eds), *Coping with Global Environmental Change, Disasters and Security* (Springer 2011) at 61.

9 Ibid.

10 See HG Brauch, 'Introduction: Globalization and Environmental Challenges: Reconceptualizing Security in the 21st Century' in Brauch HG and others (eds), *Globalization and Environmental Challenges: Reconceptualizing Security in the 21st Century* (Springer 2008) at 28.

Council entrusted with issues of ecological security;[11] while politicians in the West argued along the same line. For instance, Johan Jørgen Holst, the then Norwegian Defence Minister, pointed out that 'environment degradation may be viewed as a contribution to armed conflict in the sense of exacerbating conflicts or adding new dimensions'.[12]

Thus, in realising that the various new threats to both national and international security could not simply be addressed by looking through the military lens alone, the perception of security changed considerably.[13] The inclusion of non-military threats – the so-called 'widening' process – was accompanied by efforts to also 'deepen' security studies. Here, the approach was to regard the individual, rather than the state, as the main referent object by introducing the concept of 'human security'.[14] In 1997, the UN Development Programme's *Human Development Report* observed that

> Security is increasingly interpreted as the security of people, not just territory; security of individuals, not just of nations; security through development, not through arms; security of all people everywhere – in their homes, in their jobs, in their streets, in their communities, and in the environment.[15]

One of the consequences of the awakened political interest in this concept was, again, an increase in research on 'environmental security', arguing that environmental degradation poses a threat to international security which justifies the re-evaluation of the traditional notion of security.[16] Interestingly, it was not environmental research which drove the development at the beginning; but rather two other disciplines which spearheaded early progress. Peace research used the concept of environmental security to overcome the classic notion of a military-focused security of the individual state, while researchers of international development incorporated environmental factors in their analysis of violent conflicts in the developing world to argue for restructuring the global economy.[17] This process led to defining the environmental security of a state as the 'absence of non-conventional threats against the environmental substratum essential to the well-being of its population and to the maintenance

11 See E Shevardnadze, 'Ecology and Diplomacy' (1990) *Environmental Policy and Law*, 20, 20.

12 JJ Holst, 'Security and the Environment: A Preliminary Exploration' (1989) *Bulletin of Peace Proposals*, 20, 123.

13 *B Buzan, People, States and Fear: An Agenda for International Security Studies in the Post-Cold War Era* (2nd edn, Harvester Wheatsheaf 1991).

14 See O Brown, 'The Environment and Our Security – How Our Understanding of the Links Has Changed' (International Conference on Environment, Peace and Dialogue among Civilizations).

15 Mahbubul Haq, speaking at the launch of the UN Development Programme (UNDP), *Human Development Report* (1997), cited in Ibid. at 2.

16 See, e.g., W Scholtz, 'Collective (Environmental) Security: The Yeast for the Refinement of International Law' (2009) *Yearbook of International Environmental Law*, 19, 135 at 138.

17 L Brock, 'Environmental Conflict Research – Paradigms and Perspectives' in Carius A and Lietzmann KM (eds), *Environmental Change and Security – a European Perspective* (Springer 1999) at 37.

of its functional integrity'.[18] Evidently, it reasserts the responsibilities of a state towards its citizens, which is the logical consequence of associating 'national security' with 'quality of life' (or human security).[19] This is why other scholars put the individual in the centre of security research, arguing that 'In the field of international security, a focus on the individual as the nexus of concern enables us to understand both the broad spectrum of threats, and their interlocking nature, in any given context.'[20] While this concept does not break with the notion of national security, since 'the security of the state is necessary for human security', it nevertheless challenged the traditional thinking to become more human-centred.[21]

From this focus on human-centred security, the 'essential freedoms' discourse evolved, primarily embraced by the United Nations, which placed the security paradigm within the following fundamental freedoms: the freedom from want, the freedom from fear, the freedom to live with human dignity, and the freedom from hazardous impact.[22] Implementing these baskets of freedoms remains an obligation of states as the principal actors responsible for dealing with internal and external (international, regional and global) security challenges. In his report 'In Larger Freedom', Kofi Annan, the former Secretary-General of the United Nations, identified the 'imperative of collective action' as essential for achieving the core purposes of the UN Charter:[23]

> In a world of interconnected threats and challenges, it is in each country's self-interest that all of them are addressed effectively. Hence, the cause of larger freedom can only be advanced by broad, deep and sustained global cooperation among states. Such cooperation is possible if every country's policies take into account not only the needs of its own citizens but also the needs of others. This kind of cooperation not only advances everyone's interests but also recognizes our common humanity.[24]

Providing input to the UN Secretary-General's report, the High-Level Panel on Threats, Challenges and Change offered interesting insights into the security discourse. The panel noted that

18 M Frédérick, 'A Realist's Conceptual Definition of Environmental Security' in Deudney D and Matthew RA (eds), *Contested Grounds : Security and Conflict in the New Environmental Politics* (State University of New York Press 1999) at 100.

19 Ibid. at 94.

20 RG McRae, 'Human Security in a Globalized World' in McRae RG and Hubert D (eds), *Human Security and the New Diplomacy–- Protecting People, Promoting Peace* (McGill-Queen's University Press 2001) at 21.

21 B von Tigerstrom, *Human Security and International Law* (Hart Publishing 2007) at 50.

22 See also United Nations, A More Secure World: Our Shared Responsibility – Report of the Secretary-General's High-Level Panel on Threats, Challenges and Change (United Nations 2004) at 77.

23 K Annan, In Larger Freedom: Towards Development, Security and Human Rights for All (United Nations General Assembly 2005).

24 Ibid. at 6.

> The threats to peace and security in the twenty-first century include not just international war and conflict but civil violence, organized crime, terrorism and weapons of mass destruction. They also include poverty, deadly infectious disease and environmental degradation since these can have equally catastrophic consequences. All of these threats can cause death or lessen life chances on a large scale. All of them can undermine states as the basic unit of the international system'.[25]

The panel endorsed the central role of the United Nations in the context of a more broadly defined concept of security by insisting 'that the Charter as a whole continues to provide a sound legal and policy basis for the organisation of collective security, enabling the Security Council to respond to threats to international peace and security, both old and new in a timely and effective manner.'[26] It recommended that the United Nations be provided with 'new expertise to deal with new threats – for example, the scientific advice necessary to address questions of environmental and biological security'.[27] While recent efforts of Germany have put the threats of climate change on the agenda of the UN Security Council,[28] some states – the most vocal being Russia – remain sceptical as to whether the Council actually is the right forum for discussing the security issues caused by the rapidly changing climate.[29] In any case, one should not expect the UN to mobilise 'green helmets' as a response to climate change.[30] This is evident not only due to the rather weak formulation in the Security Council's statement that 'possible adverse effects of climate change may, in the long run, aggravate certain existing threats to international peace and security',[31] but also due to the fact that a renewed attempt in 2013 to have climate change recognised as an international security threat was also unsuccessful, as the intended formal session was downgraded to an 'Arria Formula Meeting' owing to pressure from China and Russia.[32] However, the recognition by the Security Council that the realities of the changing climate have repercussions on international peace and security is still a laudable step.

25 Ibid. at 24.

26 United Nations, *A More Secure World: Our Shared Responsibility – Report of the Secretary-General's High-Level Panel on Threats, Challenges and Change* at 93.

27 Ibid. at 91. The report also recommends the creation of a deputy Secretary-General for peace and security.

28 Statement by the President of the Security Council (20 July 2011) UN Doc S/PRST/2011/15 available at <http://www.securitycouncilreport.org/atf/cf/%7B65BFCF9B-6D27-4E9C-8CD3-CF6E4FF96FF9%7D/CC%20SPRST%202011%205.pdf>.

29 P Worsnip for Reuters, 'West, Russia Divided on U.N. Council Climate Role' (20 July 2011) <http://www.reuters.com/article/2011/07/20/us-climate-un-idUSTRE76J7QY20110720>.

30 See United Nations Environment Programme, *Greening the Blue Helmets : Environment, Natural Resources and UN Peacekeeping Operations* (United Nations Environment Programme 2012).

31 UN Security Council, 6587th Meeting (20 July 2011) UN Doc SC/10332 available at <http://www.un.org/News/Press/docs/2011/sc10332.doc.htm>.

32 What's in Blue, 'Arria Formula Meeting on Climate Change' (14 February 2013) <http://www.whatsinblue.org/2013/02/arria-formula-meeting-on-climate-change.php>.

Despite international policy developments, most governments have adopted a security paradigm which is based on the flawed premise that all kinds of insecurity can be controlled by using military force or containment. The underlying reason for states to follow this 'control paradigm' is their wish of being able to maintain the status quo.[33] Fuelled by the 9/11 attacks, many Western governments perceived terrorism to be the greatest threat. In doing so, however, valuable resources and time have been wasted by distracting from the much greater – and also much more fundamental – threats to international peace and security: global environmental change and competition over natural resources.[34]

A new approach which addresses the drivers of insecurity by 'curing the disease' rather than 'fighting the symptoms' is urgently needed.[35] Here, conjoint processes have recently led to the notions of collective and sustainable security,[36] which try to pave the way towards a mutual understanding that security can no longer be regarded as a zero-sum game between states; since a contemporary take on the notion unveils its 'common' characteristic. It has to be acknowledged that 'security anywhere depends on sustainable development everywhere';[37] hence on addressing the security challenges, we are facing in a more holistic manner. The concept of sustainable development is being considered as a strategy of conflict prevention by addressing the root causes of insecurity and ensuring lasting peace and development.[38] While it positions itself against the control paradigm, more research is needed to tease out how exactly sustainable development as a security concept (sustainable security) can have an impact in the international security discourse – otherwise it might be at risk of being overstretched due to its vagueness. However, in combining sustainable security thinking with the more advanced concept of collective security, which is being perceived as one of the core purposes of the UN Charter,[39] a promising platform for discourse could emerge – one which might be capable of facilitating a meaningful debate about how to address the security issues the international community is facing. Although states are the bedrock of the international system, and thus no collective security is possible unless it is

33 C Abbott, P Rogers and J Sloboda, *Global Responses to Global Threats – Sustainable Security for the 21st Century* (Oxford Research Group 2006) at 28.

34 See C Abbott, P Rogers and JA Sloboda, *Beyond Terror: The Truth About the Real Threats to Our World* (Rider 2007).

35 H Brock, *Competition over Resources: Drivers of Insecurity and the Global South* (Oxford Research Group 2011) at 2.

36 Scholtz, 'Collective (Environmental) Security: The Yeast for the Refinement of International Law'; C Voigt, 'Sustainable Security' (2009) *Yearbook of International Environmental Law*, 19, 163.

37 UN Secretary-General Ban Ki-moon in Time Magazine, 'The Right War' (17 April 2008) <http://www.time.com/time/specials/2007/article/0,28804,1730759_1731383_1731345,00.html>.

38 Voigt, 'Sustainable Security' at 164.

39 Annan, In Larger Freedom: *Towards Development, Security and Human Rights for All at 6; United Nations, A More Secure World: Our Shared Responsibility – Report of the Secretary-General's High-Level Panel on Threats, Challenges and Change* at 93.

based on the various perceptions of the security of states, collective security has always been expected to operate 'above and beyond' orthodox patterns of international relations – i.e., to add 'universal moral obligations' to the table of international negotiations.[40] Given the complexity of the challenges ahead, adding the perspective of sustainability to this approach seems to be a promising way forward in the pursuit of common security.

2.2 The securitisation of water

While the concept of environmental security, notwithstanding its yet undefined normative meaning, has acquired some recognition and acceptance within current international legal discourse,[41] the notion of water security is a relatively recent phenomenon. A number of interesting attempts to link environmental security with shared freshwater resources can be found in the literature,[42] but these studies have considered water more as a premise for promoting the appeal of an ecosystem-centred legal regime, rather than as a security issue in its own right. Unlike most other elements of the environment, water, however, is a multi-purpose resource of high economic and social significance, with diminishing availability and uneven distribution in space and time; and for which there is no alternative substitute. These special features make water resources open to conflicting claims of different users and uses, both domestically and across international borders. Thus, the characteristics of the global water crisis (as briefly described in the previous chapter) justify the disengagement of water security from environmental, food, energy and other 'securities', and examining it as an own subject of an independent study.[43] The conclusions drawn from this exercise, however, will most certainly fertilise the general security discourse as well and demonstrate how water security can help bring about common security for all.

2.2.1 Defusing the 'water war' scare

The fear is that if efforts to mitigate and adapt to climate change (and other drivers of the water crisis) fail, it might turn into a prime driver for violent

40 See A Orakhelashvili, *Collective Security* (Oxford University Press 2011) at 6.

41 See, e.g., S Vinogradov, 'International Environmental Security: The Concept and Its Implementation' in Carty A and Danilenko GM (eds), *Perestroika and International Law : Current Anglo-Soviet Approaches to International Law* (Edinburgh University Press 1990); G Handl, 'Environmental Security and Global Change: The Challenge to International Law' (1990) *Yearbook of International Environmental Law*, 1, 3; AS Timoshenko, 'Ecological Security: Global Change Paradigm' (1990) *Columbia Journal of International Environmental Law and Policy*, 1, 127; J Brunnée, 'Environmental Security in the Twenty-First Century: New Momentum for the Development of International Environmental Law?' (1995) *Fordham International Law Journal*, 18, 1742.

42 See J Brunnée and SJ Toope, 'Environmental Security and Freshwater Resources: A Case for International Ecosystem Law' (1994) *Yearbook of International Environmental Law*, 5, 41.

43 P Wouters, S Vinogradov and B-O Magsig, 'Water Security, Hydrosolidarity and International Law: A River Runs through It' (2009) *Yearbook of International Environmental Law*, 19, 97 at 103.

conflict.[44] This conclusion follows the reasoning that the changing climate is very likely to make poor states poorer (i.e. less able to absorb risk) and scarce natural resources, like freshwater, even scarcer. This is why the 'water war' discourse mainly revolves around the debate whether scarcity of natural resources can trigger military conflict; often drawing heavily from the rich literature on climate change and conflict.[45] While the potential link between climatic changes and conflict has been investigated extensively, the conclusions which have been drawn by the various studies are often contradictory. Some scientists, for instance, concluded that rising temperatures would cause 'a cumulative additional 393,000 battle deaths by 2030',[46] while others maintain the contrary and argue that 'countries that are affected by climate-related natural disasters face a lower risk of civil war';[47] still others strongly refute any one-to-one causality between climatic changes and conflict, stating that it is impossible to isolate single factors as the sole trigger of violence.[48] This is why the prevailing opinion which has emerged is that environmental variables, including climate change, act as 'threat multipliers', such as in the case of Mali in 2012, where the state's difficulty in providing basic resources for its people was exacerbated by droughts and led to a growing popularity of the militant group Al-Qaida in the Islamic Maghreb.[49]

Analysing these studies makes clear that the majority of current research does not suggest that climate change alone can spark conflict between states, except perhaps where rapidly deteriorating water availability cuts across already

44 L De Stefano and others, 'Climate Change and the Institutional Resilience of International River Basins' (2012) *Journal of Peace Research*, 49, 193 at 206.

45 See, e.g., D Bergholt and P Lujala, 'Climate-Related Natural Disasters, Economic Growth, and Armed Civil Conflict' (2012) *Journal of Peace Research*, 49, 147; O Brown and A Crawford, *Rising Temperatures, Rising Tensions – Climate Change and the Risk of Violent Conflict in the Middle East* (International Institute for Sustainable Development 2009); A Evans, *Resource Scarcity, Climate Change and the Risk of Violent Conflict* (World Bank 2010); NP Gleditsch, 'Whither the Weather? Climate Change and Conflict' (2012) *Journal of Peace Research*, 49, 3; D Smith and J Vivekananda, *A Climate of Conflict – the Links between Climate Change, Peace and War* (International Alert 2007); OM Theisen, H Holtermann and H Buhaug, 'Climate Wars? Assessing the Claim That Drought Breeds Conflict' (2012) *International Security*, 36, 79; J Tir and DM Stinnett, 'Weathering Climate Change: Can Institutions Mitigate International Water Conflict?' (2012) *Journal of Peace Research*, 49, 211.

46 MB Burke and others, 'Warming Increases the Risk of Civil War in Africa' (2009) *Proceedings of the National Academy of Sciences*, 106, 20670 at 20672.

47 RT Slettebak, 'Don't Blame the Weather! Climate-Related Natural Disasters and Civil Conflict' (2012) *Journal of Peace Research*, 49, 163 at 163.

48 See L Beehner for World Policy Blog, 'Don't Blame the Weather' (15 October 2012) <http://www.worldpolicy.org/blog/2012/10/15/dont-blame-weather>; J Scheffran, 'The Gathering Storm: Is Climate Change a Threat to Security?' (2009) *Security Index*, 15, 21.

49 See The Economist, 'Strife in the Sahel : A Perfect Desert Storm' (17 March 2012) <http://www.economist.com/node/21550324>; D Lewis for Reuters, 'Mali: From Democracy Poster Child to Broken State' (24 April 2012) <http://www.reuters.com/article/2012/04/24/us-mali-idUSBRE83N09Q20120424>; M Trémolières, *Security and Environmental Variables: The Debate and an Analysis of Links in the Sahel* (OECD 2010).

existing tensions and weak institutions.[50] It is this obvious link between climate and water which has drawn more and more researchers to look at water as a source of violent conflict.[51]

On the one hand, there are claims that we are currently going through a transition period from an era of oil conflicts to one of water wars, since water is now supposed to be a 'commodity as important as oil'.[52] This argument is often supported by listing various instances in the past, where water has already been used as a political tool or even a military target.[53] Prominent examples are: the poisoning of enemy's wells by the Assyrians as early as during the sixth century BC; the selection of dams and water supply infrastructure in Germany as a primary target of bombings by the British Royal Air Force in the Second World War, and the opening of dikes on the Yellow River by China during the Second Sino-Japanese War (1938) in order to slow the advance of the Japanese Army.[54] Furthermore, some proponents of the 'water war' theory argue that Israel's occupation of the Golan Heights after the Six Day War (5–10 June 1967) was a historical conflict over land and water.[55] Looking ahead, some scholars suggest that protecting a state's national water security might even become a *jus ad bellum* criterion for a 'just war' in some particular cases.[56] On the other hand, historical data is also employed to prove that there is no serious risk of a fully fledged war triggered by water scarcity, since the only known war solely fought over water occurred some 4,500 years ago between the ancient Mesopotamian city states of Lagash and Umma.[57] In an attempt to examine the history of conflict over water resources more rigorously, a study analysing every

50 World Bank, *World Development Report 2011: Conflict, Security, and Development* (World Bank 2011) at 35.

51 See, e.g., recent special issue in *International Journal of Sustainable Society* including MZ Kaiser Khan, 'Ganges Basin: An Example of Social Conflicts Regarding Water Resources Especially in Developing Countries' (2012) *International Journal of Sustainable Society*, 4, 158; B-O Magsig, 'Rising to the Challenge of Water Security: International (Water) Law in Need of Refinement' (2012) *International Journal of Sustainable Society*, 4, 28; MM Rahaman, 'Hydropower Ambitions of South Asian Nations and China: Ganges and Brahmaputra Rivers Basins' (2012) *International Journal of Sustainable Society*, 4, 131; A Swain, 'Global Climate Change and Challenges for International River Agreements' (2012) *International Journal of Sustainable Society*, 4, 72; J Warner, 'Three Lenses on Water War, Peace and Hegemonic Struggle on the Nile' (2012) *International Journal of Sustainable Society*, 4, 173.

52 J Bulloch and A Darwish, *Water Wars : Coming Conflicts in the Middle East* (Victor Gollancz 1993) at 198.

53 See, e.g., PH Gleick, 'Water and Terrorism' (2006) *Water Policy*, 8, 481.

54 DK Kreamer, 'The Past, Present, and Future of Water Conflict and International Security' (2012) *Journal of Contemporary Water Research & Education*, 149, 87 at 89.

55 M Daoudy, 'A Missed Chance for Peace: Israel and Syria's Negotiations over the Golan Heights' (2008) *Journal of International Affairs*, 61, 215 at 216.

56 See C Waddington, 'Reconciling Just War Theory and Water-Related Conflict' (2012) *International Journal of Applied Philosophy*, 26, 197.

57 SL Postel and AT Wolf, 'Dehydrating Conflict' (2001) *Foreign Policy* 60 at 60.

reported international water-related interaction (conflict and cooperation) over the past five decades concluded that the record of cooperation overwhelmed that of conflict by far.[58]

The problem with most studies analysing the possibility of water wars is their simplistic nature. It is difficult – if not impossible – to single out one factor in causing military action, since conflicts have to be understood as complex social systems.[59] Furthermore, the various steps leading towards a fully fledged war are frequently being overlooked. In order to better understand the risks imposed by conflict, the Heidelberg Institute for International Conflict Research distinguishes between five levels of hostility with increasing intensity: dispute, non-violent crises, violent crises, limited war and war.[60] The main weakness of the water wars discourse, however, is the fundamental misunderstanding of the political economy of water conflicts. While water scarcities are often portrayed as a Malthusian imbalance between supply and demand, they are actually the result of uneven patterns of economic development and severe mismanagement of natural resources.[61] Therefore, it is implausible to explain international water conflicts in state-centric terms and solely as provoked by unequally powerful states competing for dwindling freshwater resources in order to secure their respective national interests. The starting point for analysing the likelihood of international conflicts over water should not be the availability of the resources as such, but the complex dynamics triggering both scarcity and conflict.[62] Hence, it has to be concluded that the oil-water analogy is fundamentally flawed.

It seems like the recent scaremongering about the potential of water wars has moved on from the Middle East and is now focusing on Asia.[63] Given the regional preconditions and drivers, it might be apparent that the possibility conflict over water resources is growing – particularly along the borders of China, India and Pakistan. Yet again, it is not advisable 'to cry wolf', as this will only give the floor to extremist forces within those countries who, by putting water on their agenda, benefit from the fears of the population. After all, hydropolitics is what societies make of it.[64] Hence, the increasingly fierce

58 See AT Wolf, SB Yoffe and M Giordano, *International Waters: Indicators for Identifying Basins at Risk* (UNESCO 2003).

59 See S Stetter and others, 'Conflicts About Water: Securitizations in a Global Context' (2011) *Cooperation and Conflict*, 46, 441 at 442.

60 See J Deuter and others (eds), *Conflict Barometer 2011* (Heidelberg Institute for International Conflict Research 2012).

61 J Selby, 'Oil and Water: The Contrasting Anatomies of Resource Conflicts' (2005) *Government and Opposition*, 40, 200 at 200.

62 Ibid.

63 One of the most prominent contributions might well be the work by Indian security hawk B Chellaney, *Water : Asia's New Battleground* (Georgetown University Press 2011).

64 See F Julien, 'Hydropolitics Is What Societies Make of It (or Why We Need a Constructivist Approach to the Geopolitics of Water)' (2012) *International Journal of Sustainable Society*, 4, 45.

rhetoric used by some officials comes as no real surprise: Pakistan's General Ashfaq Kayani, citing water to justify his 'India-centric' military stance;[65] Bashir Ahmad warning that India 'will switch the Indus off to make Pakistan solely dependent on India. It's going to be a water bomb';[66] or Bangladeshi security expert Muniruzzaman stating that 'if there ever were a localized conflict in South Asia it will be over water'.[67]

However, despite the fact that the only true 'water war' occurred more 4,500 years ago,[68] the security implications of the global water crisis (see Chapter 1) suggest that the past may not be an adequate basis from which to make predictions about the potential for future water conflicts. While this may play into the reasoning of 'Neo-Malthusians', who believe that violent conflicts can erupt due to overexploitation of a specific resource[69] – often driven by population growth, rapid economic development and inequitable distribution of resources – 'Cornucopians' draw a much brighter picture of the future. They stress the argument that rather than being a crisis of absolute resource scarcity, the water challenge is one of management.[70] This is why, in their view, it will be resolved through 'virtual water' (embedded in traded goods), economic development and investment in infrastructure.[71] Yet the fear of interstate or even regional conflicts related to water scarcity is rather persistent. This is mainly due to three observations. Firstly, many of the 276 transboundary rivers flow between countries with a long history of (sometimes military) conflicts.[72] Secondly, many countries are heavily reliant upon the flow of freshwater from their upstream neighbours.[73] Finally, some states have already reached 'peak water' due to overexploitation, which will inevitably increase competition over the remaining (and often transboundary) freshwater resources.[74]

65 Quoted in Kreamer, 'The Past, Present, and Future of Water Conflict and International Security' at 91.

66 The Economist, 'South Asia's Water : Unquenchable Thirst' (19 November 2011) <http://www.economist.com/node/21538687>.

67 Ibid.

68 In 2,500 BC, the two Sumerian states of Lagash and Umma signed an agreement that resolved a violent dispute; see Postel and Wolf, 'Dehydrating Conflict' at 60.

69 TF Homer-Dixon, 'Environmental Scarcities and Violent Conflict: Evidence from Cases' (1994) *International Security*, 19, 5.

70 NP Gleditsch, 'Armed Conflict and the Environment: A Critique of the Literature' (1998) *Journal of Peace Research*, 35, 381.

71 T Allan, *The Middle East Water Question: Hydropolitics and the Global Economy* (I.B. Tauris 2002); T Allan, 'Global Trade: Balancing Existing and Future Regional Water Resource Deficits' in Brauch HG and others (eds), *Facing Global Environmental Change : Environmental, Human, Energy, Food, Health and Water Security Concepts* (Springer 2009); W Barnaby, 'Do Nations Go to War over Water?' (2009) *Nature*, 458, 282.

72 HPW Toset, NP Gleditsch and H Hegre, 'Shared Rivers and Interstate Conflict' (2000) *Political Geography*, 19, 971 at 971.

73 I van der Molen and A Hildering, 'Water: Cause for Conflict or Co-Operation?' (2005) *Journal on Science and World Affairs*, 1, 133 at 139.

74 PH Gleick and M Palaniappan, 'Peak Water Limits to Freshwater Withdrawal and Use' (2010) *Proceedings of the National Academy of Sciences of the United States of America*, 107, 11155.

While the academic debate has long been a bipolar one – discussing whether there is a clear link between scarcity of natural resources and violent conflict[75] – several studies have moved away from this simplistic approach and have tried to explain how the most powerful actor in a basin can impose its own policies on the weaker riparians due to their respective power asymmetries by focusing on the concept of 'hydro-hegemony'.[76] In any case, even if future conflicts over water are not likely to lead to fully fledged wars between riparian countries, early interaction between the states will help alleviate the water crisis. A discourse solely revolving around whether we will face 'water wars' in the future is not only incapable of comprehending the manifold challenges of the water crisis, but it also constitutes a 'red herring', which is distracting from the underlying issues. The fact that more than 3.5 million people die every single year because of poor water, sanitation and hygiene – far more than by all ongoing wars combined – clearly suggests the need for a wider approach to water security than the narrow military one.[77]

While often still applying violent conflict analogies, the human security imperative has been highlighted, among others, by the United Nations Development Programme (UNDP):

> The 1.8 million child deaths each year related to unclean water and poor sanitation dwarf the casualties associated with violent conflict. No act of terrorism generates economic devastation on the scale of the crisis in water and sanitation. Yet the issue barely registers on the international agenda.[78]

It has been estimated that by 2020, if the international community fails to effectively address global water insecurity, as many as 135 million preventable deaths could occur.[79] The apparent lack of willpower in addressing this global crisis has prompted warnings that the world is slowly moving towards a 'hydrocide'[80] – the 'deliberate murder of our water bodies'.[81]

75 See G Baechler, 'Environmental Degradation in the South as a Cause of Armed Conflict' in Carius A and Lietzmann KM (eds), *Environmental Change and Security – a European Perspective* (Springer 1999); C Rohloff, 'Conflict Research and Environmental Conflicts: Methodological Problems' in Carius A and Lietzmann KM (eds), *Environmental Change and Security – a European Perspective* (Springer 1999); Toset, Gleditsch and Hegre, 'Shared Rivers and Interstate Conflict'.

76 M Zeitoun and JA Allan, 'Applying Hegemony and Power Theory to Transboundary Water Analysis' (2008) *Water Policy*, 10, 3; M Zeitoun and A Jägerskog, *Influencing and Challenging Power Asymmetry in Transboundary Waters* (2009); M Zeitoun and JF Warner, 'Hydro-Hegemony : A Framework for Analysis of Trans-Boundary Water Conflicts' (2006) *Water Policy*, 8, 435.

77 CJ Schuster-Wallace and others, *Safe Water as the Key to Global Health* (United Nations University, International Network on Water, Environment and Health 2008) at 8.

78 United Nations Development Programme, Human Development Report 2006: *Beyond Scarcity: Power, Poverty and the Global Water Crisis* (Palgrave Macmillan 2006) at 3.

79 United Nations Environment Programme, *The Greening of Water Law : Managing Freshwater Resources for People and the Environment* (United Nations Environment Programme 2010) at 17.

80 First coined by J Lundqvist, 'Avert Looming Hydrocide' (1998) *Ambio*, 27, 428.

81 AK Gerlak and others, 'Hydrosolidarity and Beyond: Can Ethics and Equity Find a Place in Today's Water Resource Management?' (2011) *Water International*, 36, 251 at 257.

In addition to stressing the human security implications of the water crisis, it has to be acknowledged that conflict and cooperation always coexist – in terms of water interaction.[82] Not only does this observation limit the danger of alarmism; it also recognises that, while dissent between riparian states regarding the (re)allocation of their shared waters may not always pose a direct military threat, the transboundary mismanagement caused by the dissonances nevertheless has the potential to destabilise nation states in an already highly unstable world. Furthermore, the debate about cooperation *or* conflict over freshwater usually ignores the quality of cooperation and the different shades of conflict. Just as not all cooperation is inherently good, not every conflict is automatically bad. Too often, treaties manifest starkly inequitable situations (legalising the utilisation of freshwater which is inequitable); while at times it needs a situation of conflict (and thus renewed interest) for some underlying issues to actually be addressed. Hence, instead of focusing on the likelihood of military interstate conflicts, more and more scholars appreciate the fact that sharing transboundary waters equitably is a 'long war' we all need to fight.

While the role of the scaremonger is mainly played by the media,[83] the continuous talk of future 'water wars' is also being nourished by various political circles – making the claim more powerful and widely accepted.[84] It seems difficult to come to grips with the exact reasons for this apparent consensus, as each of the proponents of the water war hypothesis has its own selfish interest in keeping it alive. While for some ministries of defence, it may prove as a useful tool to safeguard a high level of financial resources (e.g., in the US),[85] others may try to counter a general status of confusion and lack of direction within the context of overall geopolitical decline (e.g., the UK).[86] In any case, these heavily biased processes of 'water security agenda setting' are being driven by powerful interest groups. While it can be frustrating at times, it is worthwhile to engage in the debate and try to convince the establishments that water security means much more than just the absence of war. The development of the security concept in general, portrayed in the previous section, helps to understand why choosing a wider perspective for framing water security is not only appropriate, but also inevitable.

82 M Zeitoun and N Mirumachi, 'Transboundary Water Interaction I: Reconsidering Conflict and Cooperation' (2008) *International Environmental Agreements: Politics, Law and Economics*, 8, 297; M Zeitoun, N Mirumachi and JF Warner, 'Transboundary Water Interaction II: The Influence of "Soft" Power' (2011) *International Environmental Agreements: Politics, Law and Economics*, 11, 159.

83 See, e.g., P Ponnudurai for Radio Free Asia, 'Water Wars Feared over Mekong' (30 September 2012) <http://www.rfa.org/english/east-asia-beat/mekong-09302012160353.html>.

84 National Intelligence Council, *Global Water Security : Intelligence Community Assessment* (Office of the Director of National Intelligence 2012).

85 R Floyd, *Security and the Environment: Securitisation Theory and US Environmental Security Policy* (Cambridge University Press 2010) at 84.

86 J Tomlinson, 'The Decline of the Empire and the Economic "Decline" of Britain' (2003) *Twentieth Century British History*, 14, 201 at 201.

2.2.2 The potential risks of the water security discourse

In recognising that the threat of 'water wars' is a political argument, mainly driven by the media, which often ignores the complexity of the issues involved in the transboundary water management, a different conceptual framework is needed to comprehend the global water crisis. Yet, this desperately needed change is difficult to achieve. Simply put, securitisation is a strategy for managing risk perceptions of stakeholders which aims at moving an issue to the top of the agenda in order to generate the political will needed to address it. Thus, in theory, a matter becomes a security issue when the securitising actor convinces the relevant audience that it poses an existential threat and can only be handled with exceptional effort.[87] While this would obviously support the political status of transboundary water issues, would it also automatically achieve a more peaceful management of the shared resource; or would it rather be a 'regrettable detour to a virtual blind-alley'?[88]

Certainly, there are risks involved in the securitisation of water. One is that in being at the core of a variety of other crises, and thus touching a myriad of issues on several policy levels, it might always be a highly ambiguous concept – one which will raise different expectations depending on who employs it. As a result, it could be condemned to be nothing more than an empty shell – largely meaningless, without triggering any useful debate. However, the main argument of opponents of the concept is that the 'security' component may bring up discursive absolutes which are perceived to be 'non-negotiable' between the parties; ultimately promoting disparities between riparians and enhancing 'nationalistic feelings'.[89] Egypt, for instance, appears to be following this path in the Nile basin by slowing down the negotiation process of the Cooperative Framework Agreement (CFA),[90] arguing that the provision on water security (Article 14) should focus on historical water rights and uses – which have

87 See B Buzan, O Wæver and J de Wilde, *Security: A New Framework for Analysis* (Lynne Rienner Publishers 1998).

88 DZ Mekonnen, 'The Nile Basin Cooperative Framework Agreement Negotiations and the Adoption of a "Water Security" Paradigm: Flight into Obscurity or a Logical Cul-De-Sac?' (2010) *European Journal of International Law*, 21, 421 at 421.

89 A Kibaroglu, AD Brouma and M Erdem, 'Transboundary Water Issues in the Euphrates-Tigris River Basin: Some Methodological Approaches and Opportunities for Cooperation' in Jansky L, Nakayama M and Pachova NI (eds), *International Water Security: Domestic Threats and Opportunities* (United Nations University Press 2008) at 231.

90 The provision on water security in the Draft Cooperative Framework Agreement [on file with the author] (Art 14) as formulated in the minutes of the fifteenth Nile-COM meeting (25 June 2007) reads: 'Having due regard for the provision of Articles 4 and 5, Nile Basin states recognize the vital importance of water security to each of them. The States also recognize that cooperative management and development of the waters of the Nile River System will facilitate achievement of water security and other benefits. Nile Basin states therefore, agree, in a spirit of cooperation: (a) to work together to ensure that all States achieve and sustain water security; (b) not to significantly affect the water security of any other Nile Basin State.'

been established under a legal framework based on the colonial legacy.[91] It seems like Egypt is trying to make this legacy indelible by reinforcing its right to 75 per cent of the Nile's waters under the cover of 'water security'. In doing so, it completely disregards that Ethiopia, which, due to the fact that it was never under any colonial rule, was not involved in either the 1992 or 1959 agreement, contributes nearly 85 per cent of the Nile waters.[92] While this is no doubt an example of how the concept can be misinterpreted, it should not be used as an argument to disregard it in general. Not only is the bargaining tool employed by Egypt incompatible with the fundamental basis of international water law, it also is in conflict with the contemporary understanding of security. Egypt has applied a whole arsenal of tactics not just to maintain the control over the freshwater resource, but also to be proactive in challenging the increase in power of its upstream riparians.[93] Hence, the way in which Egypt tried to include the water security discussion was a rather poor attempt to sell old wine in new bottles. One has to be aware that, after all, water security can only be what states make of it – which is even more true in the case of a hydro-hegemon like Egypt.[94]

Another interesting example of how states use the water security paradigm to their national security advantage is the US, where the need for an integrated international water strategy to avert conflicts overseas and foster cooperation has long been identified.[95] The US Water Partnership, which was launched on World Water Day 2012, is trying to give a fresh impetus to this endeavour.[96] Its declared aim is to bring together the private sector, NGOs, academia, civil society and the government to 'unite and mobilize [the] "best of U.S." expertise, resources and ingenuity to address water challenges around the globe, with a special focus on developing countries where needs are greatest'.[97] The start of the initiative was complemented by the release of the (unclassified) National Intelligence Council report on 'global water security', which, overall, is a positive contribution to understanding the complex and interrelated issues of the

91 DZ Mekonnen, 'Between the Scylla of Water Security and Charybdis of Benefit Sharing: The Nile Basin Cooperative Framework Agreement – Failed or Just Teetering on the Brink?' (2011) *Göttingen Journal of International Law*, 3, 345 at 351; P Wouters and R Moynihan, 'Water Security: Legal Frameworks and the UN Watercourses Convention' in Loures FR and Rieu-Clarke A (eds), *The UN Watercourses Convention in Force : Strengthening International Law for Transboundary Water Management* (Earthscan 2013) at 342.

92 Mekonnen, 'Between the Scylla of Water Security and Charybdis of Benefit Sharing: The Nile Basin Cooperative Framework Agreement – Failed or Just Teetering on the Brink?' at 61.

93 AE Cascão, 'Ethiopia – Challenges to Egyptian Hegemony in the Nile Basin' (2008) *Water Policy*, 10, 13 at 19.

94 See also Julien, 'Hydropolitics Is What Societies Make of It (or Why We Need a Constructivist Approach to the Geopolitics of Water)'.

95 See ER Peterson and R Posner, *Global Water Futures : A Roadmap for Future U.S. Policy* (Center for Strategic and International Studies 2008).

96 For more information, see <http://uswaterpartnership.org/>.

97 US Water Partnership, 'Best of U.S. Solutions are Available' (22 March 2012) <http://uswaterpartnership.org/>.

global water crisis.[98] The report involved consultations across government in addition to gathering expert opinions from scholars and practitioners from various sectors. It focused on seven basins which it considers to be posing potential risks to US security interests: the Amu Darya, Brahmaputra, Indus, Jordan, Mekong, Nile and Tigris-Euphrates.

According to the report, the competition for increasingly scarce freshwater resources will fuel instability in regions such as the Middle East and Asia, which are of particular importance to US national security. While a fully fledged war on water is considered unlikely in the near future, 'water in shared basins will increasingly be used as leverage; the use of water as a weapon or to further terrorist objectives also will become more likely beyond 10 years'.[99] Thus, the report acknowledges that the future may not look like the past beyond the next decade, when the intense pressure on water resources will put institutional arrangements for transboundary water sharing and resolving disputes to the test. The report did not surprise with any revolutionary findings on the water crisis and its link to security issues:

> Water shortages, poor water quality, and floods by themselves are unlikely to result in state failure. However, water problems – when combined with poverty, social tensions, environmental degradation, ineffectual leadership, and weak political institutions – contribute to social disruptions that can result in state failure.[100]

The assessment also acknowledged the relevance of international water law, stating that

> . . . many nations . . . would benefit from new or updated international agreements. Effective water agreements encourage greater cooperation and lessen the risk of regional conflicts. Today, water basin agreements often do not exist or are inadequate . . . Shortcomings in water basin agreements often further enable stronger states to preserve their influence over weaker states.[101]

It goes on in acknowledging that the UN Watercourses Convention has been used as 'the foundation for most nations regarding the governance of international transboundary water resources', but then misinterprets the Convention by claiming that due to the fact that it only offers 'general guidance' to states sharing a river basin, its 'largely ineffective practical enforcement mechanisms and a lack of international ratification limit its effectiveness'.[102]

98 National Intelligence Council, Global Water Security : Intelligence Community Assessment.
99 Ibid. at 3.
100 Ibid.
101 Ibid. at 10.
102 Ibid. at 11.

The report also makes an attempt at evaluating the management capacity – defined as 'the strength and resilience of institutional factors, such as treaties and river basin organisations that can provide stability, increase cooperation, and mitigate political grievances over water' – of the seven river basins. The assessment rates the management capacity in the Amu Darya and the Brahmaputra as 'inadequate', in the Mekong, the Tigris-Euphrates and the Nile as 'limited', and in the Indus and the Jordan as 'moderate'.[103]

It comes as no surprise that, by definition of the report, the authors adopt a US security perspective:

> . . . many countries important to the United States will experience water problems—shortages, poor water quality, or floods—that will risk instability and state failure, increase regional tensions, and distract them from working with the United States on important US policy objectives'.[104]

Hillary R. Clinton, former US Secretary of State, called the study 'a landmark document that puts water security in its rightful place as part of national security'.[105] The National Intelligence Council does not try to hide the fact that one of the main reasons for the analysis and recommendations was to pave the way for the US to lead in water security issues around the globe and 'forestalling other actors from achieving the same influence at US expense'.[106] Since this approach strictly follows US national security interests, the outcome of the engagement can be either a push for change in transboundary water cooperation or the manifestation of the hegemonic structures in the respective basin – solely depending on US policy interests. Hence, the US Water Partnership is a perfect example of how states try to use the concept of water security to bolster their national influence – at times even overseas. While this is nothing new, as power games have been played under the guise of other concepts before, one has to closely watch the impact it has on the transboundary water cooperation of the river basins it regards as critical, as imported perceptions are not always compatible with the situations on the ground. Since the National Intelligence Council, by law, cannot make policy recommendations, it will be interesting to see what actions the US Water Partnership will take, and how the initiative will shape up operationally. This will be critical for the impact the US perception of water security can have in the identified transboundary water hot spots.

103 Ibid. at V.

104 Ibid. at 1.

105 HR Clinton, 'Remarks in Honor of World Water Day' (22 March 2012) <http://www.state.gov/secretary/rm/2012/03/186640.htm>.

106 Office of the Director of National Intelligence, ODNI News Release No. 4-12, 'ODNI Releases Assessment on Global Water Security' (22 March 2012) <http://www.dni.gov/press_releases/ODNI%20Releases%20Global%20Water%20Security%20ICA.pdf>.

2.2.3 A contemporary definition of water security

Against this backdrop of a present-day understanding of 'security' and with the global water crisis in mind, the task now is to define the term 'water security'. This truly is a challenging endeavour, given the fact that today the concept is 'a more complex matter than it was when the term meant only a firm entitlement to a fixed allocation protected by the courts, other tribunals or diplomatic pressure'.[107] Current literature from various backgrounds offers a broad range of definitions:

> Water security is the availability of freshwater in the right quantity and quality, at the right times, for dependent systems.[108]

> Water security, at any level from the household to the global, means that every person has access to enough safe water at affordable cost to lead a clean, healthy and productive life, while ensuring that the natural environment is protected and enhanced.[109]

> [Water security is] linked to a safe water supply and sanitation, water for food production, hydrosolidarity between those living upstream and those living downstream in a river basin and water pollution avoidance, so that the water in aquifers and rivers remains useable, i.e. not too polluted for use for water supply, industrial production, agricultural use or the protection of biodiversity, wetlands, and aquatic systems in rivers and coastal waters.[110]

> [Water security is] adequate protection from water-related disasters and diseases and access to sufficient quantity and quality of water, at affordable cost, to meet the basic food, energy and other needs essential for leading a healthy and productive life without compromising the sustainability of vital ecosystems.[111]

> [Water security is] the reliable availability of an acceptable quantity and quality of water for health, livelihoods and production, coupled with an acceptable level of water-related risks.[112]

107 D Tarlock, 'Water Security, Fear Mitigation and International Water Law' (2008) *Hamline Law Review*, 31, 704 at 706.

108 JD Petersen-Perlman and others, 'Case Studies on Water Security: Analysis of System Complexity and the Role of Institutions' (2012) *Journal of Contemporary Water Research & Education*, 149, 4 at 4.

109 Global Water Partnership, *Towards Water Security: A Framework for Action* (Global Water Partnership 2000) at 12.

110 M Falkenmark, 'The Greatest Water Problem: The Inability to Link Environmental Security, Water Security and Food Security' (2001) *Water Resources Development*, 17, 539 at 553.

111 L Jansky, M Nakayama and NI Pachova, 'Introduction: From Domestic to International Water Security' in Jansky L, Nakayama M and Pachova NI (eds), *International Water Security: Domestic Threats and Opportunities* (United Nations University Press 2008) at 1.

112 D Grey and CW Sadoff, 'Sink or Swim? Water Security for Growth and Development' (2007) *Water Policy*, 9, 545 at 549.

[T]he notion of water security can be understood as 'the state of having secure access to water; the assured freedom from poverty of, or want for, water for life.[113]

[W]ater security is about ensuring that every person has reliable access to enough safe water at an affordable price to lead a healthy, dignified and productive life, while maintaining the ecological systems that provide water and also depend on water.[114]

In an attempt to capture these constantly evolving definitions, UN-Water recently defined water security as:

The capacity of a population to safeguard sustainable access to adequate quantities of acceptable quality water for sustaining livelihoods, human well-being, and socio-economic development, for ensuring protection against water-borne pollution and water-related disasters, and for preserving ecosystems in a climate of peace and political stability.[115]

UN-Water is hopeful that this working definition can serve as a common framework and starting point for dialogue on water security within the vast system of the United Nations; and that it may help to better consolidate the work of UN-Water and its various partners.

What becomes obvious when going through these definitions, and drawing upon the previous discussion in this chapter, is that several of them followed the lines of the general security debate and portray water security at the interface of human security and development. While this clearly points towards a convergence of the two agendas, it is unreasonable to believe that this is also evidence of a decline in the importance of water security in the arena of international relations.[116] However, since none of these definitions fully comprehend the complex challenge water insecurity is posing to the international

113 P Wouters, 'Water Security: What Role for International Water Law?' in Doddle F (ed.), *Human and Environmental Security: An Agenda for Change* (Earthscan 2005) at 168.

114 United Nations Development Programme, *Human Development Report 2006: Beyond Scarcity: Power, Poverty and the Global Water Crisis* at 3.

115 UN-Water, *Water Security and the Global Water Agenda : A UN-Water Analytical Brief* (United Nations University 2013) at 1. This definition of water security is based on the one provided in UNESCO's International Hydrological Programme's (IHP) 20th session of the Intergovernmental Council (4–7 June 2012): (Draft) Strategic Plan of the Eighth Phase of IHP (IHP-VIII, 2014–2021), available at <http://unesdoc.unesco.org/images/0021/002164/216434E.pdf>, which defines water security as 'the capacity of a population to safeguard access to adequate quantities of water of acceptable quality for sustaining human and ecosystem health on a watershed basis, and to ensure efficient protection of life and property against water related hazards – floods, landslides, land subsidence, and droughts'.

116 Contrary to the argument of J Allouche, A Nicol and L Mehta, 'Water Security: Towards the Human Securitization of Water?' (2011) *Whitehead Journal of Diplomacy and International Relations*, 12, 153 at 166.

community; or are too vague to carry any weight in deriving rules and policies from them, they play into the hands of the critics of the concept. Here, lessons have to be drawn from the human security discourse, which opponents have always described as a superfluous exercise, since 'everyone is for it, but few people have a clear idea of what it means.'[117]

Considering the wide scope water security has to cover, is it even possible to phrase it in a way which is analytically useful? The key task is to find a definition which is broad enough to fully acknowledge the complexity of the water crisis, while at the same time providing useful avenues of approaches for effectively addressing water insecurity – making the whole exercise worthwhile. While a definition is generally regarded as most useful to policy makers when it presents a single and precise interpretation, experts should avoid oversimplification in cases as complex and multi-layered as water security.[118] Here, the interlinkages between different layers and other crises are consistently being overlooked, despite the fact that sustainable freshwater management is strengthening a whole web of securities. For instance, a situation of acute water scarcity (caused by drought or mismanagement) in a developing country which is highly dependent on agriculture would certainly compromise human security (increasing poverty and affecting health), food security (domestic and, potentially, of food-importing countries), economic security (decrease in (not only) agricultural output), energy security (diminishing availability of water for production of electricity) and environmental security (putting ecosystems under stress and causing biodiversity loss) – at the local, regional and international level. Hence, an unambiguous definition, applicable to each and every instance of water insecurity, is simply elusive, and thus cannot be a prerequisite for tackling the world water crisis.

What is needed, however, is a common understanding of what water security means and, even more importantly, how we should move ahead in order to prevent the crisis getting out of hand. This is why the following definition of water security is proposed here:

> A community is water secure when it has sustainable access to freshwater of sufficient quantity and quality, or to the benefits derived therefrom, and the ability to minimise water-related risk and its various repercussions to an acceptable level – without compromising the supporting ecosystems.

This definition draws from both the widening and deepening process of the general security debate; while, at the same time, acknowledging the complexity of the water crisis. Accordingly, the definition has several advantages over previous ones.

117 Comparing the issues of defining 'human security' to the ones of defining 'sustainable development'; R Paris, 'Human Security: Paradigm Shift or Hot Air?' (2001) *International Security*, 26, 87 at 88.

118 See A Stirling, 'Keep It Complex' (2010) *Nature*, 468, 1029.

Firstly, by looking at 'communities', it is perfectly scalable to the level one wants to look at water security – local, national, international, regional, or even global. It also does justice to the fact that several levels might overlap, which in water resources management is the rule rather than the exception.

Secondly, by including the 'benefits derived' from the access to freshwater and the repercussions of water-related risks, the true complexity of the water crisis is being pulled into play. Not only are we looking at access to and threats from the resource water, but also the opportunities and issues linked (directly or indirectly) to it. Here, concepts such as virtual water and water footprint, and challenges such as coping with rapid urbanisation, changing migration patterns and 'land grabs'[119] come to mind.

Finally, by containing undetermined parameters such as 'sufficient quantity and quality of freshwater' and 'acceptable level of water-related risk and repercussions', the definition is giving the respective community the freedom of how to actually implement the concept of water security – geared to its own needs, capacities and social preferences. The open questions are important in transforming theory into action and help steering the debate within community as to which water security is being envisioned. The concept has to be perceived as a dynamic one, which will certainly be interpreted differently in different parts of the world – since it mirrors geographic, social, economic and political factors – and might change over time as several of these factors tend to change as well.[120] While opponents of the conceptualisation of water security might argue that a rather imprecise definition blurs the clear boundaries of security studies and opens it up to rather difficult questions about the security concept in general, it has to be stressed that the conceptual complexity has always been inherent to the debate about security; and thus renders multifariousness not only unavoidable, but even useful.[121] Rather than being a mere (constricting) explanation of the term 'water security', it aims at providing a platform for stimulating discourse.

2.3 Water security through a legal lens

The previous analysis has demonstrated that following a contemporary path of security, rather than applying the orthodox state-centred and military-focused

119 See, e.g., L Cotula and others, *Land Grab or Development Opportunity? Agricultural Investment and International Land Deals in Africa* (IIED; FAO; IFAD 2009); M Görgen and others, *Foreign Direct Investment (FDI) in Land in Developing Countries* (GTZ 2009); M Kugelman and SL Levenstein (eds), *Land Grab? The Race for the World's Farmland* (Woodrow Wilson International Center for Scholars 2009); J Mosley, *Peace, Bread and Land: Agricultural Investments in Ethiopia and the Sudans* (Chatham House 2012); J von Braun and R Meinzen-Dick, '"Land Grabbing" by Foreign Investors in Developing Countries: Risks and Opportunities' (2009) *International Food Policy Research Institute Policy Brief*, 13.

120 D Grey and CW Sadoff, *Water Resources, Growth and Development: A Working Paper for Discussion* (The World Bank 2005) at 7.

121 von Tigerstrom, *Human Security and International Law* at 35.

approach, is the only way to overcome the concerns about securitising water. As discussed, the perception of the concept has changed dramatically since it is no longer perceived as necessary for there to be a violent conflict over scarce resources or a military threat to the sovereignty of a state to affect the security and development of nations.[122] Yet, this perception has to be supported by a system of values which direct societies; and law must play a central role in supporting those values. During a recent High-Level Meeting, the UN General Assembly reminded us that 'our collective response to the challenges and opportunities arising from the many complex political, social and economic transformations before us must be guided by the rule of law'.[123]

International law is a particularly useful tool in promoting water security, as it: (1) defines and identifies the legal rights and obligations regarding the use of water and provides the prescriptive parameters for the management of the resource, (2) provides tools for ensuring the continuous integrity of the regime (including dispute prevention and settlement), and (3) allows for modifications of the existing regime, in order to be able to accommodate change.[124] By establishing the substantive and procedural 'rules of the game', international law aims to fulfil its primary function to promote peaceful relations between states and thus helps to prevent conflicts over transboundary watercourses.[125] While law should not be considered the only possible tool for addressing issues of water security, since science and policy play important roles,[126] owing to the fact that transboundary freshwater cooperation is largely an issue of (re)allocation, the importance of a transparent and credible legal framework cannot be overlooked.[127] Only through international law can water security move away from being merely employed as political rhetoric and obtain some normative impact.

This implies that the water security concept can only be of use in addressing the global water crisis if it is backed by a legal framework which supports the transformation of society towards the contemporary perception of security. The calls for 'de-securitising' water are being met with approval mainly

122 Brauch, 'Introduction: Globalization and Environmental Challenges: Reconceptualizing Security in the 21st Century' at 27; RH Ullman, 'Redefining Security' (1983) *International Security*, 8, 129 at 129.

123 UN General Assembly, Sixty-seventh Session, 3rd Plenary Meeting (24 September 2012) UN Doc A/RES/67/1, available at <http://unrol.org/files/Declaration%20HLM_A%20RES%2067%201.pdf>.

124 P Wouters, 'The Relevance and Role of Water Law in the Sustainable Development of Freshwater : From "Hydrosovereignty" to "Hydrosolidarity"' (2000) *Water International*, 25, 202 at 203; Wouters, Vinogradov and Magsig, 'Water Security, Hydrosolidarity and International Law: A River Runs through It . . .' at 107.

125 WJ Cosgrove, *Water Security and Peace: A Synthesis of Studies Prepared under the PCCP-Water for Peace Process* (UNESCO 2003) at 25.

126 See E Lopez-Gunn and MR Llamas, 'Re-Thinking Water Scarcity: Can Science and Technology Solve the Global Water Crisis?' (2008) *Natural Resources Forum*, 32, 228.

127 Wouters, Vinogradov and Magsig, 'Water Security, Hydrosolidarity and International Law: A River Runs through It . . .' at 107.

because of the fear that it allows issues of freshwater cooperation to be detached from any legal process trying to level the playing field. Yet, as this study will show, this does not have to be the case. International water law can be used and developed further in order to fully comprehend the advanced conception of security, which has emerged in recent years. Water insecurity is already the reality in many places of the world. While some states abuse the desperate situations they are in for pushing nationalistic agendas forward – defining water security as national security issue – international law can counter this movement. If guided by a framework which can bring about a more equitable way of transboundary water resources management, the concept of water security – as defined above – can play the important role of the long-yearned-for change agent. By considering securitisation as a reflexive, rule-altering process, it might even provide relevant insights into the transformation and development of general international law.[128]

The next chapter will deal with this issue by analysing international water law through the security lens. Not only will it show that the concept of water security actually has something new to offer in terms of legal analysis, it will also indicate that using it as an operational methodology for issues of transboundary water cooperation is beneficial. The two main questions arising in this exercise are: (1) what are the key components of water security relevant to international water law? and (2) what are the shortcomings of the current legal system?

128 See also MC Kettemann, 'The Conceptual Debate on Human Security and Its Relevance for the Development of International Law' (2006) *Human Security Perspectives*, 1, 39.

3 International law in the water security discourse

3.1 The core elements of water security

After having conceptualised water security in the previous chapter, the task now is to operationalise it. Since it is an interstitial concept, it has to be disaggregated to allow for thorough analysis from a legal perspective. In order to do so, a methodology has to be designed which teases out the core elements of water security which have to be addressed by international law. Recalling the definition of water security suggested in this book:

> . . . [a] community is water secure when it has sustainable access to freshwater of sufficient quantity and quality, or to the benefits derived therefrom; and the ability to minimise water-related risk and its various repercussions to an acceptable level – without compromising the supporting ecosystems,

a framework for operationalising water security consisting of the following four parameters (1) availability, (2) access, (3) adaptability and (4) ambit is being proposed here. This structure will provide the means for revealing the strengths and weaknesses of the current legal architecture and serve as a basis for recommendations for the future development of international water law. Ultimately, this exercise will also unfold the fundamental conceptual challenges of linking the notion of water security with public international law.

3.1.1 Availability

'Availability' relates to issues of water quantity as well as quality. Primarily, this element deals with the actual management of the resource as such – including its control and protection. While the total usable water existing on the planet is – in theory – more than enough to satisfy all human and environmental requirements,[1] the problem, however, is that water is not always available in sufficient amounts and of sufficient quality at the right time and location needed.

1 C Vörösmarty, C Lévêque and C Revenga, 'Fresh Water' in Hassan R, Scholes R and Ash N (eds), *Ecosystems and Human Well-Being : Current State and Trends* (Island Press 2005) at 171.

Over the last two centuries, population grew by a factor of four, while the amount of freshwater withdrawal increased fifteenfold.[2] Between 1960 and 2000 alone, global freshwater use increased at a rate of about 20 per cent per decade, with significant regional differences due to diverse ranges of socio-economic development.[3] Acknowledging that the world population is predicted to grow from 7 billion to more than 9 billion by 2050,[4] the magnitude of the future pressure on the world's freshwater resources becomes obvious (see Figure 3.1).

In terms of water quantity, the production of food is by far the biggest challenge for freshwater management, as agriculture accounts for around 70 per cent of global freshwater withdrawals and more than 90 per cent of its consumptive use.[5] Driven by the demand for irrigation, overall withdrawals across the Middle East and North Africa (MENA) region for instance constitute around 120 per cent of renewable accessible supplies, which means that food production already relies on non-renewable water resources here.[6] The changing diets in emerging economies add even more pressure to the availability of freshwater by moving towards livestock and horticultural products at the expense of staples.[7]

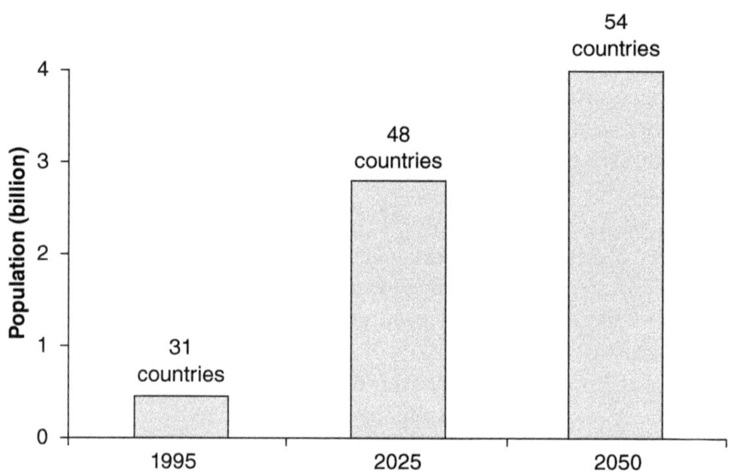

Figure 3.1 Population in water-scarce and water-stressed countries

Source: Vital Water Graphics, UNEP. http://www.unep.org/dewa/vitalwater/article141.html

2 Ibid. at 174.

3 C Ringler and others, 'Water and Food Security under Global Change' in Ringler C, Biswas AK and Cline SA (eds), *Global Change : Impacts on Water and Food Security* (Springer 2009) at 4.

4 United Nations Department of Economic and Social Affairs, *World Population Prospects: The 2010 Revision: Highlights and Advance Tables* (United Nations 2011) at xiii.

5 *FAO Land and Water Division, Coping with Water Scarcity: An Action Framework for Agriculture and Food Security* (FAO 2012) at 2.

6 Vörösmarty, Lévêque and Revenga, 'Fresh Water' at 174.

7 H Turral, J Burke and J-M Faurès, *Climate Change, Water and Food Security* (FAO 2011) at 77.

Another factor determining our water future is the increasing demand for energy, as water needs for the production of energy are set to grow at twice the rate of energy demand.[8] The reason for energy becoming an even thirstier resource is that water is key to its production – starting already with the extraction of fossil fuels. The International Energy Agency (IEA) projects a rise in energy-related water consumption of 85 per cent over the period to 2035, mainly reflecting the shift towards more water-intensive power generation (e.g., shale gas) and the expanding production of biofuels.[9] In addition, water management – from the withdrawal (especially for lifting groundwater and desalination), over the transport, to the treatment of wastewater – is also a highly energy-intensive business.[10] The need to meet a 60 per cent increase in demand for energy over the next thirty years, combined with the goals set forth in many states' climate change policy, is already making the expanding production of biofuels and increasing hydropower critical parts of the 'green economy' puzzle.[11] Since almost all of these uses not only have an effect on quantity but also quality, the need to maintain the natural integrity of the water body – by requiring environmental flows or toughening pollution control mechanisms – is being addressed under 'availability' as well.[12] Of particular concern here is, again, the water-food-energy nexus. Since water is used in various ways along the stages of fossil-fuel extraction and processing, there are also several ways in which water is regularly being contaminated with a wide variety of toxic pollutants.[13] Further, agriculture is not only a major user of water resources worldwide; it is also one of their biggest polluters due to the amounts of pesticides and fertilisers used in the production of food.[14]

Finally, the role of demand management should not be overlooked at the international level. Only with an approach addressing both demand and supply management, will we be able to achieve water security. The impacts of global

8 International Energy Agency, *World Energy Outlook 2012* (International Energy Agency 2012) at 7.

9 Ibid.

10 United Nations World Water Assessment Programme, *The United Nations World Water Development Report 4: Managing Water under Uncertainty and Risk, vol. 1* (UNESCO 2012) at 25.

11 See R Dominguez-Faus and others, 'The Water Footprint of Biofuels: A Drink or Drive Issue?' (2009) *Environmental Science & Technology*, 43, 3005; RF Service, 'Another Biofuels Drawback: The Demand for Irrigation' (2009) *Science*, 326, 516; C de Fraiture, M Giordano and Y Liao, 'Biofuels and Implications for Agricultural Water Use: Blue Impacts of Green Energy' (2008) *Water Policy*, 10, 67; MM Rahaman, 'Hydropower Ambitions of South Asian Nations and China: Ganges and Brahmaputra Rivers Basins' (2012) *International Journal of Sustainable Society*, 4, 131; MA Zentner, 'Assessing the Design of International Water Supply and Hydropower Arrangements for Managing Certain Climate Change Scenarios' (PhD, Oregon State University, 2010).

12 A Forslund and others, 'Securing Water for Ecosystems and Human Well-Being: The Importance of Environmental Flows' (2009) 24 Swedish Water House Report; M Palaniappan and PH Gleick, 'Peak Water' in Gleick PH and others (eds), *The World's Water 2008-2009* (Island Press 2009).

13 L Allen and others, 'Fossil Fuels and Water Quality' in Gleick PH and others (eds), *The World's Water Volume 7: The Biennial Report on Freshwater Resources* (Island Press 2011) at 73.

14 Organisation for Economic Co-operation and Development, *Better Policies for Development: Recommendations for Policy Coherence* (OECD Publishing 2011) at 40.

population growth, industrialisation and climate change have already caused us to exceed the limit of ecological sustainable abstraction of water for about one-third of the global population; this number will very likely rise to about half by 2030.[15] While the economic side often takes centre stage in the debate about future development paths, neglecting the pressing concerns of freshwater availability (sufficient quantity and quality) will backfire sooner rather than later.

3.1.2 Access

At the centre of the water security debate is the element of 'access', which describes the right to make use of the shared resource. It covers a broad spectrum of concerns across the increasing diversity and growing number of users and uses with regard to matters of (re)allocation. While the availability of water is of concern for some regions, physical scarcity is only one aspect of the water crisis. At the heart of the challenge are issues of political power and inequality.[16] Already, due to the uneven distribution of safe freshwater in space and time, only 15 per cent of the world's population lives with relative water abundance, while the majority has to cope with at least moderate water stress.[17]

Rapid economic development (in some places) and global population growth causes the water footprint of some regions to soar, which turns the competition for the vital but limited water resources into a serious security concern. It is the component 'access' which links the 'water security' concept to resource conflicts scholarship, as it is argued that disagreements over the allocation of water resources are causing fears over military conflicts to rise.[18] While often contradictory in their conclusions (see the previous chapter), several studies emphasised the important role of frameworks which are capable of establishing a system of determining the rules of the game.[19] The discrepancy between the surging increase in demand for freshwater with sufficient quality and its declining availability, the uneven distribution of resources and unilateral development of water projects regularly cause disruptions in co-riparian relations.[20] One example is the fact that many potential hydropower sites are situated on transboundary watercourses – and thus provide important opportunities for increased cooperation on issues of shared freshwater management between the riparian states.[21]

15 United Nations World Water Assessment Programme, *The United Nations World Water Development Report 4 : Knowledge Base*, vol. 2 (UNESCO 2012) 508.

16 United Nations Development Programme, *Human Development Report 2006: Beyond Scarcity: Power, Poverty and the Global Water Crisis* (Palgrave Macmillan 2006) at 2.

17 Vörösmarty, Lévêque and Revenga, 'Fresh Water' at 167.

18 B Chellaney, *From Arms Racing to 'Dam Racing' in Asia: How to Contain the Geopolitical Risks of the Dam-Building Competition* (Transatlantic Academy 2012) at 1.

19 See, e.g., MF Giordano, MA Giordano and TW Aaron, 'International Resource Conflict and Mitigation' (2005) *Journal of Peace Research*, 42, 47 at 53.

20 B-O Magsig, 'Rising to the Challenge of Water Security: International (Water) Law in Need of Refinement' (2012) *International Journal of Sustainable Society*, 4, 28 at 29.

21 See United Nations World Water Assessment Programme, *The United Nations World Water Development Report 4: Managing Water under Uncertainty and Risk* 32.

Hence, legal and institutional responses to the allocation of transboundary waters are essential to ensuring long-term water security.[22] In order to achieve this, the rules governing the (re)allocation of water have to be perceived as fair by all parties involved. Only if the playing field is truly levelled, will transboundary water cooperation be able to contribute towards a more sustainable common water security.

3.1.3 Adaptability

Considering that, in the majority of cases, the most important variable to the successful sharing of freshwater resources is the resilience of the legal and policy frameworks (including institutions) that govern water management, rather than absolute water scarcity,[23] a future-proof structure for transboundary watercourses has to include a fair amount of flexibility. This is vital for ensuring 'adaptability' in order to be able to address changing conditions in supply and demand – while still providing for some level of predictability. Legal certainty – a legal order which effectively attributes responsibility to others as well as delineates the limits of such responsibility – is a prerequisite if international security is to be provided for by law.[24]

Since many states depend on the waters from shared basins, they need certainty with regards to the quantities and qualities of the water they are entitled to use and required to provide – and this must take into account the reality of the ever-changing interplay between supply and demand.[25] Understanding the temporal and spatial distribution and flux of water is key for managing the resource efficiently, distinguishing it considerably from the management of any other natural resource. Hence, water-resource management plans and policies must take this variability into account in order to be viable in the long term.[26] At the same time, law has to provide for 'security of expectations' – which can be considered as one of its main functions, and proves to be crucial within transboundary water management and constantly changing societal, political and environmental needs.[27] What makes this 'legal challenge' even more

22 Leadership Group on Water Security in Asia, *Asia's Next Challenge: Securing the Region's Water Future* (Asia Society 2009) at 18.

23 G Eckstein, 'Water Scarcity, Conflict, and Security in a Climate Change World: Challenges and Opportunities for International Law and Policy' (2009) *Wisconsin International Law Journal*, 27, 409; AT Wolf, 'Troubled Waters: Conflict and Cooperation over Shared Rivers' (2009) World Politics Review 3 at 5.

24 P T Stoll, 'Responsibility, Sovereignty and Cooperation – Reflections on the "Responsibility to Protect"' in König D and others (eds), *International Law Today: New Challenges and the Need for Reform?* (Springer 2008) at 16.

25 See Magsig, 'Rising to the Challenge of Water Security: International (Water) Law in Need of Refinement'.

26 United Nations World Water Assessment Programme, *The United Nations World Water Development Report 4: Managing Water under Uncertainty and Risk* at 75.

27 M Bothe, 'Security in International Law since 1990' in Brauch HG and others (eds), *Globalization and Environmental Challenges: Reconceptualizing Security in the 21st Century* (Springer 2008).

difficult to address is the fact that the impacts of climate change, population growth and economic development are all uncertain variables which have a considerable impact on transboundary water cooperation.

Just looking at climate change makes this dilemma quite clear, as it is an extremely complex issue with several dimensions, dynamic feedbacks and interactions between different impacts.[28] Further, drawing a universally valid picture about the impacts of climate change is problematic, since some of them only occur indirectly, different ecosystems and communities may not be equally affected by the changing climate and their respective degree of adaptability may vary as well. In theory, global warming leads to increased evaporation over oceans coupled to an increase in continental precipitation, which finally leads to an increase of the global continental river runoff.[29] Yet, in most regions of the world, the climatic changes will actually increase the demand for irrigation, due to a combination of a decrease in rainfall and an increase of evaporation caused by the warmer temperatures.[30]

Besides the actual changes in water availability, the magnitude of uncertainty and the complexity of the science of global climate change pose unique challenges for resource allocation and risk management.[31] Uncertainty refers to 'a situation in which there is not a unique and complete understanding of the system to be managed' and includes epistemic uncertainty (the imperfect knowledge), ontological uncertainty (variability and unpredictability inherent in a system) and ambiguity (resulting from 'the simultaneous presence of multiple frames of reference about a certain phenomenon') – all increasing the potential of leading to multiple interpretations of a specific issue.[32] Since the ultimate aim of (transboundary) water management is to allocate the resource in a way which allows for maximising the benefits for *all* users, the affected stakeholders must be able to predict the future supply of and demand for freshwater – ideally on a seasonal basis. In the past, this has been accomplished by using historical records, which have become more and more unreliable as the uncertainties of global warming emerged.[33] Projections on future climate depend on various speculative factors like the trend of greenhouse gas (GHG) emissions and the precise effects of these emissions in the atmosphere. Hence, climate forecasts and their implied impacts are highly scenario-dependent.[34]

28 See, e.g., A Iglesias and others, 'Challenges to Manage the Risk of Water Scarcity and Climate Change in the Mediterranean' (2007) *Water Resources Management*, 21, 775.

29 D Labat and others, 'Evidence for Global Runoff Increase Related to Climate Warming' (2004) *Advances in Water Resources*, 27, 631 at 641.

30 BC Bates and others, *Climate Change and Water: Technical Paper of the Intergovernmental Panel on Climate Change* (Intergovernmental Panel on Climate Change 2008) at 60.

31 D Tarlock, 'Now, Think Again About Adaptation' (1992) *Arizona Journal of International and Comparative Law*, 9, 169 at 169.

32 M Brugnach and others, 'Toward a Relational Concept of Uncertainty: About Knowing Too Little, Knowing Too Differently, and Accepting Not to Know' (2008) *Ecology and Society*, 13, 30 at 33.

33 SE Draper and JE Kundell, 'Impact of Climate Change on Transboundary Water Sharing' (2007) *Journal of Water Resources Planning and Management*, 133, 405 at 409.

34 J Alcamo and others, 'Water and Climate: A Global Perspective' (2003) *Kassel World Water Series*, 6 at 8.

Sustainable freshwater yields may or may not be reduced in the long-term average, but they will definitely be less reliable in the future.[35] This development will result in higher costs for water infrastructure, intensified competition between water users, and in some cases – primarily in developing countries – it may also slow down economic development.[36]

In addition to the direct effect global climatic change has on exacerbating the uncertainty over freshwater availability, it also affects the demand side of water management, e.g., through its impact on energy security,[37] food security[38] and human migration patterns.[39] However, the interconnections between climate change and water demands remain heavily understudied – compared to the research on the impacts on availability. This is crucial, as water demands for some users are highly sensitive to the climate – for instance agriculture.[40] Since this sector accounts for around 70 per cent of global water use, picking a particular scenario of changes in demand will have major implications.

In negotiating transboundary water agreements, the issue of uncertainty is a determining factor. Here, the additional component of 'strategic uncertainty' comes into play, which describes the limited knowledge of the preferences and characteristics of the other negotiating states.[41] This in turn can affect the actual distribution of benefits from a water agreement; which by implication has an effect on the willingness of states to enter into an agreement in the first place, as well as on the stability of the framework created by such an agreement.[42] In practice, an atmosphere of uncertainty usually decreases the size of coalitions adopting international environmental agreements,[43] and thus hampers both the formation of coalitions and credible commitments.[44]

All these pressures will make the already highly complex hydrological variability an even bigger challenge in the struggle for water security.[45] Further, the notion of security as such is a moving target rather than an end in itself. Not only does the evolving perception of the concept correspond with the ever-changing requirements of the various stakeholders; it also depends on the

35 Draper and Kundell, 'Impact of Climate Change on Transboundary Water Sharing' at 406.

36 Alcamo and others, 'Water and Climate: A Global Perspective' at 5.

37 See, e.g., de Fraiture, Giordano and Liao, 'Biofuels and Implications for Agricultural Water Use: Blue Impacts of Green Energy'.

38 Turral, Burke and Faurès, *Climate Change, Water and Food Security*.

39 W Myron, 'Security, Stability, and International Migration' (1992) *International Security*, 17, 91.

40 See H Cooley and others, *Understanding and Reducing the Risks of Climate Change for Transboundary Waters* (2009) at 14.

41 See K Iida, 'Analytic Uncertainty and International Cooperation: Theory and Application to International Economic Policy Coordination' (1993) *International Studies Quarterly*, 37, 431.

42 CD Kolstad, 'Systematic Uncertainty in Self-Enforcing International Environmental Agreements' (2007) *Journal of Environmental Economics and Management*, 53, 68 at 72.

43 Ibid. at 69.

44 A Drieschova and I Fischhendler, *Toolkit : Mechanisms to Reduce Uncertainty in International Water Treaties* (Hebrew University of Jerusalem 2011) at 5.

45 CW Sadoff and D Grey, 'Water Security: An Adaptation Imperative' in World Bank (ed.), *Environment Matters: Climate Change and Adaptation* (World Bank 2007) at 28.

international relations between the respective countries. Thus, in order to be able to continuously adapt to the emerging challenges which are becoming more and more complex, any framework governing a transboundary watercourse has to be reasonably flexible.[46]

3.1.4 Ambit

The final element of the 4A operational methodology is 'ambit,' which delimits the scope of water security – i.e., the sphere of influence of the notion.[47] In addition to the orthodox concept of scope,[48] the approach here is to better mirror the common character of the global water crisis. So far, the main shortcoming of transboundary water cooperation has been the inability to link the diverse influencing factors in an encompassing fashion – a serious flaw which has led to widespread 'water blindness'.[49]

The scope of a transboundary water agreement usually determines (1) the waters covered by the regime,[50] (2) the range of stakeholders that are eligible to participate in the utilisation of those waters,[51] and (3) the breadth of objectives addressed.[52] However, in addition to this traditional perception of scope, the concept of ambit also does justice to the fact that water security has to be regarded as a common security issue.[53] For instance, unilateral large-scale water management of one state might not only have a negative domestic impact (e.g., through forced resettlement), but will most certainly affect other riparians as well (e.g., through reducing the flow of the watercourse). Hence, the ambit of the notion of water security has to cut across borders in a way which not only brings all affected stakeholders to the negotiation table to discuss their respective concerns, but also accepts that the complexity of the issues at hand can only be resolved by looking at the bigger picture. Due to

46 See SC McCaffrey, 'The Need for Flexibility in Freshwater Treaty Regimes' (2003) *Natural Resources Forum*, 27, 156.

47 B-O Magsig, 'Introducing an Analytical Framework for Water Security: A Platform for the Refinement of International Water Law' (2009) *Journal of Water Law*, 20, 61 at 67.

48 See P Wouters and others, *Sharing Transboundary Waters : An Integrated Assessment of Equitable Entitlement: The Legal Assessment Model* (UNESCO 2005) at 19.

49 M Falkenmark, 'The Greatest Water Problem: The Inability to Link Environmental Security, Water Security and Food Security' (2001) *Water Resources Development*, 17, 539 at 542.

50 E.g., 'water resources' (Art 4 of the UNECE Helsinki Convention), 'international watercourse' (Art 2(b) of the UN Watercourses Convention), 'international drainage basin' (Art II of the Helsinki Rules), or 'tributaries' (Art I(2) of the Indus Waters Treaty; Art 5 of the Mekong Agreement).

51 State practice has demonstrated support for applying a basin-wide approach, although, still, too many international watercourse agreements lack the inclusion of all riparians – like the Indus Waters Treaty or the Mekong Agreement – which constitutes a high political risk.

52 The extend ranges from merely quantitative agreements (like the Indus Waters Treaty) to highly sophisticated institutions (e.g., the Mekong River Commission) which also govern aspects of water quality and emergency situations; Art 11 of the Mekong Agreement.

53 Magsig, 'Introducing an Analytical Framework for Water Security: A Platform for the Refinement of International Water Law' at 67.

the role water plays in linking the various emerging crises – i.e., food, energy and environment – in this more and more interconnected world, negative repercussions may even impact apparently remote countries beyond the river basin. The times when water could be considered solely as a national security issue are long past, since the global water crisis is seriously threatening one of our most fundamental common values – international peace and security. Since water is at the heart of the interlinkages of various risks, transboundary water cooperation usually also touches several areas and levels of policy, law and management.

Although water management is, in principle, a local challenge, several of its aspects, like the 'right to water', are debated in the global arena. This indicates that the linkages between the different scales of water cooperation have become more fluid; calling for international water law to act as an interface between the various levels.[54] Not only does the effectiveness of the international rules depend on a strong support of domestic norms (and vice versa); the impact of political and legal developments outside the 'water box' – e.g., the Biodiversity Convention, the Ramsar Convention, the UN Framework Convention on Climate Change (UNFCCC) – have to be factored into the analysis as well.[55]

Remembering that the notion of water security not only encompasses water, but also the benefits derived from its usage, the concept of 'benefit sharing' seems to be relevant here.[56] However, while it has been praised as a new and promising approach in transboundary water negotiations, it does not go far enough. The 'mutual gains approach' towards negotiating agreements for transboundary watercourses is supposed to facilitate better outcomes by allowing parties to improve their chances of creating an agreement which is superior to any existing alternative.[57] A central tenet of the approach is that parties usually have more than one goal or concern when negotiating freshwater agreements, and thus more than one issue can and should be addressed in the treaty they agree on.[58] Fully exploring the mutual gains through cooperation – rather than solely analysing options of unilateral development – can arguably provide a powerful incentive to cooperate in many cases. However, while focusing on the benefits derived from utilising water, rather than on the resource as such, is surely a step into the right direction, it still does not manage to fully eliminate the perception of water cooperation as a zero-sum game, since states still quarrel

54 A Rieu-Clarke, 'The Role of Treaties in Building International Watercourse Regimes: A Legal Perspective on Existing Knowledge' (2010) *Water Policy*, 12, 822.

55 See DK Anton, '"Treaty Congestion" in Contemporary International Environmental Law' in Alam S and others (eds), *Routledge Handbook for International Environmental Law* (Routledge 2013) at 663.

56 I Dombrowsky, 'Revisiting the Potential for Benefit Sharing in the Management of Trans-Boundary Rivers' (2009) *Water Policy*, 11, 125.

57 A Grzybowski, S McCaffrey and RK Paisley, 'Beyond International Water Law: Successfully Negotiating Mutual Gains Agreements for International Watercourses' (2010) *Pacific McGeorge Global Business & Development Law Journal*, 22, 139 at 139.

58 Ibid. at 143.

over their national interests – now only in form of broader benefits, rather than the resource as such. Adding 'more' to the table alone will not change the general approach to negotiations. Going a step further would be to link shared waters (more obviously) with national freshwater resources – and thus widening the ambit of the water security concept. How states manage their national groundwater resources, rivers and lakes will ultimately affect how they manage their respective transboundary ones. Should a state not be expected to decrease its dependencies on a highly contested international source and instead manage its domestic sources more wisely?[59] This could ultimately lead to completely shifting the focus from the water resource itself, to the benefits we want to gain from its utilisation – irrespective of whether the source is national groundwater or a transboundary river.

Finally, the notion of water security has to be open to novel approaches addressing the global water crisis, and thus it has to be able to integrate concepts like 'peak ecological water' or 'virtual water', reflecting the interconnectedness of the global crises of water, food and energy.[60] This is why its aim should be to accommodate a fruitful discourse on how to strengthen transboundary water management with input from all relevant disciplines. The element of ambit, then, has to ensure that international water law keeps exploring new opportunities for achieving common water security – beyond merely meeting international legal rights and obligations. Hence, it comprises much more than the traditional notion of scope. It represents a new mindset of how international water law should address the water crisis: by moving away from the management of the resource as such towards a holistic approach which addresses the challenges at the root.

3.2 The current framework of international freshwater regimes

The previous chapters elaborated on the importance of water in our rapidly changing world and the security challenges that come along with the increasing interconnectedness of sectors and societies. Considering the integral role water plays in the international social, economic and environmental interweaving, it is astonishing how long it has been overlooked as one of the primary causes of global uncertainty and insecurity. While realising we have now reached a state of global water crisis, which already affects the security of societies in various

59 The link envisioned here is stronger than in the cascade of factors determining 'equitable and reasonable utilisation' – i.e. the 'alternatives' available.

60 T Allan, 'Global Trade: Balancing Existing and Future Regional Water Resource Deficits' in Brauch HG and others (eds), *Facing Global Environmental Change : Environmental, Human, Energy, Food, Health and Water Security Concepts* (Springer 2009); M Nakayama, 'The Implications of Domestic Security Policy for International Water Issues in the Context of "Virtual" and "Real" Water: The Aral Sea and Mekong River Basins' in Jansky L, Nakayama M and Pachova NI (eds), *International Water Security: Domestic Threats and Opportunities* (United Nations University Press 2008); Palaniappan and Gleick, 'Peak Water'.

ways and will only get more difficult to tackle in the future, it seems helpful to recall the ultimate goal of international law: to 'maintain international peace and security'.[61] The following section will look at what role international water law can actually play in achieving this fundamental goal.

3.2.1 The role of international law

Throughout history, water has been widely regarded as a national security issue. While this led to the, still prevalent, overemphasis on self-interest, the development of international law tried to counter this kind of protectionism. Especially, the relatively young area of international environmental law, which emerged as a distinct academic discipline in the 1980s, not only helped to 'green' international law;[62] it also allowed for the recognition of new security threats in the international legal system.[63] Here, international law tries to achieve two goals: (1) flesh out the notion of security by providing the normative content, and (2) lead the way towards a more common understanding of security – away from the purely 'national security' debate.

With the emergence of contemporary security threats (e.g., to human, environmental, food, energy and economic security), international law underwent a process of specialisation which progressed from general rules to specialised rules of international environmental law, and recently to the distinct field of international water law.[64] Furthermore, it steadily shifted from the traditional 'media control' approach (e.g., rivers, oceans, air and wildlife) to a 'problem control' approach (e.g., population, desertification and climate change) – trying to reflect the environment's global interconnections, long-term dimensions and the emergence of the concept of 'sustainable development'.[65] The impact of this evolution on general international law is evident: more and more states are now appreciating the necessity to support the long-term benefits of maintaining the international legal regime.[66] While there is still widespread opinion that international law remains wholly dependent upon the will of states, the fact that an international society was created based on the rule of law by the

61 Art 1(1) of the UN Charter.

62 PH Sand, 'The Evolution of International Environmental Law' in Bodansky D, Brunnée J and Hey E (eds), *The Oxford Handbook of International Environmental Law* (Oxford University Press 2007) at 37.

63 See J Barnett, 'Environmental Security' in Collins A (ed.), *Contemporary Security Studies* (Oxford University Press 2007).

64 See P Wouters and A Rieu-Clarke, 'The Role of International Water Law in Promoting Sustainable Development' (2001) *Water Law*, 12, 281.

65 D Barstow Magraw and LD Hawke, 'Sustainable Development' in Bodansky D, Brunnée J and Hey E (eds), *The Oxford Handbook of International Environmental Law* (Oxford University Press 2007); AS Timoshenko, 'Ecological Security: Response to Global Challenges' in Weiss EB (ed.), *Environmental Change and International Law: New Challenges and Dimensions* (United Nations University Press 1992).

66 JC Barker, *International Law and International Relations* (Continuum 2000) at 4.

UN Charter, and that this very society has identified new issues of concern to be dealt with at an international level, points to a different understanding.[67]

While, clearly, law cannot be considered apart from other aspects of social organisation, due to its relationship to social control, behavioural change of states and dispute avoidance strategies, it is key to achieving common (water) security. There is a strong correlation between a state's ability to ensure its own water security and the existence of a legal regime guiding the management of its shared freshwater resources. This is due to the fact that water law serves three key functions: (1) defining and identifying the legal rights and obligations regarding the use of water and providing the prescriptive parameters for the management of the resource; (2) providing tools for ensuring the continuous integrity of the regime (including dispute prevention and settlement), and (3) allowing for modifications of the existing regime, in order to be able to accommodate change.[68] While different views may exist on the nature of international water law and its actual role in preventing conflicts and ensuring the fair use of transboundary water resources,[69] the mere existence of an agreed legal regime already contributes (at least to some extent) to water security by establishing an operational system for addressing the complex issues of transboundary water cooperation. The question then arises: do the integral elements of water security – availability, access, adaptability and ambit – find expression and normative meaning in international water law?

3.2.2 Evolution and current status of international water law

Certainly, the development of international water law has helped to prevent disputes over shared watercourses,[70] as its primary role is to determine a state's entitlement to the benefits of the watercourse and to provide for basic behavioural requirements for the development of the resource.[71] This has mainly been achieved by the application of universally agreed 'rules of the game', which have evolved through state practice and doctrine. These basic principles have served as a foundation for the development of further substantive and procedural rules, both of which help to accommodate the various characteristics of each case; and create particular regimes that determine each state's legal entitlement to the benefits of the use of the shared freshwater resource.[72]

67 Ibid. at 12.

68 P Wouters, 'The Relevance and Role of Water Law in the Sustainable Development of Freshwater : From "Hydrosovereignty" to "Hydrosolidarity"' (2000) *Water International*, 25, 202 at 203.

69 D Tarlock, 'Water Security, Fear Mitigation and International Water Law' (2008) *Hamline Law Review*, 31, 704 at 719.

70 See WJ Cosgrove, *Water Security and Peace: A Synthesis of Studies Prepared under the PCCP Water for Peace Process* (UNESCO 2003) at 25.

71 S Vinogradov, P Wouters and P Jones, *Transforming Potential Conflict into Cooperation Potential: The Role of International Water Law* (UNESCO 2003) at 12.

72 Ibid.

While societies' interests have always been linked with the development of shared freshwater resources, it was not until the 1950s that customary international water law emerged.[73] Before then, two converse approaches determined the claims and counterclaims of states over their share of the resource – the theories of 'absolute territorial sovereignty' (also called the Harmon Doctrine)[74] and of 'absolute territorial integrity'. While the former favours upstream riparians, allowing the unlimited use of the waters of a transboundary watercourse located within national borders (regardless of any consequences that may occur downstream in other countries), the latter approach favours downstream states who wish to prohibit any development in an upstream state that would interfere with the natural flow of such watercourse.[75] Obviously, neither of these quite extreme positions received universal support for a number of reasons. First, watercourse states cannot be easily divided into upstream or downstream states; as states may also be midstream states, in the case of an international river which flows through three or more countries. Furthermore, some rivers may end in the state's territory, while others may originate from it.[76] History has shown that the theories of absolute territorial sovereignty and absolute territorial integrity have been merely used as strong bargaining positions – a negotiation technique known as the 'zero-sum game' – before reaching a compromise agreement.[77]

Today, the more balanced concept of 'limited territorial sovereignty' is widely accepted as the foundation upon which the rules of international water law have evolved.[78] It states that all watercourse states enjoy an equal right to the utilisation of a shared water resource, and each watercourse state has to respect the correlative rights of other watercourse states.[79] This approach serves as the framework for the two main substantive principles of present international water law: the first principle being that of 'equitable and reasonable utilisation', entitling and obliging watercourse states to an equitable and reasonable share of

73 CB Bourne, 'The Primacy of the Principle of Equitable Utilization in the 1997 Watercourses Convention' (1997) *Canadian Yearbook of International Law*, 35, 215 at 215.

74 Named after the opinion delivered by the American Attorney General Judson Harmon in 1896 concerning a water dispute between the United States and Mexico over the use of the Rio Grande.

75 SC McCaffrey, *The Law of International Watercourses* (2nd edn, Oxford University Press 2007) at 117; A Rieu-Clarke, *International Law and Sustainable Development: Lessons from the Law of International Watercourses* (IWA Publishing 2005) at 147.

76 Rieu-Clarke, *International Law and Sustainable Development: Lessons from the Law of International Watercourses* at 147.

77 A Nardini, A Goltara and B Chartier, 'Water Conflicts: An Unavoidable Challenge from the Transboundary to the Local Dimension' in Meire P and others (eds), *Integrated Water Management Practical Experiences and Case Studies* (Springer 2008) at 97.

78 McCaffrey, *The Law of International Watercourses* at 136; A Tanzi and M Arcari, *The United Nations Convention on the Law of International Watercourses: A Framework for Sharing* (Kluwer Law International 2001) at 14.

79 Rieu-Clarke, *International Law and Sustainable Development: Lessons from the Law of International Watercourses* at 148.

the benefits of the uses of the transboundary resource; and the second principle being the obligation of states 'not to cause significant (transboundary) harm'.

The relationship between these rules has been cause for extensive debates.[80] Downstream states tend to favour the 'no harm' rule, as it protects their existing uses from adverse effects caused by upstream developments; while upstream states tend to favour the principle of equitable and reasonable utilisation, as it allows for a broader use of the shared resource for developments that may impact co-riparians.[81] Today, the principle of equitable and reasonable utilisation can be considered as predominant over the rule not to cause significant harm, due to the fact that the latter determines harm as a 'legal' injury rather than 'factual' harm.[82] Thus, the no harm rule cannot be applied as some kind of 'veto right' against later development of a watercourse state, which would basically mean that all uses that caused significant 'factual' harm would be prohibited, regardless of other factors and circumstances.[83] States are merely obliged not to utilise a transboundary watercourse in a manner that is inequitable; i.e. causing 'legal' injury. What constitutes an equitable and reasonable use depends on each case. The competing interests of states have to be balanced and weighted, taking into account all relevant factors and circumstances (e.g., population, social and economic uses, environmental issues and alternative sources).[84]

The evolution of international water law, in general, was heavily influenced by several international bodies, including the UN International Law Commission (ILC),[85] the International Law Association (ILA),[86] and l'Institut

80 PW Birnie, AE Boyle and C Redgwell, *International Law and the Environment* (3rd edn, Oxford University Press 2009) at 307; SC McCaffrey, 'Second Report on the Law of the Non-Navigational Uses of International Watercourses' in UN International Law Commission (ed.), *Yearbook of the International Law Commission 1986 Volume 2, Part 1, Documents of the 38th Session* (UN 1988) at 133.

81 D Freestone and SMA Salman, 'Ocean and Freshwater Resources' in Bodansky D, Brunnée J and Hey E (eds), *The Oxford Handbook of International Environmental Law* (Oxford University Press 2007) at 351.

82 Bourne, 'The Primacy of the Principle of Equitable Utilization in the 1997 Watercourses Convention' at 230; McCaffrey, 'Second Report on the Law of the Non-Navigational Uses of International Watercourses' at 133.

83 Rieu-Clarke, *International Law and Sustainable Development: Lessons from the Law of International Watercourses* at 170.

84 J Rainne, 'The Work of the International Law Commission on Shared Natural Resources: The Pursuit of Competence and Relevance' (2006) *Nordic Journal of International Law*, 75, 321 at 325; A Rieu-Clarke, R Moynihan and B-O Magsig, *UN Watercourses Convention : User's Guide* (IHP-HELP Centre for Water Law, Policy and Science 2012) at 111.

85 1994 International Law Commission Draft Articles on the Law of the Non-Navigational Uses of International Watercourses, UN Doc A/49/49 (1994) [hereinafter ILC Draft Articles].

86 See 1966 Helsinki Rules on the Uses of International Rivers (adopted by the International Law Commission (ILA) at the 52nd Conference, Helsinki, August 1966) [hereinafter Helsinki Rules], reprinted in S Bogdanović, *International Law of Water Resources : Contribution of the International Law Association (1954–2000)* (Kluwer Law International 2001). 2004 Berlin Rules on Water Resources (adopted, with dissenting views, by the ILA at the Seventy-First Conference, Berlin, August 2004) available at <http://www.cawater-info.net/library/eng/1/berlin_rules.pdf> [hereinafter Berlin Rules].

de droit international.[87] As a result of these efforts to codify and progressively develop customary international water law further, and following some thirty years of rigorous study by the ILC, in 1997 the UN General Assembly adopted the United Nations Convention on the Law of the Non-Navigational Uses of International Watercourses (UN Watercourses Convention),[88] which is the most important multilateral legal instrument in this area. This document codified and progressively developed the substantive and procedural rules that govern transboundary waters and is reviewed in more detail later in this book. Even though it only entered into force recently, the UN Watercourses Convention has always had considerable influence on state practice – demonstrating the early and continued relevance of this global instrument.[89]

This leads us to the role of treaties in transboundary water management, which is, arguably, the most important source of international water law. As of today, more than 3,600 treaties have been concluded between co-riparian states.[90] Although most of them relate to navigation, the number of regimes governing non-navigational issues of water management – including flood control, hydropower production, water quality, or allocation – has increased steadily. In the area of water resources, they regulate the quantity and quality of water between basin states, often by fixing the amount of water the upstream state has to deliver downstream.[91] As the subject matter of these treaties varies, so does their scope and their procedural obligations. Nevertheless, they all aim for one goal: giving relevant content to the rather vague principles of international water law, by creating a basin-specific framework for cooperation and interpretation, ultimately leading to improved exploitation of the watercourse and stable hydropolitics.[92] However, despite the undisputed benefits of entering into freshwater agreements, the number of adopted treaties has slowed down considerably in recent years (see Figure 3.2).

87 See Resolution on the Utilization of Non-Maritime International Waters (except for Navigation), adopted by the Institute of International Law at its Session at Salzburg (4–13 September 1961) *Annuaire de l'Institut de Droit International*, 49, Tome II 381 (1961); also P Wouters, *Rivers of the World: Water Law, State Practice and Current Issues* (International Waters Association forthcoming).

88 United Nations Convention on the Law of the Non-Navigational Uses of International Watercourses, UN Doc A/51/869 (21 May 1997; in force 17 August 2014) reprinted in 36 ILM 700 (1997) [hereinafter UN Watercourses Convention].

89 For a more detailed analysis, see FR Loures and A Rieu-Clarke (eds), *The UN Watercourses Convention in Force : Strengthening International Law for Transboundary Water Management* (Earthscan 2013); A Rieu-Clarke, 'The Role and Relevance of the UN Convention on the Law of the Non-Navigational Uses of International Watercourses to the EU and Its Member States' (2008) *The British Yearbook of International Law*, 78, 389. Also SC McCaffrey, 'An Overview of the UN Convention on the Law of the Non-Navigational Uses of International Watercourses' (2000) *Journal of Land, Resources, and Environmental Law*, 20, 57.

90 Vinogradov, Wouters and Jones, *Transforming Potential Conflict into Cooperation Potential: The Role of International Water Law* at 14.

91 I Fischhendler, 'Legal and Institutional Adaptation to Climate Uncertainty: A Study of International Rivers' (2004) *Water Policy*, 6, 281 at 282.

92 A Swain, 'Water Wars: Fact or Fiction?' (2001) *Futures*, 33, 769 at 772.

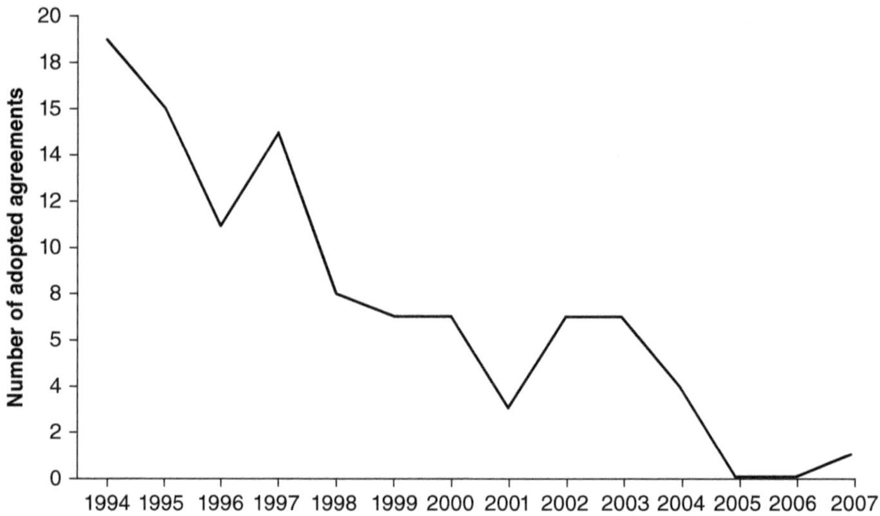

Figure 3.2 Adoption of international freshwater agreements

Source: Transboundary Freshwater Dispute Database, Department of Geosciences, Oregon State University.

Water treaties are often capable of stabilising international relations, by adding an element of predictability and certainty to the general principles of international water law.[93] Another advantage is that they put pressure on the contracting parties to comply with their obligations, and thus, in theory, improve the resource management in times of increasing water stress.[94] Yet they can also be used by hydro-hegemons to determine their own rules of the game.[95] One should not forget that treaties have the ability to 'hide' issues by pretending cooperation. Thus, cooperation is not always as positive as it is perceived, since research on the actual quality of cooperation is sparse.

3.2.3 Applying the 4A operational methodology

The primary role of international water law is to determine a state's entitlement to the benefits of the watercourse (substantive rules) and to establish certain requirements for states' behaviour while jointly developing the resource

93 McCaffrey, 'The Need for Flexibility in Freshwater Treaty Regimes' at 157.

94 Swain, 'Water Wars: Fact or Fiction?' at 776.

95 See, e.g., DZ Mekonnen, 'From Tenuous Legal Arguments to Securitization and Benefit Sharing: Hegemonic Obstinacy – the Stumbling Block against Resolution of the Nile Waters Question' (2010) *Mizan Law Review*, 4, 232; AE Cascão, 'Ethiopia – Challenges to Egyptian Hegemony in the Nile Basin' (2008) *Water Policy*, 10, 13; J Brunnée and SJ Toope, 'The Changing Nile Basin Regime: Does Law Matter?' (2002) *Harvard International Law Journal*, 43, 105.

(procedural rules).[96] Since cooperation in transboundary freshwater management is not merely an option but an imperative necessity, the question arises: how well does international water law actually address the challenges thrown up by the global water crisis? The following section will address this question by examining how the core elements of water security – availability, access, adaptability and ambit – are translated into the regime of international water law.

3.2.3.1 Availability

This facet of water security primarily deals with the resource as such – its quantity and quality. International law offers a broad spectrum of rules and concepts that may be used in addressing the issue of hydrological and physical aspects, including the control and protection (sustainability) of the resource. Human interference with transboundary waters is regulated primarily through the body of substantive rules (i.e. rules setting out requirements for specific uses, quantities or quality of water), through procedural rules (e.g., the requirements for prior notification of new or increased uses,[97] consulting on changes to the regime,[98] and exchanging information in the event of planned measures)[99] and, through the remit and activities of institutional mechanisms,[100] such as river basin organisations or basin commissions).[101]

Legal rules regarding the quantitative aspects are numerous and can be found in various treaties where states aim to specify the basic principles of international water law.[102] In trying to spread the risk of water stress among all riparians, states often allocate water corresponding to percentage and time of flow, rather than a fixed amount.[103] Furthermore, states often negotiate so-called

96 Vinogradov, Wouters and Jones, *Transforming Potential Conflict into Cooperation Potential: The Role of International Water Law* at 12.

97 UN Watercourses Convention, Arts 12–16 and Arts 18–19. These provisions cover a range of issues – from timing of notification, response to notification, and what should occur in the absence of notification, or where there is need for urgent implementation of planned measures.

98 Ibid., Art 17.

99 Ibid., Art 11.

100 Ibid., Art 24 provides: 'Watercourse States shall, at the request of any of them, enter into consultations concerning the management of an international watercourse, which may include the establishment of a joint management mechanism. For the purposes of this article, "management" refers, in particular, to: (a) Planning the sustainable development of an international watercourse and providing for the implementation of any plans adopted; and (b) Otherwise promoting the rational and optimal utilization, protection and control of the watercourse.'

101 For example, the International Commission for the Protection of the Rhine (ICPR).

102 See, e.g., Treaty between India and Pakistan Regarding the Use of the Waters of the Indus (19 September 1960; entered into force 1 April 1960) 419 UNTS 125 (1960) [hereinafter Indus Waters Treaty]; Art 1 of the Treaty between His Majesty's Government of Nepal and the Government of India concerning the Integrated Development of the Mahakali River including Sarada Barrage, Tanakpur Barrage and Pancheshwar Project (12 February 1996; entered into force June 1997) reprinted in 36 ILM 531 (1997) [hereinafter Mahakali Water Treaty].

103 Fischhendler, 'Legal and Institutional Adaptation to Climate Uncertainty: A Study of International Rivers'.

'escape clauses', which allow countries suffering from water scarcity to deliver less water than they would have to under normal circumstances.[104]

However, examples in transboundary water treaties for obligations regarding pollution control and prevention are rather few. Examples can be found in both framework instruments, such as EC Directive 2000/60 Establishing a Framework for Community Action in the Field of Water Policy (EC Water Framework Directive)[105] and the UN Economic Commission for Europe's (UNECE) Convention on the Protection and Use of Transboundary Watercourses and International Lakes (UNECE Helsinki Convention),[106] and in basin-specific documents such as the Convention on the Protection of the Rhine (Rhine Convention)[107] and the 1909 Treaty between Great Britain and the United States Relating to Boundary Waters, and Questions Arising between the United States and Canada (Boundary Waters Treaty).[108] Together, these rules identify the duties and obligations of riparian states on water quality issues, an integral element of the 'availability of water' security concern. Yet, in many cases, water for the environment has still no priority in water management practices, which has caused tremendous environmental pressures in numerous places around the world.[109] In China, for instance,

104 Art 4(B)(d) of the Treaty between the United States of America and Mexico relating to the Utilization of the Waters of the Colorado and Tijuana Rivers and of the Rio Grande (Colorado-Rio Grande Treaty) (14 November 1944; entered into force 8 November 1945) available at <http://ocid.nacse.org/tfdd/tfdddocs/55ENG.htm>.

105 EC Directive 2000/60 Establishing a Framework for Community Action in the Field of Water Policy, Official Journal of the European Communities L 327/1 (22 December 2000) [hereinafter EU Water Framework Directive]; Art 10 provides for a combined approach for tackling point and diffuse sources of pollution.

106 UNECE Convention on the Protection and Use of Transboundary Watercourses and International Lakes (17 March 1992; entered into force 6 October 1996) reprinted in 31 ILM 1312 (1992) [hereinafter UNECE Helsinki Convention]; Art 3(3), obliges its parties to define 'water-quality objectives and adopt water-quality criteria for the purpose of preventing, controlling and reducing transboundary impact'. Art 1(2) defines 'transboundary impact' broadly to include 'any significant adverse effect on the environment resulting from a change in the conditions of transboundary waters caused by a human activity'.

107 Convention on the Protection of the Rhine (22 January 1998; entered into force 12 April 1999) available at <http://faolex.fao.org/docs/pdf/mul17477.pdf> [hereinafter Rhine Convention]; Art 3(1)(a) states:' . . . avoiding, reducing or eliminating as far as possible pollution due to hazardous substances and nutrients from point sources . . . from diffuse sources equally passing by the groundwater and shipping.'

108 Treaty between Great Britain and the United States Relating to Boundary Waters, and Questions Arising between the United States and Canada (1 January 1909; entered into force 5 May 1910) available at <http://www.ijc.org/rel/agree/water.html#text> [hereinafter Boundary Waters Treaty]; under Art IV, the parties 'agreed that the waters herein defined as boundary waters and waters flowing across the boundary shall not be polluted on either side to the injury of health or property on the other'.

109 United Nations Environment Programme, *The Greening of Water Law : Managing Freshwater Resources for People and the Environment* (United Nations Environment Programme 2010) at ix. For the link between the environment and water management, see X Fuentes, 'International Law-Making in the Field of Sustainable Development: The Unequal Competition between Development and the Environment' (2002) *International Environmental Agreements: Politics, Law and Economics*, 2, 109; O McIntyre, *Environmental Protection of International Watercourses under International Law* (Ashgate 2007).

70 per cent of the rivers and lakes are significantly contaminated, while 50 per cent of its cities only have access to polluted groundwater resources – not only affecting businesses and communities in China, but also other countries further downstream.[110]

Another aspect of 'availability' is the mitigation of the destructive force of water-related natural disasters (i.e., floods and droughts); which is, above all, stipulated by rules of emergency preparedness and response.[111] Furthermore, the need to maintain the natural integrity of the freshwater resource – by calling for environmental flows or introducing terms like 'peak ecological water' – is being addressed in the sphere of 'availability' as well.[112] International water law provides a framework to ensure the protection and sustainability of shared water resources. Under the UN Watercourses Convention, for example, watercourse states are required to use and develop their shared waters 'with a view to attaining optimal and sustainable utilization . . . consistent with adequate protection of the watercourse' and to 'protect and preserve the ecosystems of international watercourses'.[113] The UNECE Helsinki Convention is more specific, requiring state parties to

> . . . take all appropriate measures: . . . [t]o ensure that transboundary waters are used with the aim of ecologically sound and rational water management, conservation of water resources and environmental protection; . . . [t]o ensure conservation and, where necessary, restoration of ecosystems.[114]

The EU Water Framework Directive is aimed at achieving good-quality status of surface and ground waters through early action and stable long-term planning of protective measures.[115] Other examples of international water law rules to protect and sustain the resource can be found in, *inter alia*, the Convention on Cooperation for the Protection and Sustainable Use of the Danube River,[116] the Rhine Convention[117] and numerous other river basin agreements.

The various examples of state practice show that new thinking in the sustainable management of water resources has finally emerged which at least puts

110 See PH Gleick, 'China and Water' in Gleick PH and others (eds), *The World's Water 2008–2009* (Island Press 2009); L Carmody, *Water in China: Issues for Responsible Investors* (Responsible Research 2010) at 4.

111 E.g., Art 5(4)(e) of the Rhine Convention.

112 Forslund and others, 'Securing Water for Ecosystems and Human Well-Being: The Importance of Environmental Flows'; Palaniappan and Gleick, 'Peak Water'.

113 UN Watercourses Convention, Arts 5 and 20.

114 UNECE Helsinki Convention, Art 2(2).

115 EU Water Framework Directive, Art 1(e).

116 Convention on Cooperation for the Protection and Sustainable Use of the Danube River (29 June 1994; entered into force 22 October 1998) [hereinafter Danube Convention] available at <http://www.ecolex.org/server2.php/libcat/docs/multilateral/en/TRE001207.txt>.

the environmental protection and sustainability of transboundary watercourses on the table; international water law provides the basic tools for effectively addressing those challenges.

3.2.3.2 Access

The issue of access, which describes the right to use the shared freshwater resource, is at the centre of the water security discourse and covers a wide spectrum of concerns across an ever expanding range of users and uses. The matter of access is addressed by international law in a number of ways, but, essentially, through the legal rules related to the (re)allocation of the resource and is linked to the cornerstone principle of 'equitable and reasonable utilisation'.

The principle determines the right of a state to use the transboundary water resources in two distinct ways. First, it lays out the objective to be achieved (an equitable and reasonable use), which then specifies the legitimacy of the new or increased utilisation. Second, it entails an important operational function, since it requires all relevant factors and circumstances to be considered when determining what exactly qualifies as an equitable and reasonable use.[118] This obligation to balance all the interests of the various stakeholders is essential to the notion of access.[119] In order to assist in the implementation of this relatively vague principle, the UN Watercourses Convention provides a (non-exhaustive) list of factors to be considered in each specific case – all the factors being principally equal in weight; although there might be a priority of use with respect to vital 'human' and 'environmental' needs.[120] Issues of (re)allocation, then, are determined through identifying and considering all relevant factors and reaching a conclusion arrived at on the basis of the whole.

From the water security perspective, the issue of access must be considered within this flexible and broadly inclusive and evolving process, inherent to the rule of equitable and reasonable use, which is designed to address and respond to the changing circumstances in the development, use and management of transboundary waters.[121] The rule has been codified in a number of international agreements, including, *inter alia*, the South African Development Community's Revised Protocol on Shared International Watercourses (which seeks to 'advance the sustainable, equitable and reasonable utilization of the shared watercourses')[122] and the 1992 UNECE Helsinki Convention ('to

117 Arts 3, 5(1) of the Rhine Convention.

118 See, e.g., Art 6 of the UN Watercourses Convention.

119 P Jones, 'The Application of Equitable and Reasonable Utilisation to Transboundary Water Resources Disputes: Lessons from International Practice' (PhD Thesis, University of Dundee, 2009).

120 Arts 6, 10, 21 of the UN Watercourses Convention. See also Rieu-Clarke, Moynihan and Magsig, *UN Watercourses Convention : User's Guide* at 111.

121 See P Wouters, 'The Legal Response to International Water Conflicts: The UN Watercourses Convention and Beyond' (1999) 42 German Yearbook of International Law 293.

122 Art 2(b) of the SADC Revised Protocol on Shared International Watercourses (7 August 2000; entered into force 22 September 2003) reprinted in 40 ILM 321 (2001) [hereinafter SADC Revised Protocol].

ensure that transboundary waters are used in a reasonable and equitable way, taking into account their transboundary character'),[123] to cite but a few examples.

Despite the fact that the principle of equitable and reasonable utilisation has been widely accepted as the basic principle of international water law, the issue of fairness of access continues to divide riparian states in a number of international river basins, such as, for example, the Nile river. Here, despite more than a decade of negotiations, which has resulted in a draft legal framework instrument,[124] a basin-wide agreement remains elusive. The Nile basin states are divided over the draft's cornerstone, and most controversial, substantive provision (Article 14) on water security.[125] All efforts to overcome this impasse, including a proposed recommendation that the meaning of the contested provision be determined by the institutional body established under the agreement, failed when Egypt objected with a proposed reservation to the provision. The Nile Basin Initiative reported that

> Egypt registered a reservation to this adoption. Egypt's position remained that, Article 14(b) which relates to historical water rights and uses should be formulated with a Committee of Ministers from the Eastern Nile, the Equatorial Lakes region, Egypt and Sudan and one or two experts from international organizations to formulate an acceptable text within six months and present it to the NILE-COM members.[126]

This shows that the complex issue of access will continue to be one of the most difficult challenges for achieving water security. International water law addresses this through an identifiable body of substantive and procedural rules, founded essentially upon the notions of equity and reasonableness. However, questions still remain about the relationship between law and equity, which can be seen as a counterpoint to the classical insistence on the formal equality of states and as providing a compromise between permanent sovereignty over natural resources and a common security issue – like water.[127]

123 Art 2(c) of the UNECE Helsinki Convention.

124 See M Abseno, 'How Can the Work of the General Assembly and the ILC on the Law of Non-Navigational Uses of International Watercourses Contribute Towards Basin-Wide Legal Framework for the Nile Basin' (LLM Dissertation, University of Dundee, 2009).

125 Draft Cooperative Framework Agreement [on file with the author]. The provision on water security (Art 14) as formulated in the minutes of the fifteenth Nile-COM meeting (25 June 2007) reads: 'Having due regard for the provision of Articles 4 and 5, Nile Basin states recognize the vital importance of water security to each of them. The States also recognize that cooperative management and development of the waters of the Nile River System will facilitate achievement of water security and other benefits. Nile Basin states therefore, agree, in a spirit of cooperation: (a) to work together to ensure that all States achieve and sustain water security; (b) not to significantly affect the water security of any other Nile Basin State.'

126 Nile Basin Initiative, 'Positive Steps towards Establishing a Permanent River Basin Commission' (2011) <http://www.nilebasin.org/index.php?option=com_content&task=view&id=131&Itemid=102>.

127 D Shelton, 'Equity' in Bodansky D, Brunnée J and Hey E (eds), *The Oxford Handbook of International Environmental Law* (Oxford University Press 2007) at 653.

Hence, despite the fact that the last war over water occurred some 4,500 years ago,[128] disputes over international waters are both common[129] and current.[130] This is why one of the most important functions of international law is to prevent, manage and peacefully resolve actual conflicts, including conflicts-of-use scenarios,[131] through the use of available dispute settlement mechanisms and techniques. International law deals with this problem in a number of ways – from using procedures aimed at conflict avoidance, to formal mechanisms designed to resolve international disputes. In cases where disputes nevertheless arise, international water law offers a framework for the peaceful resolution of the differences, which is fully embraced by the UN Watercourses Convention.[132] This is consistent with the UN Charter requirements that its members resolve their disputes peacefully,[133] through 'negotiation, enquiry, mediation, conciliation, arbitration, judicial settlement, resort to regional agencies or arrangements, or other peaceful means'.[134]

In addition, the UN Watercourses Convention introduced an innovative approach to dispute settlement – compulsory fact-finding[135] – which deserves broader attention, especially in regions without agreements governing shared watercourses. The UN Watercourses Convention, as a framework instrument, also promotes consultation and the creation of joint water commissions as cooperative activities, which support preventive diplomacy and leaves it to the watercourse states to devise their own mechanisms for managing shared waters.[136]

The extensive range of treaties and state practice demonstrate the benefits of including mechanisms for compliance verification (an important element of

128 A treaty ended the water war between the ancient Mesopotamian city states of Lagash and Umma. See SL Postel and AT Wolf, 'Dehydrating Conflict' (2001) *Foreign Policy* 60 at 60.

129 See PH Gleick, *Water Conflict Chronology* (Pacific Institute for Studies in Development, Environment, and Security 2008). The most recent version is available at <http://worldwater.org/conflictchronology.pdf>.

130 See Wouters, 'The Legal Response to International Water Conflicts: The UN Watercourses Convention and Beyond'.

131 Conflict-of-use scenarios have been defined as situations where there may not be sufficient amounts of water of adequate quality to satisfy competing needs. See B Schreiner, 'Issues of Balancing International, Environmental and Equity Needs in a Situation of Water Scarcity' in Dinar A and Albiac J (eds), *Policy and Strategic Behaviour in Water Resource Management* (Earthscan 2009).

132 See Art 33 of the UN Watercourses Convention; Rieu-Clarke, Moynihan and Magsig, *UN Watercourses Convention : User's Guide* at 234.

133 Art 2(3) of the UN Charter.

134 Art 33 of the UN Charter.

135 UN Watercourses Convention, Art 33(3) and (4) provides that the dispute shall be submitted to 'impartial fact-finding' where the parties are unable to resolve the matter through diplomatic means. The procedure is more akin to compulsory conciliation, rather than open-ended fact-finding. Under Art 33(8), 'The Commission shall adopt its report by a majority vote, unless it is a single-member Commission, and shall submit that report to the Parties concerned setting forth its findings *and the reasons therefore and such recommendation and it deems appropriate for an equitable solution of the dispute, which the Parties concerned shall consider in good faith*' [emphasis added].

136 See UN Watercourses Convention, Arts 4 and 8(2).

dispute avoidance) and dispute settlement within international agreements.[137] A number of water-related cases have been contested between riparian states by means of international arbitration and adjudication, including the Territorial Jurisdiction of the International Commission of the River Oder (United Kingdom, Czechoslovakia, Denmark, France, Germany, Sweden v. Poland) (River Oder Case),[138] the Lake Lanoux Arbitration (France v. Spain),[139] the Case Concerning the Gabčíkovo-Nagymaros Project (Hungary v. Slovakia),[140] and the recently decided Case Concerning Pulp Mills on the River Uruguay (Argentina v. Uruguay).[141] International law has developed a range of options in addressing issues related to conflict avoidance under the sphere of 'access' and it offers numerous mechanisms for resolving these disputes peacefully. However, the rulings of the ICJ often leave much to be desired when it comes to applying a certain degree of determinacy to a customary norm. For example, in the famous Gabčíkovo-Nagymaros Case, the Court held that the former Czechoslovakia's unilateral decision to proceed with its part of the project, which in effect diverted between 80 and 90 per cent of the river's flow, deprived 'Hungary of its right to an equitable and reasonable share of the natural resources of the Danube' – though without specifying what should be considered an equitable and reasonable share here.[142] Further, since both states were found to have violated international law, they were sent back to the negotiation table where the issue still lies – 17 years after the judgment. In the recent Pulp Mills Case between Argentina and Uruguay, the ICJ held that Uruguay had breached duties to notify and negotiate in both the relevant treaty between the two states and customary international environmental law.[143] Due to its recognition of the customary status of the requirement to undertake an Environmental Impact Assessment (EIA) whenever there is risk of transboundary pollution, the judgment will certainly win 'jurisprudential fame'.[144] Yet, the Court did not dare to specify the minimum scope and content of such an EIA.[145] This issue

137 See UNECE second Meeting of the Parties to the Water Convention, Geneva Strategy and Framework for Monitoring Compliance with Agreements on Transboundary Waters: Elements of a Proposed Compliance Review Procedure, Expert's Report, UN Doc MP.WAT/2000/5 and Add. 1.

138 Territorial Jurisdiction of the International Commission of the River Oder (United Kingdom, Czechoslovakia, Denmark, France, Germany, Sweden v. Poland) (Judgment) PCIJ (ser A) No. 23 (1929).

139 Lake Lanoux Arbitration (France v. Spain) 24 ILR 101 (1957).

140 Case Concerning the Gabčíkovo-Nagymaros Project (Hungary v. Slovakia), General List no. 92 (1997); reprinted in 37 ILM 162 (1998).

141 Case Concerning Pulp Mills on the River Uruguay (Argentina v. Uruguay), Judgment of 20 April 2010, ICJ Reports 2010, 14; available at <http://www.icj-cij.org/docket/index.php?p1=3&p2=3&code=au&case=135&k=88>.

142 International Court of Justice, Gabčíkovo-Nagymaros Project (Hungary v. Slovakia) Judgment (25 September 1997) ICJ Reports 1997, para 85.

143 Case Concerning Pulp Mills on the River Uruguay (Argentina v. Uruguay) Judgment of 20 April 2010, ICJ Reports 2010, 14, paras 143–50.

144 P Merkouris, *Case Concerning Pulp Mills on the River Uruguay (Argentina v. Uruguay): Of Environmental Impact Assessments and "Phantom Experts"* (2010) at 11.

145 O McIntyre, 'The World Court's Ongoing Contribution to International Water Law: The Pulp Mills Case between Argentina and Uruguay' (2011) *Water Alternatives*, 4, 124 at 141.

of indeterminacy is not limited to ICJ cases dealing with water or other natural resources and has triggered a general debate about the effectiveness, role and relevance of the Court, which is too extensive to be discussed here.[146]

From this it follows that, while providing a foundation for weighing and balancing of issues surrounding access, customary international water law falls short of striking a new path towards compatibility between the concepts of permanent sovereignty and common water security. This shortcoming, however, is not limited to the realm of water or the environment, as it constitutes a rather fundamental issue of general international law.

3.2.3.3 Adaptability

Undisputedly, the likelihood of conflict increases in scenarios where an enormous and/or rapid change occurs in demand or supply, and where the institutional settings are not capable of dealing with this change.[147] Hence, the question now arises: is the cornerstone of international water law – the customary principle of equitable and reasonable utilisation – capable of dealing with the security challenge of adaptability? In theory, equitable and reasonable utilisation is flexible enough to cope with future factual hydrological changes,[148] because it is able to implement an adaptive management approach relatively smoothly in order to deal with constant change.[149] However, it may even be too flexible to provide for the predictability and certainty needed by the states sharing a watercourse under stress. In the case of a dispute, both sides are trying to justify their opposing claims by referring to the principle of equitable utilisation.[150] This is evident regarding the non-exhausting variety of non-prioritised circumstances of each case, which have to be weighted and balanced to reach an equitable solution. As one author described it: 'The absence of constraining rules (or "criteria") transforms settlement into *ad hoc* legislation'.[151] Although flexibility and future readjustment may be implicit in the principle of equitable and reasonable utilisation, the lack of specific guidance about how to actually apply such readjustment minimises its potential.[152]

This is why states have entered into freshwater agreements, trying to limit the flexibility of the legal regime to a more useful level. However, water treaties have

146 See, e.g., ABILA Committee on Intergovernmental Settlement of Disputes, 'Reforming the United Nations: What About the International Court of Justice?' (2006) *Chinese Journal of International Law*, 5, 39; J Kammerhofer, 'Uncertainty in the Formal Sources of International Law: Customary International Law and Some of Its Problems' (2004) *European Journal of International Law*, 15, 523.

147 AT Wolf, 'Possible Futures for Transboundary Water Resources' (2010) *World Politics Review*.

148 McCaffrey, 'The Need for Flexibility in Freshwater Treaty Regimes' at 157.

149 JC Neuman, 'Adaptive Management: How Water Law Needs to Change' (2001) *Environmental Law Reporter*, 31, 11432 at 11433.

150 Rainne, 'The Work of the International Law Commission on Shared Natural Resources: The Pursuit of Competence and Relevance' at 326.

151 M Koskenniemi, 'Peaceful Settlement of Environmental Disputes' (1991) *Nordic Journal of International Law*, 60, 73 at 81.

152 G Goldenman, 'Adapting to Climate Change: A Study of International Rivers and Their Legal Arrangements' (1990) *Ecology Law Quarterly*, 17, 741 at 796.

one shortcoming: they are often perceived as rather rigid instruments. This is due to the fact that these regimes can only be modified according to their terms, within the boundaries of progressive interpretation,[153] or by mutual agreement.[154] Hence, if a treaty lacks flexible tools and a situation of water stress occurs, one party to the agreement may have to reduce its water consumption in order to be able to comply with its international obligations. If it fails to do so, disputes over the shared watercourse are likely to ensue.[155] In the case that water stress causes asymmetric harm, the more severely harmed state may want to terminate the agreement, while the co-riparian may want to stick to it, as it still benefits from the treaty.[156] In its judgment in the Gabčíkovo-Nagymaros Case, the ICJ concluded that 'the stability of treaty relations requires that the plea of fundamental change of circumstances be applied only in exceptional cases'.[157] The Court further stated that new developments or changing conditions should be dealt with on the level of implementation of the treaty, not by terminating it.[158] Hence, a treaty is only as static as its specific terms require. None the less, even if the parties agree to renegotiate their water agreement, this sensible diplomatic process may be too lengthy to effectively adapt to rapid climate change.[159]

The question arises whether this more rigid form of international water law can still be adapted to changing circumstances imposed by global warming. In order to answer this question, several studies have been conducted which all come to the same conclusion: the majority of freshwater treaties will have to be modified or even renegotiated in order to include more flexible climate-uncertainty mechanisms.[160] They either completely lack those mechanisms, or the implemented provisions are weak in actual substance. The most prominent failure in allocating freshwater is the assumption of a fixed (sometimes even too optimistic), perpetual water supply and flow allocation regime.[161] In a case where

153 See Art 33(3)(c) of the Vienna Convention on the Law of Treaties (23 May 1969; entered into force 27 January 1980) 1155 UNTS 331; available at <http://www.refworld.org/docid/3ae6b3a10.html>. See also, Permanent Court of Arbitration, Award in the Matter of the Iron Rhine Arbitration (Belgium v. Netherlands) (24 May 2005) at 23; available at <http://www.pca-cpa.org/upload/files/BE-NL%20Award%20corrected%20200905.pdf>; Permanent Court of Arbitration, Partial Award in the Matter of the Indus Waters Kishenganga Arbitration (Pakistan v. India) (18 February 2013) available at <http://www.pca-cpa.org/showfile.asp?fil_id=2101>.

154 McCaffrey, 'The Need for Flexibility in Freshwater Treaty Regimes' at 157.

155 Fischhendler, 'Legal and Institutional Adaptation to Climate Uncertainty: A Study of International Rivers' at 284.

156 McCaffrey, 'The Need for Flexibility in Freshwater Treaty Regimes' at 157.

157 International Court of Justice, Gabčíkovo-Nagymaros Project (Hungary v. Slovakia) Judgment (25 September 1997) ICJ Reports 1997, para 104.

158 Ibid., para 112.

159 Goldenman, 'Adapting to Climate Change: A Study of International Rivers and Their Legal Arrangements' at 769.

160 See McCaffrey, 'The Need for Flexibility in Freshwater Treaty Regimes'; Goldenman, 'Adapting to Climate Change: A Study of International Rivers and Their Legal Arrangements' at 802.

161 D Tarlock, 'How Well Can International Water Allocation Regimes Adapt to Global Climate Change?' (2000) *Journal of Land Use and Environmental Law*, 15, 423 at 425.

no provisions are made for future changes in circumstances, the contracting parties are likely to lose sight of the fact that aquatic ecosystems and the dependencies on them are constantly changing, and that this matter of fact is becoming even more challenging with the uncertainty added by global climate change.

There are several ways for the incorporation of more flexibility into freshwater agreements. Depending on their purposes and political relations, negotiating or contracting parties should choose the method most appropriate for them.[162] First of all, the allocation of water according to percentage and time of flow, rather than a fixed amount, is a way to enhance treaty flexibility.[163] While spreading the risk of water stress among all parties, this mechanism still puts downstream users at particular risk if developmental changes occur upstream, as their share in the water they receive will almost certainly diminish.[164] Another method of designing a flexible watercourse regime is to enter into a general framework agreement that requires the parties to conclude more specific periodic agreements regarding water use and management.[165] Obviously, a high level of cooperation between the basin states and good political relations are the preconditions for this kind of technique.[166]

Special treaty provisions can also introduce flexibility. The most popular among policy makers is the 'escape clause'. It allows countries suffering from water stress to deliver less water than they would have to under normal conditions, thereby allowing them to respond to unpredicted circumstances while not infringing the treaty itself.[167] Since downstream states often oppose the use of such a clause, as it implies that they will receive less water during times of drought, it is often accompanied by a deficit mechanism, compelling the upstream state to return the amount of water shortfall once the drought ends.[168] In order to prevent disputes regarding its application, it is essential that this provision is drafted unambiguously.[169]

162 McCaffrey, 'The Need for Flexibility in Freshwater Treaty Regimes' at 159.

163 Fischhendler, 'Legal and Institutional Adaptation to Climate Uncertainty: A Study of International Rivers' at 283.

164 This is the fear of Egypt regarding the Nile basin, as all the upstream riparians have not exploited their developmental potential yet.

165 See, e.g., Art 2 Syr Darya Agreement, Agreement between the Governments of the Republic of Kazakhstan, the Kyrgyz Republic, and the Republic of Uzbekistan on the Use of Water and Energy Resources of the Syr Darya Basin (17 March 1998), English version available at <http://ocid.nacse.org/cgi-bin/qml/tfdd/treaties.qml>.

166 McCaffrey, 'The Need for Flexibility in Freshwater Treaty Regimes' at 159.

167 Fischhendler, 'Legal and Institutional Adaptation to Climate Uncertainty: A Study of International Rivers' at 283.

168 See, e.g., Art 4(B)(d) Colorado-Rio Grande Treaty, Treaty between the United States of America and Mexico relating to the Utilization of the Waters of the Colorado and Tijuana Rivers and of the Rio Grande (14 November 1944; entered into force 8 November 1945) available at <http://ocid.nacse.org/cgi-bin/qml/tfdd/treaties.qml>.

169 In the case of the 1944 Colorado-Rio Grande Treaty, the term 'extraordinary drought' is not defined, which led to tensions between the two parties and an accumulated deficit of Mexico which reached 1.5 million acre-feet in October 2002; Fischhendler, 'Legal and Institutional Adaptation to Climate Uncertainty: A Study of International Rivers' at 287.

Two other formal methods proposed by McCaffrey are rather suboptimal. He suggests a provision allowing for termination of the agreement upon a given period of notice; or giving the water treaty a short life while providing for its automatic renewal unless one party objects.[170] Although both certainly provide for more flexibility, they cannot be considered as serious options, since consistent long-term management is needed to anticipate and adapt to the dynamic and changing conditions of transboundary watercourses. The two main advantages of an international water treaty – increased stability and predictability – would be lost.

Although the rules of customary international law do not (yet) require watercourse states to establish joint institutions,[171] state practice demonstrates that the majority of international freshwater regimes provide for such mechanisms – varying vastly in terms of purpose, size and responsibilities.[172] The overall aim of a joint institution is to foster the implementation of the water treaty, promote basin-wide cooperation and prevent disputes.[173] To achieve this goal they deal with operational matters, provide for monitoring and reviewing, establish information pools, and may also serve as a forum for dispute resolution. Although in most of the cases decisions are merely advisory in the form of recommendations, they are generally adopted in practice.[174]

It seems like joint institutions offer the greatest potential of all the flexibility mechanisms. However, in order to effectively meet the challenges of global climate change, they must be able to respond in an appropriate way.[175] The needed flexibility can be incorporated when the joint body has a broad functional and geographic framework, is independent from governmental structures, and is authorised by the treaty creating it to amend the basic freshwater regime in order to keep it up to date.[176] Only if the joint institution holds these qualities, will the watercourse states be able to respond to the uncertain future challenges of water insecurity.

3.2.3.4 Ambit

The make-or-break issue with regard to international water security is the concept of ambit, which, in this context, describes and delimits the scope of water security – i.e., the sphere of influence of the notion.

170 McCaffrey, 'The Need for Flexibility in Freshwater Treaty Regimes' at 159.

171 Art 8(2) of the UN Watercourses Convention generally recommends to watercourse states to 'consider the establishment' of joint bodies, but leaves the particulars to be determined by the parties.

172 E.g., Rhine, Danube, Niger, Nile, Mekong, Indus, US-Canada, US-Mexico; For a comparative overview about the most comprehensive joint institutions, see Burchi S and Spreij M, *Institutions for International Freshwater* (Paris: UNESCO – International Hydrological Programme, 2003).

173 N Ely and A Wolman, 'Administration' in Garretson AH, Hayton RD and Olmstead CJ (eds), *The Law of International Drainage Basins* (Oceana Publications 1967) at 137.

174 Ibid.

175 Tarlock,''Now, Think Again About Adaptation' at 173.

176 McCaffrey, 'The Need for Flexibility in Freshwater Treaty Regimes' at 161.

Regarding the hydrological extent of the waters covered by a regime, various terms have been employed; such as 'watercourse',[177] 'international watercourse',[178] 'shared watercourse',[179] 'international drainage basin',[180] 'aquifer',[181] 'water resources',[182] 'tributary',[183] and so forth. International practice has demonstrated increasing support for adopting a basin-wide approach to managing transboundary waters,[184] which has important implications related to 'ambit'. For example, if the 'international watercourse' under consideration is determined to be the territorial scope of the applicable legal regime, all states that 'share' this particular system of surface and groundwaters should have identifiable and enforceable legal entitlements and obligations related to the development and management of the entire watercourse – a situation that might affect river basins where there are no international watercourse agreements or where such agreements do not include all watercourse states.[185] The issue of scope also determines the range of legal actors eligible to participate in the watercourse utilisation (for example, the definitions of 'watercourse state', 'watercourse agreement', and 'parties to a watercourse agreement' from the 1997 UN Watercourses Convention). Another issue which falls under the matter of 'ambit' is the breadth of objectives covered by a regime. Here, the extent ranges from merely quantitative agreements to highly sophisticated institutions

177 Art 2(a) of the UN Watercourses Convention defines 'watercourse' as 'a system of surface waters and groundwaters constituting by virtue of their physical relationship a unitary whole and normally flowing into a common terminus'.

178 Art 2(b) of the UN Watercourses Convention, defines 'international watercourse' as 'a watercourse, parts of which are situated in different States'.

179 Art 1(1) of the SADC Revised Protocol.

180 Helsinki Rules, Art II.

181 Art 2(a) of the ILC Draft Articles on the Law of Transboundary Aquifers defines 'aquifer' as 'a permeable water-bearing geological formation underlain by a less permeable layer and the water contained in the saturated zone of the formation' <http://untreaty.un.org/ilc/texts/instruments/english/draft%20articles/8_5_2008.pdf>; see also F Daibes-Murad, 'A Progressive Multidisciplinary Approach for Resolving the Palestinian-Israeli Conflict over Transboundary Groundwater: What Lessons from International Law?' (PhD Thesis, University of Dundee, 2004); F Daibes-Murad, *A New Legal Framework for Managing the World's Shared Groundwaters : A Case Study from the Middle East* (IWA Publishing 2005); X Fuentes, 'The Utilization of International Groundwater in General International Law' in Goodwin-Gill GS and Talmon S (eds), *The Reality of International Law: Essays in Honour of Ian Brownlie* (Clarendon Press 1999).

182 See, e.g., Art 3(8)(vi) of the SADC Revised Protocol; Art 2(2)(b) of the UNECE Helsinki Convention; Art 4 of the Mekong Agreement.

183 See, e.g., Treaty between India and Pakistan Regarding the Use of the Waters of the Indus (19 September 1960; entered into force 1 April 1960) 419 UNTS 125 (1960), Art I(2) [hereinafter Indus Waters Treaty]; Preliminary Article of the Boundary Waters Treaty.

184 See Commentary to the Draft Articles on the Law of the Non-Navigational Uses of International Watercourses, Adopted on Second Reading, in International Law Commission, 'Report of the International Law Commission on the Work of Its Forty-Sixth Session' (1994) *Yearbook of the International Law Commission*, 2, at 93.

185 For example, the Mekong Agreement, which includes only four of the six riparian states – China and Myanmar being absent, and the Indus Waters Treaty, which only includes India and Pakistan, while China and Afghanistan are also river basin states.

(e.g., the Rhine Convention), which also govern aspects of water quality and emergency situations. The most effective management of transboundary watercourses, for the benefit of the whole basin, can only be achieved through a truly joint strategy involving all sectors and disciplines across borders.[186]

Recently, there has been a chance to strengthen international water law considerably – with the adoption of the Draft Articles on the Law of Transboundary Aquifers by the International Law Commission (ILC).[187] While it was an opportunity to bring the global frameworks governing transboundary groundwaters and surface waters closer together, instead they go separate ways on very fundamental issues. The UN Watercourses Convention can be seen as a framework for at least trying to level the playing field and overcome state-centrism, whereas Article 3 of 2008 Draft Articles speaks a different language, stating that 'Each aquifer State has sovereignty over the portion of a transboundary aquifer or aquifer system located within its territory'. This perception of sovereignty is inconsistent with the doctrine of 'limited territorial sovereignty' and its outflow – the principle of equitable and reasonable utilisation. Furthermore, by focusing primarily on the geological formation, the aquifer, the draft 'invites confusion as to whether the geological formation (rock) or its content (water) is the primary subject of legal regulation'.[188] Hence, the question must be asked, whether the 2008 Draft Articles have actually added anything new to the area of international water law; or whether they may have even made a negative contribution to the development of international law? It seems like the 2008 Draft Articles have moved away from the concept of distributive equity, which traditionally has been used to translate the uniqueness of the resource water into international law, towards a narrow approach based on national and absolute sovereignty.[189]

Thus, water governance at the international level is still missing the fact that water is not merely a resource which has to be well managed to avoid conflicts – it is a means to an end as well. Users generally do not care where the water comes from (confined aquifer, connected groundwater, or surface water) as long as it is of sufficient quality and quantity to satisfy their needs. Here, international water law is lacking in tools to conceptualise this understanding. When analysing the scattered approaches to transboundary water management, with many treaties merely focusing on quantitative issues, it becomes clear that most legal frameworks lack full support of the notion of ambit. This politically short-sighted behaviour – focusing on one's own national interests and

186 See Ely and Wolman, 'Administration' at 124.

187 Report of the International Law Commission on the Work of Its Sixtieth Session, UN GAOR, 62d Sess., Supp. No. 10, at 19, UN Doc A/63/10 (2008) [hereinafter 2008 Draft Articles].

188 SC McCaffrey, 'Current Developments : The International Law Commission Adopts Draft Articles on Transboundary Aquifers' (2009) 103 American Journal of International Law 272 at 283.

189 O McIntyre, 'International Water Resources Law and the International Law Commission Draft Articles on Transboundary Aquifers: A Missed Opportunity for Cross-Fertilisation?' (Transboundary Aquifers and International Law: The Experience of the Guarani Aquifer System) at 25.

security at the cost of international security – will inevitably backfire. Water cooperation is still seen as zero-sum conflict with a fixed-pie outcome – rather than a perpetual process to achieve the more sustainable common security. With the help of international law, the concept of water security has to create a space which transcends national boundaries (real and imaginary) and put water high on the agenda.[190] International water law, then, has to provide a legal environment that fully comprehends the ambit of water security.

3.3 Water security as a challenge to international law

International water law has often been interpreted as focusing merely on the (re)allocation of water; and thus strengthening the argument that riparian disputes should be perceived as zero-sum games.[191] While it is also true that law governing transboundary waters does not provide a clear hierarchy for the competing claims of riparian countries, it does introduce important principles for developing a sound framework for international cooperation. The previous section has shown that international water law does – at least to some extent – provide guidance on the four core issues of water security: availability, access, adaptability and ambit. The 4A operational methodology offers the necessary breakthrough for the further development of international water law, by pinpointing the main flaws of the current legal regime. Challenged by the water security concept, the shortcomings of international water law become clearly visible.

While the recognition of the principle of equitable and reasonable utilisation as a customary rule of international law is indeed a great achievement, it is often ignored in practice. The processes of adjudicating international water disputes at the ICJ, which requires the consent of disputing states, plays its part here. This is why two fundamental challenges remain. First, the principle as such does little in overcoming state-centrism. Second, it fails in truly levelling the playing field of transboundary water cooperation, since the hydro-hegemon still holds all the cards in the transboundary water game. The most powerful riparians are often willing to take unilateral action, as the risk that their action will be subsequently found inequitable and unreasonable is rather low. In most cases, the hegemon has the incentive to utilise the water first and worry little about the (unlikely) consequences it might face in the future – especially in basins where no treaty exists. This is why we still see countless examples of states not sharing their transboundary watercourses equitably; e.g., in the Nile basin, Central Asia and the Tigris-Euphrates. Here, hydropolitics based on power still determine the rules of the game.

190 A Turton, 'Water and State Sovereignty: The Hydropolitical Challenge for States in Arid Regions' (1999) 5 MEWREW Occasional Paper.

191 CW Sadoff and D Grey, 'Beyond the River: The Benefits of Cooperation on International Rivers' (2002) *Water Policy*, 4, 389 at 397.

In addition, concepts like benefit sharing have not been able to soothe the tension between maximising the overall benefit and the relative benefits of states. Since water is the source of growth, it is often considered as a strategic national resource. This is why states are constantly worried about the relative gains of their co-riparians. They are very cautious about the impacts any freshwater cooperation might have with regard to the power interplay of the respective actors. This usually leads to the pursuit of 'maximised individual benefits' rather than looking at how to gain the most from the management of the shared resource in absolute terms. It is correct that states are obliged to protect their national interests – and always will be. However, many of the interests that have previously been perceived as national interests are no longer merely national. As we have seen in the previous chapters, the intertwinement of water security issues with other crises (i.e., food, energy and environment) is changing the dynamics of international relations on a global scale.

It is surprising that, despite the need to increase both the adaptability and ambit of water agreements in order to cope with water stress, riparian states find it difficult to do so. The number of flexible and multilateral frameworks initially negotiated shows that the current inability of water-sharing regimes to address water insecurity is not an issue of awareness – it is rather due to political obstacles.[192] States are often reluctant to implement rules that limit their sovereignty. Thus, many international water treaties remain dead-letter regimes – in some cases negotiated with good intentions, but ineffective in reality. This dilemma will get even worse in many hot spots around the world, since the less harmonious the political relations are between the parties, the more difficult it is to agree on complex policies.

The perceived threat of losing national sovereignty often increases the political costs of implementing flexible mechanisms.[193] However, when excluding these measures, policy makers must necessarily also consider the potential benefits their implementation would have had. In basing decisions on optimistic water availability scenarios and low-resource sensitivity forecasts, the reasons for including flexible mechanisms are being reduced; thus, their non-implementation seems justified.[194] The bottom line is that by stressing the immediate political costs instead of the future social and environmental benefits, the implementation of mechanisms addressing uncertainty seems unreasonable, and thus they are often excluded. Today, the level of flexibility of water-sharing regimes still hugely depends on the political will of the co-riparians.

There is a growing need for international freshwater regimes to meet the challenges of constantly changing demands and environmental settings.

192 Fischhendler, 'Legal and Institutional Adaptation to Climate Uncertainty: A Study of International Rivers' at 284.

193 Ibid. at 298.

194 Ibid. at 295.

At its current stage, customary international water law is providing the needed flexibility, but lacks in predictability and stability. Watercourse states try to address these shortcomings by concluding freshwater treaty regimes, which are more precise, but also much more rigid tools of resource management. In addition to some formal options, the establishment of a joint institution can be considered the most effective approach for providing the crucial flexibility required in freshwater agreements. Although these joint bodies are desperately needed, their implementation often founders on political hurdles. It might be helpful to raise the awareness of policy makers that freshwater treaties should be seen as a long-term process of involving stakeholders in water resources management, rather than an ultimate outcome.[195] Only then can the immediate political costs and the future social and environmental benefits be properly weighted.

The prevailing 'react-and-correct' approach of international water law is not adequate anymore. What we desperately need is one of 'foresee-and-prevent'.[196] Such an approach would fully comprehend the concept of 'common' water security, which is inherently preventative compared to the conservative understanding of security as a reactive control paradigm. Hence, international water law has to strive for addressing the potential causes of instability and international conflict well before their effects are being felt. While not being without flaws, by no means can the current legal framework governing transboundary freshwater resources be described as 'poorly developed, contradictory, and unenforceable'.[197] Yes, international water law has to be developed further based on a more common and regional normative basis – and water security serves as a suitable concept to study the progressive development of the legal framework.

With the help of international law, the notion of water security can create a 'space' which transcends national boundaries (real and imaginary), put water high on the political agenda and trigger real change in transboundary freshwater cooperation. However, in order to be able to do so, international law has to accept the challenge posed by the concept of water security. While some authors still consider this to be highly improbable and ask for desecuritising water,[198] the momentum created by the water security discourse can certainly assist with the further development of international water law. It kick-starts a process which otherwise would not exist; one looking beyond water – and beyond nation states. How this process can come about, and upon what normative foundation such an approach should be based, is examined in the next two chapters.

195 Ibid. at 298.

196 See Timoshenko, 'Ecological Security: Response to Global Challenges'.

197 Wolf, 'Troubled Waters: Conflict and Cooperation over Shared Rivers' at 4.

198 See C Leb and P Wouters, 'The Water Security Paradox and International Law: Securitisation as an Obstacle to Achieving Water Security and the Role of Law in De-Securitising the World's Most Precious Resource' in Lankford B and others (eds), *Water Security: Principles, Perspectives and Practices* (Routledge 2013).

4 Hydrosolidarity – the answer to state-centrism?

In realising that the current legal framework governing transboundary watercourses is not able to overcome state-centrism and truly level the playing field, the question arises: which conceptual change is needed in order to help international water law move towards this aim? Is it possible to carve out an alternative approach to challenge the orthodox strategy in transboundary water cooperation? Would such an approach have to follow a rather radical path of recognising our freshwater resources as 'hydro-commons'[1] or even consider the duty to ensure 'water for all' as an obligation *erga omnes* shared by all states?[2]

While it is certainly not sensible to expect states' willingness to break with the current system overnight, there are signs that new – and less sovereignty-invasive – concepts are emerging, which can at least alter traditional orthodoxy in such a way as to overcome the challenges state-centrism is posing to the management of transboundary watercourses. With regard to water, the notion of 'hydrosolidarity' seems promising; since its overall aim is to shift the focus from competing national interests to common benefits. This chapter will trace the origins of the concept of hydrosolidarity, outline its changing perceptions and discuss why it still lacks implementation at a wider scale – despite the fact that its relevance to the water crisis is evident. The analysis contributes to one of the key debates of transboundary water cooperation by focusing on the role and relevance of international law in promoting solidarity and simultaneously providing specific guidance on the parameters of hydrosolidarity.

1 D Tarlock and P Wouters, 'Reframing the Water Security Dialogue' (2009) *Journal of Water Law*, 20, 53 at 58.

2 See Tams' comments on Judge Weeramantry's decision in the Gabčíkovo-Nagymaros Case: CJ Tams, *Enforcing Obligations Erga Omnes in International Law*, vol. 43 (Cambridge University Press 2005) at 190. The interesting position that under Articles 20 and 23 of the 1994 Draft Articles, any watercourse state – even if not directly harmed – could have be considered 'injured', has to be negated, as the Articles 7 and 21(2) of the 1994 Draft Articles adhere to the long-established understanding pursuant to which harm only triggers enforceable rights where it actually affects another watercourse state: J Brunnée and SJ Toope, 'Environmental Security and Freshwater Resources: A Case for International Ecosystem Law' (1994) *Yearbook of International Environmental Law*, 5, 41 at 65.

The value-driven principle with its strong ethical underpinning might just be the key ingredient to successfully support water security in creating a forum for discussing freshwater interaction which transcends national boundaries and leads towards a truly joint approach.[3]

4.1 Hydrosolidarity

Following from the discussion in the previous chapter, it is unrealistic to expect that the existing legal order will easily allow for a move fully away from state-oriented transboundary freshwater management. Thus, a sensible path would be to follow less sovereignty-invasive concepts, which can at least modify traditional orthodoxy in such a way as to make it more responsive to the complex challenges of water security. Here, the concept of hydrosolidarity offers a fresh perspective – and potentially an operational platform for implementing the notion of water security. The chief objective of hydrosolidarity is to inject a common understanding, based on the ideas of collective action, interdependence and ethics, into (transboundary) water cooperation, which for too long has been focused on technical variables and engineering solutions to the challenge of managing freshwater resources sustainably.[4] Ultimately, following an approach of solidarity in transboundary water cooperation implies that reconciliation of conflicts over water have to be based on solidarity among all water users. In concert with an evolving understanding of sovereignty, it could do justice to the ambit of water security – bringing together a community of states and ensuring the truly joint management of shared water resources.

4.1.1 The history of hydrosolidarity

The concept of hydrosolidarity arose as a countermove to the notion of hydroegoism, which describes the state-centred approach prevalent in the management of transboundary watercourses. The argument which hydroegoism follows is that satisfying geopolitical self-interests (e.g., national, sectoral and political) should be the underlying principle guiding water allocation between riparian countries. This view, of course, proves to be incompatible with the aim of a holistic and socially responsible development and management of water resources. Malin Falkenmark, a strong proponent of integrated water resources management (IWRM), devised a new conceptual framework in the attempt to challenge the predominant approach.[5] In 1996, she presented

3 K Wellens, 'Solidarity as a Constitutional Principle: Its Expanding Role and Inherent Limitations' in Macdonald RSJ and Johnston DM (eds), *Towards World Constitutionalism: Issues in the Legal Ordering of the World Community* (Martinus Nijhoff Publishers 2005) at 5.

4 A Gerlak, R Varady and A Haverland, 'Hydrosolidarity and International Water Governance' (2009) *International Negotiation*, 14, 311 at 312.

5 Falkenmark was awarded the 1998 Volvo Environmental Prize and the 2005 Rachel Carson Prize (among other awards) which recognised her innovative approaches to sustainable freshwater management.

her initial ideas at the World Conservation Congress.[6] Two years later, she first introduced the term in her Volvo Prize Lecture in Brussels. Falkenmark described the process of drawing away from what she calls 'water blindness' by addressing the need for 'water solidarity',[7] and ultimately rising above our inherited ways of addressing the global water challenge, which are heavily based on sectorisation and fragmentation.[8] According to her, this attempt should be paired with the concepts 'green water'[9] and 'virtual water', in order to be most effective. Virtual water – i.e., the water involved in the production of goods – is being transferred from one region (usually water rich) to another region (usually more water scarce) with a demand in the respective goods.[10] The idea of virtual water is especially relevant for equity-related issues in water-short areas, since it tries to reveal hidden or unintended transfers of water.[11] Here, 'water solidarity' would open the eyes of the 'water world' to novel ideas of management, in calling for: (1) human water obligations to deserve the same respect as other human rights to safe household water, (2) the recognition that 'upstream/downstream issues related to sharing water' must take precedence, and (3) the support from ethical and philosophical circles to incorporate water ethics.[12]

The term originally coined 'water solidarity' by Falkenmark subsequently underwent a process of evolution as scholars and water managers adopted and refined the concept, shaping it into what today is known as hydrosolidarity.[13] The concept now entails five key elements: (1) motivating stakeholders and decision-makers to use broad information, (2) designing organisational structures for finding compromises, (3) making public participation socially acceptable, (4) addressing social implications of resource use, and (5) redressing the use of resources that damages the interest of other uses.[14] Dukhovny argues for the inclusion of four additional elements: (1) including state governance in the principle of national hydrosolidarity, (2) public involvement in the promotion

6 Proceedings available at <http://data.iucn.org/dbtw-wpd/edocs/WCC-1st-003.pdf>.

7 M Falkenmark, 'Forward to the Future: A Conceptual Framework for Water Dependence – Volvo Environment Prize Lecture 1998' (1999) *Ambio*, 28, 356 at 356.

8 M Falkenmark, 'The Greatest Water Problem: The Inability to Link Environmental Security, Water Security and Food Security' (2001) *Water Resources Development*, 17, 539 at 539.

9 'Green water' is the fraction of rainwater that is available as soil moisture; while water stored in surface water bodies and aquifers has been coined 'blue water'; see FAO Land and Water Division, *Coping with Water Scarcity: An Action Framework for Agriculture and Food Security* (FAO 2012) at 48.

10 See M Falkenmark and C Folke, 'The Ethics of Socio-Ecohydrological Catchment Management: Towards Hydrosolidarity' (2002) *Hydrology and Earth System Sciences*, 6, 1.

11 For a discussion about the concept see E Ansink, 'Refuting Two Claims About Virtual Water Trade' (2010) *Ecological Economics*, 69, 2027.

12 Falkenmark, 'Forward to the Future: A Conceptual Framework for Water Dependence – Volvo Environment Prize Lecture 1998' at 360.

13 Gerlak, Varady and Haverland, 'Hydrosolidarity and International Water Governance' at 313.

14 VA Dukhovny, 'Big Challenges and Unlimited Opportunities: What Are Constraints for Co-Operation?' (From *Conflict to Cooperation in International Water Resources Management: Challenges and Opportunities*) at 121.

of moral awareness, (3) creation of a regulating system of laws and provisions, and (4) forecasting.[15] These should be applied directly to negotiations involving transboundary watercourses and their sustainable management. Here, high regard should be given to the fact that water has to be understood as a component of vital importance to society and the environment, rather than merely a technical issue.[16]

Ultimately, in Falkenmark's view, it remains vital to institutionalise the existing interdependencies in each river basin in order to achieve hydrosolidarity.[17] She argues that

> The basis should be general solidarity with focus on beneficial sharing of the joint water resource – that is, the rainfall caught within the water divide. Solidarity means the willingness to restrain one's freedom. Adaptation to the hydro-climatic constraints of a catchment will demand that all the interested parties are prepared to compromise. Principles and rules for sharing will have to be found for the unavoidable compromises between incompatible water interests in a certain catchment.[18]

While the focus of this work is on the international level, the concept of hydrosolidarity (just like water security) can be applied to different scales as well – i.e., the (sub)catchment level or the national scale.[19]

It becomes clear that the notion of hydrosolidarity intends to serve as an ethical basis for wiser water governance and provides the backdrop for balancing upstream and downstream claims for water utilisation, as well as human and ecosystem needs. Philosophically, it can be described to be the opposite of 'hydroegoism', the 'all-too-prevalent fragmented and sectoral approach to water management, where the strongest lobbyists tend to win'.[20] This paints a picture of an increasingly integrated approach to water resources management, heavily relying on public participation and coordination among various stakeholders. The ultimate aim of hydrosolidarity then is the truly cooperative,

15 Ibid.

16 Falkenmark supports this argument by stating that water serves three crucial functions: '(1) it acts as a silent messenger and a unique solvent continuously on the move through the landscape, in incessant contact with the ecosystems; (2) it is a key component of land productivity and plant production, and (3) it has many different functions for societal human life: for health; for food production; for industrial production and the generation of income; for energy production; for navigation; and so on.' Falkenmark, 'The Greatest Water Problem: The Inability to Link Environmental Security, Water Security and Food Security' at 541.

17 See M Falkenmark and J Lundqvist, 'Towards Water Security: Political Determination and Human Adaptation Crucial' (1998) *Natural Resources Forum*, 22, 37; Falkenmark and Folke, 'The Ethics of Socio-Ecohydrological Catchment Management: Towards Hydrosolidarity'.

18 M Falkenmark and J Rockström, *Balancing Water for Humans and Nature: The New Approach in Ecohydrology* (Earthscan 2004) at 214.

19 Stockholm International Water Institute (SIWI), *The History of 'Hydrosolidarit'*, (2002) at 18.

20 SIWI, *Hydrosolidarity through Catchment Based Balancing of Human Security and Ecological Security* (SIWI 2003) at 4.

unified management of shared freshwater resources, whether at the local, national, or transboundary level. While hydrosolidarity 'originated as a deliberate attempt to inject mutual understanding, common good and ethics in relation to shared waters',[21] the question arises: how can the key elements of the concept – including law, governance, stakeholder involvement and resource protection – play a more concerted role?[22]

4.1.2 A new consensus in the water community?

Despite the somewhat enthusiastic reception of the notion of hydrosolidarity, some scholars and practitioners are rather pessimistic when it comes to the applicability of the concept. To be useful, they argue, hydrosolidarity needs a set of metrics which can serve as a benchmark for its effectiveness.[23] Necessary for the development of such metrics, however, is having set boundaries and mutually agreed guidelines which can then be used to apply the concept of hydrosolidarity at the various levels of water management.[24]

Thus, in order for hydrosolidarity to become the ethical underpinning of transboundary water interaction, it has to be based on a mutual understanding of how to translate the concept into practice. The following section will tease out traces of hydrosolidarity in recent developments in the water arena and analyse whether the global water community has reached a common ground. The processes picked here all flowed into the UN Conference on Sustainable Development (UNCSD) which was held in Rio de Janeiro in June 2012. The main goal of the summit, also known as 'Rio+20', was the evaluation of the achievements of the landmark UN Conference on Environment and Development (UNCED) held in Rio de Janeiro twenty years before.[25] The importance of the UNCSD process for getting water on the global political agenda becomes clear when realising the disappointing inclusion of water issues in global climate change negotiations. While freshwater resources play a central role in climate change mitigation and adaptation efforts,[26] the UNFCCC Conferences of the Parties (COPs) and Conferences and Meetings of the Parties to the Kyoto Protocol (CMPs) consistently fail to acknowledge this fact and solely focus on the, not unimportant, issue of greenhouse gas emissions targets. This is why the best hope for the global water community to push water up the political agenda and arrive at a common understanding of hydrosolidarity is through the UNCSD process.

21 Gerlak, Varady and Haverland, 'Hydrosolidarity and International Water Governance' at 312.

22 See Dukhovny, 'Big Challenges and Unlimited Opportunities: What Are Constraints for Co-Operation?'.

23 See, e.g, Gerlak, Varady and Haverland, 'Hydrosolidarity and International Water Governance'.

24 Ibid. at 315.

25 For follow-up-to information on the Rio+20 Summit, see <http://sustainabledevelopment.un.org/>.

26 UN Water, *Climate Change Adaptation: The Pivotal Role of Water* (UN Water 2010).

4.1.2.1 Mechanisms for galvanising the global water community

Several governmental and non-governmental processes are aimed at promoting the peaceful management of transboundary freshwater resources. In this section the most prominent ones which contributed to the UNCSD are being analysed as to how they interpret hydrosolidarity and whether they elevate the concept to finally become the ethical underpinning of transboundary water cooperation – as the creators of the notion envisioned.

One of the most important gatherings of water experts, the annual World Water Week (which began as the Stockholm Water Symposium in 1991), is organised by the Stockholm International Water Institute (SIWI). Its mission is to generate knowledge and inform policy makers towards water-wise decisions – focusing on five thematic areas: (1) water governance, (2) transboundary water management, (3) water and climate change, (4) the water-energy-food nexus, and (5) water economics.[27] Each year, the World Water Week attracts over 2,500 participants and around 200 collaborating institutions from all over the world.[28] During the event in 2011 (21–27 August), the World Water Week Statement to the Rio+20 Summit was published with the aim to get water on the global political agenda.[29]

The document contains some interesting statements relevant for this analysis. In recognising that 'water, energy, and food are interlinked and interdependent', it stresses the fact that water is more than just a resource at risk of being overexploited; it is at the heart of several other resource security risks. This clearly calls for cross-fertilisation between water governance and other policy sectors – confirming the need for an ambit of water security which is significantly wider than the prevalent 'water box'. While falling short of demonstrating ways of how to put such an approach into practice, the statement argues that the integration of water, energy and food security issues in a holistic manner has to recognise 'the carrying capacity of the planet' (i.e., the planetary boundaries), which resonates with the definition of water security proposed in Chapter 2 of this study. In calling for 'a universal provisioning of safe drinking water, adequate sanitation and modern energy services by 2030' to achieve the Millennium Development Goals,[30] the focus of the Stockholm Statement clearly lies in the realm of human security. Interestingly, the document also recommends the creation of an institutional framework for sustainable development. However, in being rather poor in content, it merely reiterates vague

27 SIWI, 'Vision' (2012) <http://www.siwi.org/about/vision/>.

28 SIWI, 'World Water Week in Stockholm' (2012) <http://www.siwi.org/prizes/worldwaterweek/>.

29 The Stockholm Statement to the 2012 United Nations Conference on Sustainable Development in Rio de Janeiro (Rio+20 Summit) (27 August 2011) available at <http://www.worldwaterweek.org/documents/WWW_PDF/2011/2011-Stockholm-Statement.pdf>.

30 For more information on the MDGs, see United Nations Department of Economic and Social Affairs, *The Millennium Development Goals Report 2012* (United Nations Department of Economic and Social Affairs 2012); R Lenton, K Lewis and AM Wright, 'Water, Sanitation and the Millennium Development Goals' (2008) *Journal of International Affairs*, 61, 247.

and widely agreed-upon suggestions – e.g., 'policy and institutional reforms that create an enabling environment for the coherent and integrated management of water, energy and food', 'national legislation that guarantees access to water and sanitation for all and protect freshwater ecosystems', and 'cross-cutting frameworks that bridge ministries and sectors, leading the way to water, energy and food security in a green economy'. Finally, the Statement calls on the participants of the Rio+20 Summit to commit to achieving five main targets by 2020:

- 20 per cent increase in total food supply-chain efficiency,
- 20 per cent increase in water efficiency in agriculture,
- 20 per cent increase in water use efficiency in energy production,
- 20 per cent increase in the quantity of water reused, and
- 20 per cent decrease in water pollution.

While these goals surely are noble ones, they read more like a publicity campaign than serious policy recommendations based on empirical analysis. Despite having been supported by UN-Water, the German Federal Ministry for the Environment and endorsed by several international organisations (e.g., Conservation International, International Water Management Institute, Wateraid and Worldwide Fund for Nature),[31] both the language and content of the document remind us of what it actually is: a policy statement. The positive aspects of such policy language are that it is accessible to a broad audience and concepts are, generally, easy to grasp. The negative aspect of such broad language and seemingly randomly selected goals is that they are problematic for the practical, legal and institutional realities of implementing such goals. Even so, considering Falkenmark's role as Senior Scientific Advisor to SIWI, it seems astonishing that the statement did not mention the notion of hydrosolidarity even once in order to promote it at the global level. Given the fact that the concept is neither referred to in the post-event documentation of the following World Water Week,[32] nor in the call for papers and events for the most recent events,[33] the question arises whether SIWI still has the intention to promote hydrosolidarity, or whether it has given up due to the lack of significant uptake?

Organised by the World Water Council (WWC) since 1997, the triennial World Water Forum is the largest gathering of water professionals. The WWC is an international multi-stakeholder platform which was founded in 1996 in response to increasing concerns from water experts and international

31 SIWI, 'World Water Week closes with "Stockholm Statement" to the Rio+20' (27 August 2011) <http://www.worldwaterweek.org/sa/node.asp?node=1269>.

32 See SIWI, *2012 World Water Week Workshop Highlights* (SIWI 2012).

33 SIWI, '2013 Call for Abstracts and Event Proposals – World Water Week in Stockholm : Water Cooperation: Building Partnerships' <http://www.worldwaterweek.org/documents/WWW_PDF/2013/2013_Call_for_abstracts_event_proposals_web.pdf>.

organisations about the world water crisis. According to its mission statement, its goal is to

> . . . promote awareness, build political commitment and trigger action on critical water issues at all levels, including the highest decision-making level, to facilitate the efficient conservation, protection, development, planning, management and use of water in all its dimensions on an environmentally sustainable basis for the benefit of all life on earth.[34]

One of the main tools to achieve this is the provision of a debating and knowledge exchange platform in order to 'reach a common strategic vision on water resources and water services management amongst all stakeholders in the water community'.[35] In supporting this process, the World Water Forum can be considered the main catalyst. The most recent Forum (12–17 March 2012) was held in Marseilles and attracted around 35,000 participants from more than 145 countries.[36] The goal of the meeting – billed as 'Time for Solutions' – was to make 'progress on the cause of water and sanitation through concrete solutions and commitments'.[37] Endorsed by 84 government ministers from around the world, the Ministerial Declaration calls for a 'new approach' to water policy ahead of Rio+20.[38] With its 32 articles, the Declaration tries to explain what this new approach is and how it should be implemented.

Regarding the debate revolving around water security and hydrosolidarity, a few points seem to be of particular relevance. It acknowledges the interlinkages of water, food and energy by calling for a new approach to better understand their interaction in decision-making and planning processes, since this would release new potential in improving the 'production and sustainable management of these scarce resources'.[39] Further, it argues that since there will be no food security without water, 'water and food security policies need to be integrated'.[40] While these recommendations point towards a wider ambit of water security, as proposed in this study, the Declaration falls short in demonstrating feasible pathways of implementing such an endeavour.

Article 24, then, acknowledges the principles of the 1992 Rio Declaration on Environment and Development and the fact that 2013 has been declared

34 World Water Council, 'Vision, Mision, Strategy' (12 November 2012) <http://www.worldwatercouncil.org/about-us/vision-mission-strategy/>.

35 Ibid.

36 World Water Forum, 'The World's Largest Meeting around Water' (12 March 2012) <http://www.worldwaterforum6.org/en/the-forum/about/>.

37 World Water Council, *Hydro-Diplomacy in Motion: World Water Council 2010–2012* (World Water Council 2012) at 21.

38 Ministerial Declaration of the 6th World Water Forum, 12–17 March 2012, Marseille (13 March 2012) <http://www.worldwaterforum6.org/fileadmin/user_upload/pdf/Ministerial_Declaration_Final_EN.pdf >.

39 Art 10 of the Ministerial Declaration.

40 Art 12 of the Ministerial Declaration.

the International Year of Water Cooperation by the UN General Assembly. Hence, with regard to transboundary water interaction, the Declaration stressed the commitment to

> . . . enhance cooperation across and beyond water, taking into account the interests of all riparian States concerned, to foster peace and stability. We appreciate cooperative efforts in the field of transboundary waters. We intend to further promote and encourage coordinated, equitable, reasonable and optimal water utilisation in transboundary basins, with a view to deepening mutual trust among riparian countries and achieve sound cooperation.[41]

This is a step backwards from customary international law, which requires, rather than encourages, equitable and reasonable water utilisation. Furthermore, this section does not mention the global framework treaty on water management, the UN Watercourses Convention, directly (let alone call for its ratification or accession), nor does it promote any legal principles in particular. Furthermore, the provision on human right to water has been criticised by activists as well, since it falls short in formally defining water and sanitation as human rights.[42] The Declaration's focus on investment and technology comes as no surprise, given the World Water Council has always been seen as having close links with multilateral water corporations and financial institutions.[43] However, fears that the Declaration is actively promoting privatisation policies could have been addressed by including guiding principles of ethics, equity and justice – like the concept of hydrosolidarity. However, this opportunity was not taken.

The whole Declaration is rather bland with vague statements and references to undisputed figures, owing to the fact that the hosts are usually rather keen to avoid controversy.[44] There are only a few points (like the (non-)reference to the human right to water) which could be contested. Who, for instance, would argue against the statement that 'Accounting for water use in energy production and for energy use in the water and sanitation sector can improve water and energy efficiency', or that 'Investment in sustainable multi-purpose water storage, the utilisation of wastewater as a source of renewable energy as well as the use of renewable energy, such as solar and wind, in water supply and sanitation, need to be promoted'?[45]

41 Art 24 of the Ministerial Declaration.

42 See C Provost for the *Guardian*, 'World Water Forum Declaration Falls Short on Human Rights, Claim Experts' (14 March 2012) <http://www.guardian.co.uk/global-development/2012/mar/14/world-water-forum-declaration-human-rights>.

43 M Barlow and T Clarke, *Blue Gold: The Fight to Stop the Corporate Theft of the World's Water* (W.W. Norton 2002) at 157.

44 J Lane, 'Global Water Conferences: A Personal Reflection' in Biswas AK and Tortajada C (eds), *Impacts of Megaconferences on the Water Sector* (Springer 2009) at 107.

45 Art 15 of the Ministerial Declaration.

Given the lack of content-related substance, the question arises: what is the impact of the Declaration? While it clearly does not have any direct legal effect, as the World Water Council is devoid of any legitimacy under international law, the results of the World Water Forum are still sending out signals as to where discussions around water management are heading. However, the Ministerial Declaration should not be mistaken for a serious multilateral statement on the future global water policy.

International organisations and research institutes were not the only actors in drafting policy recommendations ahead of the UNCSD and putting water security high on the global political agenda. The Bonn2011 Conference, for example, convened by the German Federal Ministry for the Environment, Nature Conservation and Nuclear Safety (BMU) and the German Federal Ministry for Economic Cooperation and Development (BMZ) in November 2011, was organised as a stepping stone for the discussions around the specific contribution Germany could make towards Rio+20. Dedicating the whole conference to the water-energy-food security nexus is definitely an important step in the recognition of the water security concept. The underlying objective of the international event was to develop policy recommendations based on a multi-stakeholder consultation process, while promoting the water-energy-food 'nexus perspective' as an important dimension within the Rio+20 process. In addition, the aim was to also launch concrete initiatives to address the water-energy-food security challenges in a coherent manner.[46]

The policy recommendations aim to illuminate how the approach can help achieve sustainable development.[47] The document starts off with a detailed description of why 'failing to recognize the consequences of one sector on another can lead to notable inefficiencies in the system'.[48] According to the Bonn Recommendations, the main challenges to achieving water, energy and food security are 'weak governance systems, limited awareness, distortions from perverse subsidies and unsustainable investments', which can worsen unintended consequences.[49] It claims that only a new nexus-oriented approach can effectively address impending resource constraints and thus promote common security.[50] This clearly takes to heart the notion of ambit, which is an integral part of the water security paradigm proposed in this study. Only by taking a wider perspective at the complex challenges ahead can we identify policy responses which are mutually beneficial and provide an informed framework for determining the paths for meeting demands 'without compromising

46 Federal Government of Germany, 'Bonn2011 Nexus Conference – Initiating Integrated Solutions for the Green Economy' (2011) <http://www.water-energy-food.org/en/conference.html>.

47 Bonn2011 Conference: The Water, Energy and Food Security Nexus – Solutions for a Green Economy (13 February 2012) <http://www.water-energy-food.org/documents/bonn2011_policyrecommendations.pdf> [hereinafter Bonn Recommendations].

48 Bonn Recommendations at 2.

49 Ibid. at 3.

50 Ibid.

sustainability and exceeding environmental tipping points'.[51] The following section assesses the most interesting recommendations discussed during Bonn2011 with regard to international water law and policy.

One of the main goals of the conference was to find ways to increase policy coherence, in order to ensure that development pathways explicitly account for the inter-dependency between water, energy and food. With regard to international freshwater management, it was seen as important to promote collaborative transboundary and basin-wide approaches.[52] Taking into account that decisions on resource management in one part of the world may affect resource (re)allocation in another, the Bonn Recommendations see 'opportunities of regional integration to enhance markets, trade and financing to promote optimal resource use, more equitable distribution and sustainable outcomes', while also warning that unilateral development of shared rivers and aquifers can have a negative effect on a whole region.[53] Here, the role of international water agreements is being stressed as being of paramount importance for the nexus, which can only be addressed genuinely when the legal framework is being expanded to also 'influence responses to food and energy drivers and the wider political economy'.[54] This, again, strengthens the argument for striving for an ambit of water security which is as comprehensive as possible.

In supporting this argument, the document calls for considering the 'transnational consequences and externalities of trade policy on water, energy and food security'[55] – the concept of virtual water. While this notion is nothing new,[56] the Bonn Recommendations also propose collecting data which helps in better understanding the effect trade in food and other products has on the management of natural resources; for instance with the help of water, energy and land-use footprints.[57] Furthermore, it calls for the ratification or accession of the UN Watercourses Convention (where appropriate); moving from the concept of water sharing to also include benefit sharing; and establishing a coordinated approach to implementation of multilateral environmental agreements and other treaties related to the water-energy-food nexus.[58]

In terms of a contemporary understanding of water security, the most interesting point in the document is the proposal to promote transboundary cooperation beyond the boundaries of a river basin.[59] On this suggestion, however,

51 Ibid.
52 Ibid. at 8.
53 Ibid.
54 Ibid.
55 Ibid. at 18.
56 See, e.g., AY Hoekstra, 'Water Security of Nations: How International Trade Affects National Water Scarcity and Dependency' in Jones JAA, Vardanian TG and Hakopian C (eds), *Threats to Global Water Security* (Springer 2009).
57 See also AY Hoekstra and others, *The Water Footprint Assessment Manual: Setting the Global Standard* (Earthscan 2011).
58 Bonn Recommendations at 19, 20.
59 Ibid. at 19.

the Bonn Recommendations only elaborate slightly as to how this could be achieved. While the document does not mention the concept of hydrosolidarity explicitly, it nevertheless touches upon several important elements of it – mainly in the form of widening the ambit of the security approach and fostering cooperation which goes beyond the basin. Hence, the Recommendations have to be considered as an important contribution to the UNCSD in terms of putting hydrosolidarity high on the political agenda and proposing steps to actually achieve water, energy and food security.

4.1.2.2 New opportunities through the Rio+20 process?

Despite the recent disappointing experiences with large events trying to alter the course of our relationship with the environment, for instance, the 15th session of the Conference of the Parties (COP 15) to the UNFCCC on climate change negotiations held in Copenhagen,[60] the Rio+20 Conference had awakened the hope for fundamental change: 'The stakes are rising . . . One hundred days to a once-in-a-generation opportunity. We must agree on sustainable solutions to build the future we want.'[61] Hence, one of the main objectives of Rio+20 was to renew the political commitment of states to sustainable development to be forearmed against the emerging challenges. In doing so, it was hoped to be able to give key principles, decided on in Rio in 1992, more substance – such as the principle not to cause transboundary harm,[62] the right to development,[63] common but differentiated responsibilities,[64] public participation,[65] the precautionary principle[66] and the polluter pays principle.[67] With regard to the concept of water security – and the underlying ethical principle of hydrosolidarity – expectations were that Rio+20 would acknowledge the complexities of the global water crisis and reflect them in its declaration.[68] Since water security is being seen as a major political issue in the quest for sustainable development, for the summit to be called a success, it had to fully acknowledge the nexus approach and the central role water plays in linking various other securities.

60 See P Christoff, 'Cold Climate in Copenhagen: China and the United States at COP15' (2010) *Environmental Politics*, 19, 637.

61 Ban Ki-moon, 'Rio+20: Social Media Countdown to UN Sustainable Development Forum Kicks Off' (12 March 2012) <http://www.un.org/apps/news/story.asp?NewsID=41519&Cr=sustainable+development>.

62 Principle 2 of the 1992 Rio Declaration on Environment and Development (14 June 1992) UN Doc A/CONF.151/26 (Vol. I), available at <http://www.un.org/documents/ga/conf151/aconf15126-1annex1.htm> [hereinafter 1992 Rio Declaration].

63 Principle 3 of the 1992 Rio Declaration.

64 Principle 7 of the 1992 Rio Declaration.

65 Principle 10 of the 1992 Rio Declaration.

66 Principle 15 of the 1992 Rio Declaration.

67 Principle 16 of the 1992 Rio Declaration.

68 See JJ Bogardi and others, 'Water Security for a Planet under Pressure: Interconnected Challenges of a Changing World Call for Sustainable Solutions' (2012) *Current Opinion in Environmental Sustainability*, 4, 35 at 36.

In the process of leading up to the gathering, UNEP published a report with the aim to provide an update on how the world has changed – geopolitically, economically and environmentally – over the last twenty years since the Earth Summit. In terms of freshwater management, it again mentions effective water-sharing agreements between riparian states as a determining factor in the sustainable protection of freshwater ecosystems.[69] The report also notices the increase in states signing multilateral environmental agreements (e.g., the Convention on Biological Diversity, the Ramsar Convention and the Kyoto Protocol) and argues that this trend is proof of a rising political awareness of global environmental challenges.[70] However, the vagueness of many international treaties, together with the general lack of guidance on implementation and compliance, reveals a gap between legal scholarship and developments on the ground.[71] This is why, despite the numerous agreements negotiated since the 1972 Stockholm Conference and the 1992 Earth Summit in Rio, the UNEP report has to conclude that 'with limited progress on environmental issues achieved, and few real "success stories" to be told, all components of the environment – land, water, biodiversity, oceans and atmosphere – continue to degrade'.[72] This raises the question of whether the new deal struck in Rio during the UNCSD in 2012 will be able to put the community of states on track to develop the desperately needed cooperative frameworks based on solidarity, which are flexible enough to deal with the persistent environmental challenges which will only become more complex in the future.

In a move to include the public in the process, major non-governmental organisations and other stakeholders were invited to contribute to a compilation document used by the Secretariat of the UNCSD to prepare the Zero Draft of the outcome document.[73] This draft was supposed to be preliminary and transitional when it had been released in January 2012. It comes as no surprise that its language is rather vague and preambular, since the aim of the Zero Draft was to provide a point of departure for the debate on a common vision of how to implement sustainable development. The final statement from Rio, *The Future We Want*, is a 283-paragraph-long document which 'reaffirms', 'recognizes' and 'acknowledges' apparently every green initiative and environmental problem.[74] The wide spread of issues raised, as well as the type

69 United Nations Environment Programme, *Keeping Track of Our Changing Environment : From Rio to Rio+20* (United Nations Environment Programme 2011) at 43.

70 Ibid. at 55.

71 For an interesting analysis on why some international environmental regimes succeed while others fail, see EL Miles and others, *Environmental Regime Effectiveness : Confronting Theory with Evidence* (MIT Press 2002).

72 United Nations Environment Programme, *Keeping Track of Our Changing Environment: From Rio to Rio+20* at 90.

73 Secretariat of the 2012 United Nations Conference on Sustainable Development, *The Future We Want : Zero Draft* (10 January 2012) available at <http://www.uncsd2012.org/content/documents/370The%20Future%20We%20Want%2010Jan%20clean%20_no%20brackets.pdf>.

74 United Nations, Agenda Item 10 : Outcome of the United Nations Conference on Sustainable Development (UNCSD) Rio de Janeiro, Brazil (22 June 2012) UN Docs A/CONF.216/L.1, available at <https://rio20.un.org/sites/rio20.un.org/files/a-conf.216l-1_english.pdf.pdf> [hereinafter called 'The Future We Want'].

of language employed, prevents incorporating any substance as to how the global community should tackle the emerging crises. Hence, it is up to the governments to adapt and embed the vague language of *The Future We Want* in their respective national legal frameworks. The ambiguity does not break with the patchwork approach, and thus will not help to establish the global sustainable standards desperately needed for strengthening cooperative action.

With regard to the management of freshwater resources, the document reserves one section especially for the issues of 'water and sanitation'.[75] In paragraph 119, it 'recognises' that

> . . . water is at the core of sustainable development as it is closely linked to a number of key global challenges. We therefore reiterate the importance of integrating water in sustainable development and underline the critical importance of water and sanitation within the three dimensions of sustainable development.

The Future We Want then addresses the human security dimension of water by reaffirming

> . . . the commitments made in the Johannesburg Plan of Implementation and the Millennium Declaration regarding halving by 2015 the proportion of people without access to safe drinking water and basic sanitation and the development of integrated water resource management and water efficiency plans, ensuring sustainable water use. We commit to the progressive realization of access to safe and affordable drinking water and basic sanitation for all, as necessary for poverty eradication, the empowerment of women and to protect human health, and to significantly improve the implementation of integrated water resource management at all levels as appropriate. In this regard, we reiterate the commitments to support these efforts, in particular for developing countries, through the mobilization of resources from all sources, capacity-building and technology transfer.[76]

Regarding the human right to safe drinking water and sanitation, the document reaffirms earlier commitments made by states, without proposing actual steps as to its realisation.[77] Interesting here from an international law perspective is the mentioning of giving 'full respect for national sovereignty' in the process of achieving this goal. Paragraph 122 mentions the 'key role that ecosystems play in maintaining water quantity and quality'. Again, rather than committing to concrete actions or agreeing on minimum standards and rules

75 Paras 119–24 of *The Future We Want.*

76 Para 120 of *The Future We Want.*

77 Para 121 of *The Future We Want.*

with respect to maintaining healthy aquatic ecosystems – e.g., by fleshing out the obligation to conduct environmental and social impact assessments in a transboundary setting – it even limits its support to actions within 'respective national boundaries'.[78] The last two paragraphs of the section on water and sanitation underline the need to address issues of water quality (e.g., pollution and wastewater) and quantity (floods and droughts) with the help of mobilising financial resources, private investment in infrastructure, as well as through international assistance and cooperation.[79]

While some of the aims of Rio+20 were to push for the implementation of the original Rio Principles and to add detail to the Zero Draft in terms of content, rather than providing concrete goals and timelines, *The Future We Want* merely provides commitments to discuss further, hold more conferences and evaluate potential future commitments.[80] According to the final document of the UNCSD, sustainable development should be designed at the local and national levels. While there is nothing wrong with idea of 'act locally', marginalising the critical need to 'think globally' is counterproductive, given that the majority of local and national policies will certainly have an impact on transboundary ecosystems. While hopes were high that the summit could counteract the prevailing nationalism in addressing environmental problems, it did little to challenge the orthodox system and failed to promote the change needed to implement sustainable development practices across national borders. This is particularly obvious in the brief section on water and sanitation, with the mention of 'full respect for national sovereignty' and 'national boundaries'.[81] Hence, the Rio+20 summit, at least in terms of promoting an understanding of international law which comprehends the complexities of water security and the need for hydrosolidarity, has to be called a disappointment and a step backwards when compared to the 1992 Rio Declaration on Environment and Development and the Agenda 21.

This raises the question of the implications of *The Future We Want* for international law in general. Many NGOs have a purely negative impression of the overall outcome of the UNCSD, with the WWF calling it a process 'without content', bringing about a 'squandered opportunity' by producing an agreement which misses the chance to set the international community on a 'path toward sustainable development';[82] Greenpeace labelled it a 'failure of epic

78 Para 122 of *The Future We Want*.

79 Paras 123, 124 of *The Future We Want*.

80 See, e.g., paras 255, 256 of *The Future We Want* on establishing an intergovernmental committee to 'assess financing needs, consider the effectiveness, consistency and synergies of existing instruments and frameworks, and evaluate additional initiatives, with a view to preparing a report proposing options on an effective sustainable development financing strategy to facilitate the mobilization of resources and their effective use in achieving sustainable development objectives'.

81 Paras 121,122 of *The Future We Want*.

82 WWF, 'WWF Rio+20 Closing Statement' (21 June 2012) <http://wwf.panda.org/wwf_news/?205343/WWF-Rio20-closing-statement>.

proportions'.[83] However, it is important to put Rio+20 into perspective, as the expectations of many were based on the (relative) success of the Rio Earth Summit (UNCED) in 1992. Back then, the political and economic atmosphere was completely different to the one we are experiencing right now. Rather than being heavily influenced by an environment where the recent global economic crisis is still determining the agenda of international politics, UNCED happened at a time which looked much more promising for the future development of international environmental law.[84]

In analysing the legal impact of the document, one must not forget that, just like its predecessors (the 1972 Stockholm Declaration,[85] the 1992 Rio Declaration[86] and the 2002 Johannesburg Declaration[87]), *The Future We Want* is not a legally binding instrument. It does make reference to conventions and other international agreements touching the realm of sustainable development; but only with the objective of reaffirming existing commitments – rather than making new law.[88] For instance, it urges parties to the United Nations Framework Convention on Climate Change (UNFCCC),[89] the Convention on Biological Diversity (CBD)[90] and the United Nations Convention to Combat Desertification (UNCCD)[91] to fully implement their commitments

83 Greenpeace, 'Press Statement: Rio+20 Summit – A Failure of Epic Proportions' (22 June 2012) <http://www.greenpeace.org/international/en/press/releases/Greenpeace-Press-Statement-Rio20-Earth-Summit-a-failure-of-epic-proportions>.

84 See, e.g., J Delbrück and UE Heinz (eds), *The Future of International Law Enforcement : New Scenarios, New Law?* (Duncker & Humblot 1993); M Pallemaerts, 'International Environmental Law from Stockholm to Rio: Back to the Future?' in Sands P (ed.), *Greening International Law* (Earthscan 1993); PH Sand, 'International Environmental Law after Rio' (1993) *European Journal of International Law*, 4, 377.

85 Declaration of the United Nations Conference on the Human Environment, 5–16 June 1972 in Stockholm (16 June 1972) UN Doc A/CONF.48/14 [hereinafter 1972 Stockholm Declaration]; available at <http://www.unep.org/Documents.multilingual/Default.asp?DocumentID=97&ArticleID=1503>.

86 Declaration of the United Nations Conference on Environment and Development, 3–14 June 1992 in Rio de Janeiro (14 June 1992) UN Doc A/CONF.151/26 (Vol. I) [hereinafter 1992 Rio Declaration]; available at <http://www.un.org/documents/ga/conf151/aconf15126-1annex1.htm>.

87 Johannesburg Declaration on Sustainable Development (4 September 2002) UN Doc A/CONF.199/20 [hereinafter 2002 Johannesburg Declaration]; available at <http://www.un-documents.net/jburgdec.htm>.

88 A Powers, 'The Rio+20 Process: Forward Movement for the Environment?' (2012) *Transnational Environmental Law*, 1, 403 at 408.

89 United Nations Framework Convention on Climate Change (9 May 1992; entered into force 21 March 1994) 1771 UNTS 107; UN Doc A/AC.237/18 (Part II)/Add.1; reprinted in 31 ILM 849 (1992) available at <http://unfccc.int/resource/docs/convkp/conveng.pdf>.

90 Convention on Biological Diversity (5 June 1992; entered into force 29 December 1993) 1760 UNTS 79; reprinted in 31 ILM 818 (1992) available at <http://www.cbd.int/doc/legal/cbd-en.pdf>.

91 United Nations Convention to Combat Desertification in Countries Experiencing Serious Drought and/or Desertification, Particularly in Africa (17 June 1994; entered into force 26 December 1996) 1954 UNTS 3; UN Doc A/AC.241/27; reprinted in 33 ILM 1328 (1994) available at <http://www.ecolex.org/server2.php/libcat/docs/TRE/Multilateral/En/TRE001200.pdf>.

under those legal instruments.[92] Furthermore, *The Future We Want* underlines the importance of the rule of law at both national and international levels,[93] and reaffirms that the states 'continue to be guided by the purposes and principles of the Charter of the United Nations, with full respect for international law and its principles'.[94] However, there is little in the declaration which urges new binding obligations; nor are there any clues of a wider vision for the future development of international environmental law – which differentiates Rio+20 from the foresight that inspired the 1992 Rio Principles.[95] Ultimately, no major legal shifts were triggered by the UNCSD, and no significant impetus for the further development of international environmental law. Again, the role of the UN summits is not to produce new legal agreements or principles, but rather to communicate a universal declaration of intention on a wide range of issues concerning sustainable development. It remains to be seen whether *The Future We Want*, like the 1992 Rio Declaration and Agenda 21, will become a soft law basis for legal arguments on various issues of international environmental law.[96] While it may have promoted the concept of sustainable development by, at least, agreeing on the lowest common denominator of international norms and by strengthening the increasingly important role of non-state actors (business and civil society),[97] it did not create a real sense of urgency about the need for a radical transformation in the way we manage our shared water resources.

Despite the fact that Rio+20 as such can only be called a disappointment regarding legal commitments concerning water security and hydrosolidarity, the Post-2015 Development Agenda Consultation on Water might be a useful platform for future debates on how the global community should tackle the water crisis.[98] The UN started this open consultation process after the UNCSD, in order to identify priorities from citizens around the world for the post-2015 development agenda, since the Millennium Development Goals will reach their target date in 2015. However, while this process is an important one, it lacks any legitimacy and legal impact – a chance missed at Rio+20.

4.1.2.3 Observations

As already mentioned earlier, for hydrosolidarity to be useful as an ethical underpinning of water security, it has to establish boundaries through mutually agreed guidelines. The analysis of recent developments in the water arena raises the question of whether the 'global water community' has a clear and common vision of the 'future it wants'.

92 Para 17 of *The Future We Want.*
93 Paras 8, 10, and 252 of *The Future We Want.*
94 Para 7 of *The Future We Want.*
95 Powers, 'The Rio+20 Process: Forward Movement for the Environment?' at 409.
96 See Ibid. at 410.
97 Ibid.
98 For more detailed information on the initiative, see <http://www.worldwewant2015.org/water>.

There are good reasons for negating the question. First of all, one has to be aware of the diversity within the water community. While it may have a common goal – the sustainable and peaceful management of the world's freshwater resources – each discipline has its own list of issues and its very own manner of debating the concepts and methodologies it deems useful in addressing them. This in turn means that each forum has its own agenda as well, since they are being influenced by different disciplines in very different ways. While the fact that no single discipline can offer an effective answer to the water crisis on its own seems to be widely acknowledged, the question of which discipline is allowed at the negotiation table and at what stage still seems to divide the various camps. The evolution of transboundary freshwater management has revolved around some key themes, including integrated water resources management (IWRM),[99] good water governance[100] and stakeholder involvement, to name a few.[101] Common to these is the need for adequate legal frameworks which support the peaceful utilisation and development of shared water resources and which promote regional cooperative approaches recognising the interdependencies and common interests. Over the past decade alone, the world community has elevated water as a global political issue,[102] through various streams – like the World Water Forums, the World Water Week and others. However, these initiatives do not necessarily attach the same level of importance to the development of hydrosolidarity, since they all follow their own agendas.

The focus on how to solve the global freshwater crisis has for too long been on technical solutions – fuelled by the hope of being able to innovate ourselves out of water insecurity. While science and technology are of prime importance to an effective solution, one has to remember that they have to be 'grounded in the equitable and efficient allocation of water'.[103] The prevalent piecemeal approach in the global water arena is costly – both in resources and time. We have an unprecedented opportunity to make hydrosolidarity reality by working across boundaries and tearing down silo thinking. While striving towards hydrosolidarity is a noble task, the concept can only be of any benefit if it is being supported by an effective legal framework.[104] The issue here is

99 See, e.g., Global Water Partnership and International Network of Basin Organizations, *A Handbook for Integrated Water Resources Management in Basins* (GWP; INBO 2009).

100 See C Tortajada, 'Water Governance: Some Critical Issues' (2010) *International Journal of Water Resources Development*, 26, 297.

101 P Wouters, S Vinogradov and B-O Magsig, 'Water Security, Hydrosolidarity and International Law: A River Runs through It . . . ' (2009) *Yearbook of International Environmental Law*, 19, 97 at 128.

102 See RG Varady and M Iles-Shih, 'Global Water Initiatives: What Do the Experts Think? Report on a Survey of Leading Figures in the World of Water' in Biswas AK and Tortajada C (eds), *Impacts of Megaconferences on the Water Sector* (Springer 2009).

103 E Lopez-Gunn and MR Llamas, 'Re-Thinking Water Scarcity: Can Science and Technology Solve the Global Water Crisis?' (2008) *Natural Resources Forum*, 32, 228 at 236.

104 P Wouters, 'The Relevance and Role of Water Law in the Sustainable Development of Freshwater : From "Hydrosovereignty" to "Hydrosolidarity"' (2000) *Water International*, 25, 202.

that there is no guiding principle in international water law which provides a framework for the concept to thrive. This disconnect between aspiration and the legal system is immense; this is even more distressing given the fact that the international community needs to work together across boundaries to address the complex water challenges. Here, global and regional hydrosolidarity should be the guiding concept at the policy level and a driver in the future evolution of international legal regimes.

Collective action, based upon cooperative mechanisms – reaching and implementing agreements, establishing and supporting transboundary institutional mechanisms, collecting and sharing scientific data and information, engaging with civil society and ensuring public participation – is the prerequisite for achieving common water security, addressing both the imperative to maintain the integrity of the resource and the need to meet social and economic development objectives.[105] The hydrosolidarity paradigm spans the spectrum of actors and uses, and calls for a new understanding of collective action, including the benefits of global cooperation[106] and enhanced water governance,[107] especially within the context of transboundary freshwater resources. Unfortunately, the views on, and interpretations of, hydrosolidarity within the highly diverse group of water experts varies tremendously – the main reason being the lack of legal force behind the notion. This is why the substitution of one concept with a new one, which seems to have gathered traction in the global water arena, is becoming commonplace. The issue with such an approach is that paradigms which are promising in adding something new to the discussion on sustainable freshwater management will not always be examined and acknowledged in the way they should. Instead of thorough analysis and implementation of paradigms, like hydrosolidarity, we are witnessing the emergence and disappearance of buzzwords at an increasing pace.

In order to achieve hydrosolidarity, 'Principles and rules for sharing will have to be found for the unavoidable compromises between incompatible water interests'.[108] This endeavour seems unattainable to many, especially given the increasingly short-sighted transboundary water policies, which have become more frequent with the changing role business plays in the thematic discussions in the various global water initiatives. Does this ultimately label hydrosolidarity as a utopian paradigm – or is it still a useful concept which has merely been neglected? The next section will address this question by looking at the relationship between other fields of international law and solidarity.

105 E Benvenisti, 'Collective Action in the Utilization of Shared Freshwater: The Challenges of International Water Resources Law' (1996) *American Journal of International Law*, 90, 384 at 389.

106 See S Barrett, *Why Cooperate? The Incentive to Supply Global Public Goods* (Oxford University Press 2007); M Byers, 'Conceptualising the Relationship between Jus Cogens and Erga Omnes Rules' (1997) *Nordic Journal of International Law*, 66, 211.

107 Gerlak, Varady and Haverland, 'Hydrosolidarity and International Water Governance' at 324.

108 Falkenmark and Rockström, *Balancing Water for Humans and Nature: The New Approach in Ecohydrology* at 214.

4.2 The role of international law in overcoming '(hydro) egoism'

Since solidarity is a value-laden notion and its definition is highly subjective, the implementation of the concept often proves elusive – especially in a regime based on consent like international law. Here, new legal concepts which strengthen international cooperation are key to better coping with common security challenges. The development of structures and instruments of cooperation has to facilitate more meaningful obligations based on solidarity. Hence, it seems appropriate to infer that cooperation as such already entails an element of solidarity.[109]

In social sciences, the concept of solidarity is by no means a novel one, as it is inseparably linked with the development of societies. If law is perceived as the 'formal instrument of orderly change in society',[110] it has to address questions of solidarity as well. In a national setting, this can be observed quite frequently – especially in countries following the 'social state principle'.[111] How is the concept brought into play in a more complex and multifaceted global environment? As Insensee stated correctly, solidarity requires specific commonalities in order to emerge, e.g., correlating interests and spatial proximity.[112] It would seem natural, then, that with an increase in distance between the subjects, the strength of their solidarity would decrease. This reasoning is even more plausible considering the horizontal relationship between sovereign states. Yet the following section will demonstrate that the concept of solidarity did indeed find its way into public international law and will show how it materialised.

Just as the structure of international law has been changing over time,[113] so has the role solidarity is playing here. This evolution has led to the realisation that international law has moved from a mere 'law of coexistence' to a 'law of cooperation'.[114] However, this rather simplified view ignores that most areas of international law are still ruled by the regime of coexistence; while in some specific fields, cooperation has grown into something even

109 P-T Stoll, 'Responsibility, Sovereignty and Cooperation – Reflections on the "Responsibility to Protect"' in König D and others (eds), *International Law Today: New Challenges and the Need for Reform?* (Springer 2008) at 14.

110 IF Shihata, 'Preface: Good Governance and the Role of Law in Economic Development' in Seidman AW, Seidman RB and Waelde TW (eds), *Making Development Work : Legislative Reform for Institutional Transformation and Good Governance* (Kluwer Law International 1999) at xvii.

111 See, e.g., Art 20(1) of the Basic Law for the Federal Republic of Germany (23 May 1949; last amended 11 July 2012) stating that 'The Federal Republic of Germany is a democratic and social federal state.'

112 J Isensee, 'Solidarität – Sozialethische Substanz Eines Blankettbegriffs' in Isensee J (ed.), *Solidarität in Knappheit : Zum Problem der Priorität* (Duncker & Humblot 1998) at 113.

113 See W Friedmann, *The Changing Structure of International Law* (Columbia University Press 1964).

114 P Hilpold, 'Solidarität Als Rechtsprinzip: Völkerrechtliche, Europarechtliche und Staatsrechtliche Betrachtungen' (2007) *Jahrbuch des öffentlichen Rechts*, 55, 195 at 196.

bigger: institutionalised solidarity. These distinct realities have been described as 'islands of cooperation'[115] in an ocean of coexistence and 'islands of solidarity'[116] in an ocean of cooperation. Where, then, can we find these islands of solidarity, how did they evolve, and is solidarity in international law actually more than just a catchword in need of concretisation?

Law is supposed to be applied to all of its subjects without discrimination – ultimately treating like cases alike and enabling dissimilar cases to be distinguished from each other. While governments constantly disagree on what exactly constitutes relevant differences, differentiation is a widely accepted practice in international negotiations – i.e., with contextual and differential obligations.[117]

Norms are 'contextual' when they provide for obligations which are on their face identical for all states, yet their application takes into account varying characteristics of the countries.[118] The most prominent example here may be the principle of equitable and reasonable utilisation discussed in the previous chapter. By allowing for weighing and balancing, contextual norms seem to be easier to agree on, but lack certainty in the outcome. The vagueness of the provisions regularly leads to intense arguments about compliance and non-compliance.

In contrast, 'differential' norms provide for apparently different, and in most of the cases also more beneficial, standards for one group of states compared to the others.[119] One example is the allowance for delayed compliance in the Montreal Protocol, where developing countries are entitled to postpone the phasing-out of certain ozone-depleting substances for ten years.[120] The following sections provide an overview of how international law is trying to implement the concept of solidarity.

4.2.1 Linking solidarity with principles of international law

The concept of solidarity finds expression in *erga omnes* obligations, which have been established through an *orbiter dictum* by the ICJ in 1970 in the Barcelona Traction case.[121] Here, the Court made clear that

115 G Abi-Saab, 'Whither the International Community?' (1998) *European Journal of International Law*, 9, 248 at 255.

116 K Wellens, 'Discussion Following the Presentation by Karel Wellens' in Wolfrum R and Kojima C (eds), *Solidarity: A Structural Principle of International Law* (Springer 2010) at 10.

117 D Shelton, 'Equity' in Bodansky D, Brunnée J and Hey E (eds), *The Oxford Handbook of International Environmental Law* (Oxford University Press 2007) at 641.

118 DB Magraw, 'Legal Treatment of Developing Countries: Differential, Contextual, and Absolute Norms' (1990) *Colorado Journal of International Environmental Law and Policy*, 1, 69 at 74.

119 Ibid. at 73.

120 Art 5(1) of the Montreal Protocol on Substances that Deplete the Ozone Layer (16 September 1987; entered into force 1 January 1989) 1522 UNTS 3; reprinted in 26 ILM 1550 (1987).

121 Case Concerning Barcelona Traction, Light and Power Company, Limited (Belgium v. Spain), Judgement of 5 February 1970, ICJ Reports 1970, 3 [hereinafter Barcelona Traction].

> . . . an essential distinction should be drawn between the obligations of a state towards the international community as a whole, and those arising vis-à-vis another State in the field of diplomatic protection. By their very nature the former are the concern of all states. In view of the importance of the rights involved, all States can be held to have a legal interest in their protection; they are obligations *erga omnes*.[122]

Examples of this category include the outlawing of acts of aggression and of genocide, and the protection from slavery and racial discrimination.[123] Today, the concept is claimed to be solidly grounded in modern international law.[124]

While both *erga omnes* and solidarity are often being challenged due to their content-related vagueness, their link may shine a light on their significance in international law.[125] It is periodically stated that violations of obligations *erga omnes* can be sanctioned or brought before the ICJ by any other state. This in turn would tie a strong bond of solidarity around the international community – transforming it into an inseparable 'community of fate'.[126] In the realm of common interests, every state would be obliged to remind the wrongdoing member of society of its going astray and, if necessary, call on the ICJ – without the requirement of any individual interest of the plaintiff in the matter; and giving no effect to the argument of state sovereignty of the defendant. While this seems to be an appealing theoretical construct, it does not describe the actual reality of enforcement under international law. As Bruno Simma stated correctly, 'Viewed realistically, the world of obligations *erga omnes* is still the world of the "ought" rather than of the "is;" the concept marks the direction in which international law will have to move rather than a clear course already steered today.'[127] However, given the pace at which not only the international society, but also international law is evolving, we should not close our minds to further research on how this concept can play a role in achieving water security. One prominent example is the visionary reasoning by Judge Weeramantry in his separate opinion in the Gabčíkovo-Nagymaros

122 Barcelona Traction, Judgement, ICJ Report 1970, 3at 32.

123 Ibid; also Case Concerning Military and Paramilitary Activities in and Against Nicaragua (Nicaragua v. United States of America), Merits, Judgment of 27 June 1986, ICJ Reports 1986, 14 at 100; Case Concerning East Timor (Portugal v. Australia), Dissenting Opinion of Judge Weeramantry, ICJ Reports 1995, 90 at 172, 204.

124 Tams, *Enforcing Obligations Erga Omnes in International Law* at 190.

125 See M Ragazzi, 'International Obligations Erga Omnes: Their Moral Foundation and Criteria of Identification in Light of Two Japanese Contributions' in Goodwin-Gill GS and Talmon S (eds), *The Reality of International Law: Essays in Honour of Ian Brownlie* (Clarendon Press 1999).

126 Hilpold, 'Solidarität Als Rechtsprinzip : Völkerrechtliche, Europarechtliche und Staatsrechtliche Betrachtungen' at 197.

127 B Simma, 'Does the UN Charter Provide an Adequate Legal Basis for Individual or Collective Responses to Violations of Obligations Erga Omnes?' in Delbrück J and Heinz UE (eds), *The Future of International Law Enforcement : New Scenarios, New Law?* (Duncker & Humblot 1993) at 125.

Case, where he argues for 'sustainable development' to be regarded as an obligation *erga omnes*.[128]

While the acceptance of the concept can be regarded as universal, most scholars tend to water down their examination of obligations *erga omnes* by merely referring to linked concepts which are more straightforward to analyse.[129] In addition, one can observe the tendency to minimise the debate about the concept to the, beyond doubt important, element of solidarity; without showing the same attention for another feature of *erga omnes* obligations: universality – i.e. all states, without exception, are bound by them. This shortcoming is all the more unfortunate, since universality seems to be incompatible with the current structure of international society – comprised of sovereign states on a consensual basis – which in turn raises a fundamental theoretical dilemma.[130] The result of the rather incomplete discourse is that the concept of *erga omnes* remains for the most part 'very mysterious indeed'.[131] For the purpose of this section, however, it may suffice to conclude that obligations *erga omnes* have a moral foundation – one which is based on solidarity.

The most apparent manifestation of solidarity between nations can be found in the realm of development assistance. Here, in recent decades, a process of concretisation took place by which the formerly spontaneously expressed demonstrations of solidarity initiated the formation of some legal principles.[132] While there is (still) no legal right to development aid, the UN General Assembly set a standard that – at least indirectly – applies pressure on those states which are better off. Already back in 1970, the target was set to spend 0.7 per cent of GNI on aid for developing countries. However, only a few states kept their promise. Most countries are far away from reaching this goal anytime soon, with an average rate of 0.30 per cent in 2002, while still endorsing it.[133] This does not speak for the effectiveness of solidarity in the area of development assistance. In fact, international law of development aid did fail not least because here the

128 Case Concerning the Gabčíkovo-Nagymaros Project (Hungary v. Slovakia) General List no. 92 (1997) reprinted in 37 ILM 162 (1998) Rep 7, separate opinion of Vice-President Weeramantry, at C(c).

129 One of the few exceptions which discusses the implications of *erga omnes* rules in international environmental law thoroughly is F Orrego-Vicuña, 'State Responsibility, Liability, and Remedial Measures under International Law: New Criteria for Environmental Protection' in Brown Weiss E (ed.), *Environmental Change and International Law : New Challenges and Dimensions* (United Nations University Press 1992)

130 See Ragazzi, 'International Obligations Erga Omnes: Their Moral Foundation and Criteria of Identification in Light of Two Japanese Contributions' at 459.

131 I Brownlie, 'To What Extent Are the Traditional Categories of Lex Lata and Lex Ferenda Still Available?' in Cassese A and Weiler J (eds), *Change and Stability in International Law-Making* (De Gruyter 1988) at 71.

132 Hilpold, 'Solidarität Als Rechtsprinzip : Völkerrechtliche, Europarechtliche und Staatsrechtliche Betrachtungen' at 201.

133 See OECD, 'Net ODA in 2013 – As a Percentage of GNI' (8 April 2014) <http://www.oecd.org/dac/stats/documentupload/ODA%202013%20Tables%20and%20Charts%20En.pdf>.

concept of solidarity has been exploited and strained.[134] It has been stretched beyond its limit, due to the fact that one-way foreign aid only reinforced the dependencies of the past, which in turn caused a demanding attitude which became unquenchable. Further, it has been misused by promoting financial aid instead of the much more sustainable approach of pushing for true integration of developing countries into the global economy.[135] It is this disregard for one of the fundamental principles of public international law – the sovereign equality of states – which caused the failure of effective incorporation of solidarity into development aid law. In this sense, measures of solidarity should not create or reinforce dependencies; instead, they have to overcome the hierarchy prevalent in the international community, and promote a future of political independence and economic self-sufficiency.[136]

In the realm of international humanitarian law, solidarity has to be considered a mainstay. Again, the principle of reciprocity only takes limited effect. Contrary to the law of war, which focuses on imposing mutual restrictions, the main goal here is to further develop a humanitarian standard,[137] which has been recognised as a legal principle by the ICJ in the Nicaragua Case.[138] It is this realisation which explains why the principles of humanitarian law have been applied in cases of civil war as well, despite the fact that they are primarily directed at international armed conflicts.[139] From an ethical point of view, this surely is a welcome development; its dogmatic derivation and reasoning are, however, questionable.[140]

Another sub-discipline of international law conceptually close to humanitarian law is refugee law, which came into being in the face of the humanitarian disaster following the Second World War and the subsequent flows of refugees caused by mass expulsions. While the 1951 UN Convention Relating to the

134 Hilpold, 'Solidarität Als Rechtsprinzip : Völkerrechtliche, Europarechtliche und Staatsrechtliche Betrachtungen' at 202.

135 See N Birdsall, H Kharas and R Perakis, *The Quality of Official Development Assistance Assessment 2009: Is Aid Quality Improving?* (Brookings 2012).

136 Hilpold, 'Solidarität Als Rechtsprinzip: Völkerrechtliche, Europarechtliche und Staatsrechtliche Betrachtungen' at 202.

137 MN Shaw, *International Law* (6th edn, Cambridge University Press 2008) at 1167.

138 'The Court however sees no need to take a position on that matter, since in its view the conduct of the United States may be judged according to the fundamental general principles of humanitarian law; in its view, the Geneva Conventions are in some respects a development, and in other respects no more than the expression, of such principles . . . There is no doubt that, in the event of international armed conflicts, these rules also constitute a minimum yardstick, in addition to the more elaborate rules which are also to apply to international conflicts; and they are rules which, in the Court's opinion, reflect what the Court in 1949 called "elementary considerations of humanity" . . . '; see Case Concerning Military and Paramilitary Activities in and Against Nicaragua (Nicaragua v. United States of America), Merits, Judgment, ICJ Reports 1986, 14 at para 218.

139 The Prosecutor v. Dusko Tadic (Jurisdiction of the Tribunal) Decision of 2 October 1995 in Case No.IT-94-1-AR72; reprinted in 35 ILM (1996) 32.

140 See P Hilpold, 'Gewaltverbot und Selbstverteidigung – Zwei Eckpfeiler Des Völkerrechts Auf Dem Prüfstand' (2006) *Juristische Arbeitsblätter*, 38, 234.

Status of Refugees[141] did not live up to the expectations in addressing this catastrophe (since it merely includes the principle of non-refoulement), several enactments of national legislation did go beyond this standard by including an actual right of asylum.[142] Over the last decades, the set of problems surrounding refugees has changed dramatically. The international community is now also confronted with high numbers of economic migrants,[143] internally displaced persons[144] and environmental migrants.[145] Refugees and internally displaced persons (IDPs) have tripled in the last thirty years.[146] The United Nations High Commissioner for Refugees (UNHCR) reported a total of 51.2 million forcibly displaced people at the end of 2013 – divided into 16.7 million refugees, 1.2 million asylum-seekers (pending cases) and 33.3 million internally displaced people.[147]

The latter category has found special treatment in the African Union Convention for the Protection and Assistance of Internally Displaced Persons in Africa.[148] While the Convention has not yet entered into force and is only a regional framework, its implications for the concept of solidarity in international law are nevertheless noteworthy. The Convention calls upon states – for the first time – to recognise the rights of internally displaced persons to humanitarian assistance, and defines the obligations states as well as armed groups have towards the protection of uprooted citizens.[149] Furthermore, it is remarkable that the Convention not only applies to those who are put in danger by armed conflict, but also by natural disasters.[150] However, given the magnitude

141 United Nations Convention Relating to the Status of Refugees (28 July 1951; entered into force 22 April 1954) 189 UNTS 137.

142 Examples include Art 16(a)(1) of the Basic Law for the Federal Republic of Germany: 'Persons persecuted on political grounds shall have the right of asylum.'

143 In general, economic migrants can only expect a low degree of solidarity. See J Seabrook, 'The Migrant in the Mirror' (2000) *New Internationalist* 34.

144 SE Davies and L Glanville (eds), *Protecting the Displaced: Deepening the Responsibility to Protect* (Martinus Nijhoff Publishers 2010).

145 See, e.g., J McAdam and B Saul, 'An Insecure Climate for Human Security? Climate-Induced Displacement and International Law' (2008) *Sydney Law School Legal Studies Research Paper*, 8, Also: LR Brown, *Plan B 4.0 : Mobilizing to Save Civilization* (W.W. Norton 2009) at 51.

146 World Bank, *World Development Report 2011: Conflict, Security, and Development* (World Bank 2011) at 5.

147 United Nations High Commissioner for Refugees, *UNHCR Global Trends 2013: War's Human Cost* (UNHCR 2014) at 2.

148 African Union Convention for the Protection and Assistance of Internally Displaced Persons in Africa (23 October 2009; not yet entered into force) <http://www.au.int/en/content/african-union-convention-protection-and-assistance-internally-displaced-persons-africa>.

149 SE Davies and L Glanville, 'Protecting the Displaced: Introduction' in Davies SE and Glanville L (eds), *Protecting the Displaced : Deepening the Responsibility to Protect* (Martinus Nijhoff Publishers 2010) at 1.

150 Art 1(k) of the African Union Convention for the Protection and Assistance of Internally Displaced Persons in Africa: '"Internally Displaced Persons" means persons or groups of persons who have been forced or obliged to flee or to leave their homes or places of habitual residence, in particular as a result of or in order to avoid the effects of armed conflict, situations of generalized violence, violations of human rights or natural or human-made disasters, and who have not crossed an internationally recognized State border.'

of humanitarian disaster caused by the recent uprising in various North African states, questions about the level of solidarity in the international society and its effective implementation of international legal frameworks remain – not only in this particular region. Whose responsibility is it to protect displaced people when their home country no longer feels obliged to? What is the role of the broader international community in assuring such migrants protection when their respective home nation refuses to do so? How to overcome the 'shield of sovereignty' in order to pursue the greater good of solidarity?

While the definition of a refugee according to the UN High Commissioner on Refugees does not include the environment as a reason to flee,[151] the issues linked to environmental migrants will only grow in complexity and significance. The number of such 'refugees' has been estimated to be 25 million people,[152] with the UN projecting the numbers to increase to 50 million by 2020.[153] These massive figures alone deserve a debate about broadening the UNHCR's mandate to 'persons of concern' and the nature and scope of the international refugee regime in general.[154] The term 'environmental refugees' was first popularised by Lester Brown,[155] founder of the Worldwatch Institute and the Earth Policy Institute, and has been defined as 'persons who no longer gain a secure livelihood in their traditional homelands because of what are primarily environmental factors of unusual scope'.[156] While the concept as such has been heavily criticised for being vaguely defined, legally irrelevant and rather confusing,[157] migration due to factors such as water scarcity, land and water pollution, flooding and rising sea levels is already a widespread phenomenon which demonstrates quite vividly that the changes in the earth's physical conditions are heavily impacting regional peace and security.[158] This is why

151 Adapted from Art 1(a) of the United Nations Convention Relating to the Status of Refugees, which defines a refugee as a person who 'owing to a well-founded fear of being persecuted for reasons of race, religion, nationality, membership of a particular social group, or political opinion, is outside the country of his nationality, and is unable to or, owing to such fear, is unwilling to avail himself of the protection of that country'.

152 N Myers, 'Environmental Refugees: A Growing Phenomenon of the 21st Century' (2002) *Philosophical Transactions of the Royal Society of London Series B, Biological Sciences*, 357, 609 at 609.

153 Cristina Tirado at the annual meeting of the American Association for the Advancement of Science (AAAS): 'In 2020, the UN has projected that we will have 50 million environmental refugees', available at <http://www.physorg.com/news/2011-02-million-environmental-refugees-experts.html>.

154 See R Black, *Environmental Refugees: Myth or Reality?* (United Nations High Commissioner for Refugees 2001).

155 Brown, *Plan B 4.0: Mobilizing to Save Civilization* at 51.

156 N Myers and J Kent, *Environmental Exodus: An Emergent Crisis in the Global Arena* (Climate Institute 1995) at 18.

157 See, e.g., J McGregor, 'Refugees and the Environment' in Black R and Robinson V (eds), *Geography and Refugees: Patterns and Processes of Change* (Belhaven Press 1993); G Kibreab, 'Migration, Environment and Refugeehood' in Zaba B and Clarke J (eds), *Environment and Population Change* (Derouaux Ordina Editions 1994).

158 See R Matthew, M Halle and J Switzer (eds), *Conserving the Peace: Resources, Livelihoods and Security* (International Institute for Sustainable Development 2002).

more and more scholars are calling on the international community to properly address what they consider to be one of today's most crucial governance needs – the issue of so-called 'climate refugees'. Global environmental change will affect the lives of millions of people all over the world, forcing them to leave their homes and to seek refuge elsewhere – a crisis which will most likely surpass all previously known refugee crises.[159] It is this area which will test how seriously the international community is taking the cry for greater solidarity and which concrete steps it will implement in order to make the international refugee regime future-proof.[160]

4.2.2 Solidarity in international environmental law

The concept of solidarity shares a close link with international environmental law – in particular with the notion of sustainable development.[161] This paradigm evolved through efforts to simultaneously factor in concerns regarding socio-economic development and the protection of the environment – as an attempt to address the constantly changing perception of the environment vs economic activity dilemma.[162] While there is general agreement about the value of sustainable development as an overarching framework, there is still strong disagreement about its specifics and implications. Policy makers have long tried to overcome the environment/development conundrum by treating the parties differently. The underlying expectation of such a differentiation is that it will lead to equity, which is vital for any international agreement in order to be perceived as fair, and thus, ultimately, become self-enforcing. The international community has attempted to solve this puzzle with the concept of 'common but differentiated responsibilities' (CBDR) – which arose during the New International Economic Order (NIEO) period in the area of international economic law and is increasingly being recognised in international law.[163]

159 F Biermann and I Boas, 'Preparing for a Warmer World: Towards a Global Governance System to Protect Climate Refugees' (2010) *Global Environmental Politics*, 10, 60 at 61.

160 See B Mayer, 'The International Legal Protection of Climate (or Environmental) Migrants at the Crossroads: Fraternity, Responsibility and Sustainability' (2012) *Supreme Court Law Review*, 56, 723.

161 For a detailed analysis of the concept and its linkages with international water law, see A Rieu-Clarke, *International Law and Sustainable Development: Lessons from the Law of International Watercourses* (IWA Publishing 2005).

162 See DB Magraw and LD Hawke, 'Sustainable Development' in Bodansky D, Brunnée J and Hey E (eds), *The Oxford Handbook of International Environmental Law* (Oxford University Press 2007).

163 CD Stone, 'Common but Differentiated Responsibilities in International Law' (2004) *American Journal of International Law*, 98, 276 at 276. An example for the explicit adoption of the expression is the United Nations Framework Convention on Climate Change, Art 3(1). Other conventions do not adopt the term, but do in fact differentiate, including the Adjustments and Amendments to the Montreal Protocol on Substances That Deplete the Ozone Layer (29 June 1990) reprinted in 30 ILM 537, 541 (1991). Still others employ more veiled variants, like the Convention on Biological Diversity.

The main objective of CBDR is to differentiate (mostly) between developed and developing countries in defining the degree of each state's responsibility to address a certain environmental problem – i.e., the management of a risk-related public good (e.g., climate, ozone layer, peace, or public health).[164] Therefore, it has become a touchstone for the equity debate in international environmental law.[165] Since the various competing perceptions of equity are the main obstacle to progress in international environmental negotiations, it is necessary to know exactly what the concept of CBDR implies. Although the term 'CBDR' is quite recent, implementing differentiated responsibilities in international treaties is not. The Treaty of Versailles (1919) was the first one recognising the fact that differences make uniformity difficult. Another prominent example is the General Agreement on Tariffs and Trade (GATT), which allows for 'differential and more favourable' treatment.[166] However, it is the area of international environmental law which has been proved the most fruitful for the adoption of non-uniform obligations. The so-called 'modern era' of international environmental law can be traced back to the UN Conference on the Human Environment held in 1972 in Stockholm. Here, one could witness a deep divide between developing and industrialised countries. While developing states focused on the developmental needs of their countries, the already industrialised nations were urged to develop some kind of global environmental ethic.[167] This dissonance was apparently resolved with a compromise enshrined in the 1972 Stockholm Declaration on the Human Environment.[168]

On the one hand, the preamble acknowledged that environmental protection was a 'major issue' and the 'urgent desire of the peoples of the whole world and the duty of all governments'.[169] It further states that 'The environment should be handled in a cooperative spirit by all countries on an equal footing.'[170] On the other hand, in keeping with the developing countries' focus on development, a distinction was made between the 'pollution of poverty' (caused by lack of financial resources) and the 'pollution of affluence' (originating from rapid industrialisation).[171] This is why the preamble of the Stockholm Declaration reads:

164 Ibid. at 277; M Weisslitz, 'Rethinking the Equitable Principle of Common but Differentiated Responsibility: Differential Versus Absolute Norms of Compliance and Contribution in the Global Climate Change Context' (2002) *Colorado Journal of International Environmental Law and Policy*, 13, 473 at 476.

165 M Cazorla and M Toman, 'International Equity and Climate Change Policy' (2000) *Resources for the Future – Climate Issue Brief*, 27, at 1.

166 General Agreement on Tariffs and Trade (15 April 1994; entered into force 1 January 1995) 1867 UNTS 187; reprinted in 33 ILM 1153 (1994).

167 L Rajamani, *Differential Treatment in International Environmental Law* (Oxford University Press 2006) at 55.

168 Declaration of the United Nations Conference on the Human Environment, 5 to 16 June 1972 in Stockholm (16 June 1972) UN Doc A/CONF.48/14 [hereinafter 1972 Stockholm Declaration].

169 Preamble of the 1972 Stockholm Declaration.

170 Principle 24 of the 1972 Stockholm Declaration.

171 Rajamani, *Differential Treatment in International Environmental Law* at 56.

> in the developing countries most of the environmental problems are caused by underdevelopment . . . The developing countries must direct their efforts to development, bearing in mind their priorities and the need to safeguard and improve the environment . . . [and] the industrialized countries should make efforts to reduce the gap between themselves and the developing countries.

Further, the 'state sovereignty over natural resources' principle also strikes a balance between national sovereignty and environmental responsibility:

> States have, in accordance with the Charter of the United Nations and the principles of international law, the sovereign right to exploit their own resources pursuant to their own environmental policies, and the responsibility to ensure that activities within their jurisdiction or control do not cause damage to the environment of other States or of areas beyond the limits of national jurisdiction.[172]

These wordings point out that the link between environment and development supported by the developing countries was increasingly being recognised.

Consequently, the next environmental conference was entitled the UN Conference on Environment and Development (UNCED), held in 1992 at the Rio Earth Summit. Twenty years after Stockholm, the dissonance between developing and industrialised countries had not weakened. The developed nations tried to emphasise the threat of global environmental issues, seen as a result of affluence, whereas the developing countries focused on local issues, thought to be caused by poverty.[173] While the industrialised world traced the degradation of the global environment back to population growth in the developing world, developing countries blamed it on the consumption levels of industrialised states.[174] The resulting Rio Declaration again tried to balance between these competing claims.[175] Whilst some of the adopted key principles are in favour of the developed countries' position (e.g., the 'polluter pays' principle and the precautionary approach), others tried to meet the requirements of developing countries (e.g., the right to development, poverty alleviation and the recognition of common but differentiated responsibilities).[176]

Although both conferences tried to resolve the quandary between environment and development, the approach of Rio was somehow novel, as a shift

172 Principle 21 of the 1972 Stockholm Declaration.

173 See Pallemaerts, 'International Environmental Law from Stockholm to Rio: Back to the Future?'.

174 L Rajamani, 'From Stockholm to Johannesburg: The Anatomy of Dissonance in the International Environmental Dialogue' (2003) *Review of European Community & International Environmental Law*, 12, 23 at 25.

175 Declaration of the United Nations Conference on Environment and Development, 3 to 14 June 1992 in Rio de Janeiro (14 June 1992) UN Doc A/CONF.151/26 (Vol. I)

176 Principles 16, 15; and Principles 3, 5, 7 of the 1992 Rio Declaration.

from international environmental law to the international law of sustainable development could be noticed.[177] The most notable indicator of change is the slightly different wording of the principle regarding a state's sovereignty over natural resources. Recalling that the Stockholm Declaration recognised the sovereign right of states 'to exploit their own resources pursuant to their own *environmental* policies',[178] the Rio Declaration grants the sovereign right of states 'to exploit their own resources pursuant to their own *environmental and developmental* policies'.[179] This demonstrates quite clearly that the boundaries between environmental and developmental law are floating, and that both areas are now enclosed in the sphere of international law of sustainable development.[180] Further, Principle 3 of the Rio Declaration stipulates the 'right to development', which has to take into account the developmental and environmental needs of present and future generations; while Principle 7 points out that industrialised countries bear a responsibility in the international pursuit of sustainable development, and that 'in view of the different contributions to global environmental degradation, states have common but differentiated responsibilities.' It was the first time the notion of CBDR found its way into an international document. This raises the question of what exactly is meant by 'common but differentiated responsibilities' – e.g., in the realm of global climate change policy.

Due to the fact that global environmental problems need to be addressed by common action, it is beyond debate that an international agreement aimed at addressing climatic changes fails to accomplish its goal if it does not involve the whole international community.[181] This is even more the case since formerly domestic concerns (e.g., forestry) are now being perceived as international ones (forests' function as carbon sinks). Yet, universal participation faces a major handicap: lack of resources of developing countries. Due to the fact that they need to channel a majority of their resources towards the alleviation of poverty, developing states do not have the same ability to address environmental problems as their industrialised counterparts.[182] This rationale was also implemented in the Rio Declaration which states that 'The special situation and needs of developing countries . . . shall be given special priority.'[183] Thus, their lower financial and institutional capabilities justify differentiation within the area of international environmental law. Another argument for differentiation

177 Rajamani, *Differential Treatment in International Environmental Law* at 59.

178 Principle 21 of the 1972 Stockholm Declaration (emphasis added).

179 Principle 2 of the 1992 Rio Declaration (emphasis added).

180 Pallemaerts, 'International Environmental Law from Stockholm to Rio: Back to the Future?'; Rajamani, *Differential Treatment in International Environmental Law* at 61.

181 D French, 'Developing States and International Environmental Law: The Importance of Differentiated Responsibilities' (2000) *International and Comparative Law Quarterly*, 49, 35 at 45.

182 Weisslitz, 'Rethinking the Equitable Principle of Common but Differentiated Responsibility: Differential Versus Absolute Norms of Compliance and Contribution in the Global Climate Change Context' at 478.

183 Principle 6 of the 1992 Rio Declaration.

is the different level of culpability, since not all countries contributed equally to global environmental degradation.[184] Acknowledging that industrialised nations have done most of the polluting, developing countries should be given leeway in environmental policies. These three domains of CBDR – need, capability and responsibility – can be directly traced back to the three principles of equity.

4.2.2.1 Differential treatment under the climate regime

For the first time in international environmental law, the concept of CBDR was made the explicit basis for the different commitments of developed and developing states in the UNFCCC.[185] Based on this notion, the UNFCCC entails a balance of commitments between states by stipulating that 'The parties should protect the climate system . . . on the basis of equity and in accordance with their common but differentiated responsibilities and capabilities.'[186] CBDR as codified by the UNFCCC is backed by the so-called 'leadership principle', implying that developed nations must lead the way in tackling global warming by subjecting themselves to stringent emission cuts; and transferring technology and financial resources to the needy developing countries, allowing them to also address the issue.[187]

Although the UNFCCC also includes other concepts and principles – like intergenerational equity, the precautionary principle and the right to sustainable development – these principles only have a guiding role, yet with some legal effect, as they are relevant for interpreting, implementing and developing the Convention further.[188] Hence, CBDR can be regarded as the underlying concept which the UNFCCC follows. This is why under the Convention, developing countries assumed no obligations to stabilise their emissions, only reporting obligations, and they should receive financial assistance and technology transfers from the industrialised world.[189] The first Conference of Parties concluded with the Berlin Mandate stating that the negotiation process for a future protocol shall be guided by, *inter alia*, Article 3(1) UNFCCC – i.e., the concept of CBDR.[190] This process lead to the Kyoto Protocol, which contains CBDR in its most rigid form. Article 10 reaffirms the concept 'without introducing any new commitments for parties not included in Annex I'.[191]

184 M Brookman, 'Book Review: Equality among Unequals in International Environmental Law' (2000) *Columbia Journal of Environmental Law*, 25, 369 at 371.
185 PW Birnie, AE Boyle and C Redgwell, *International Law and the Environment* (3rd edn, Oxford University Press 2009) at 524.
186 Art 3(1) of the UNFCCC.
187 Weisslitz, 'Rethinking the Equitable Principle of Common but Differentiated Responsibility: Differential Versus Absolute Norms of Compliance and Contribution in the Global Climate Change Context' at 483.
188 Birnie, Boyle and Redgwell, *International Law and the Environment* at 525.
189 Art 4(1) of the UNFCCC.
190 Rajamani, *Differential Treatment in International Environmental Law* at 181.
191 Art 10 of the UNFCCC.

Developing countries did again successfully hesitate to limit aspects of their contribution to climate change, since they feared binding emission targets would infringe on their state sovereignty.[192] They also succeeded in arguing that any limitations on their greenhouse gas (GHG) emissions would irrevocably damage their economies.[193] Consequently, only the industrialised countries were bound by strict GHG limitations.

The concept of CBDR was implemented within the climate change regime through differential norms of two categories. First, under the 'leadership principle', industrialised nations must lead the way in fighting climate change. In order to set an example, developed states are obliged to agree on GHG stabilisation in the atmosphere before developing states are asked to do so.[194] The same reasoning is true for providing funds. That is why the leadership principle constitutes a differential norm of contribution.[195] Since developing countries do not face any binding emissions reduction obligations while developed states do, this can be described as differential norms of compliance. Hence, the international effort to tackle climate change is based on norms that are differentiated in both compliance and contribution.

4.2.2.2 The boundaries of common but differentiated responsibilities

The reasoning behind the concept of CBDR is the 'tragedy of the climate'. Proponents argue that equal treatment is neither equitable nor politically feasible, since developing countries would never enter into international environmental agreements that do not bear in mind the differences between states.[196] However, the fruitlessness of the current climate regime calls for a critical assessment of CBDR, as it has, thus far, not produced the hoped-for results. The question arises as to whether the morally noble idea of differentiation in obligations to mitigate emissions really helps to achieve the goal of the UNFCCC.

The main flaw of CBDR is the entailed downgrading of environmental issues in the legal discourse.[197] The underlying goal of the UNFCCC is to prevent dangerous anthropogenic interference with the climate system.[198] Yet, instead of pushing forward the development of a low-carbon world economy, the UNFCCC squanders away time by continuously discussing what exactly

192 Brookman, 'Book Review: Equality among Unequals in International Environmental Law' at 370.

193 Weisslitz, 'Rethinking the Equitable Principle of Common but Differentiated Responsibility: Differential Versus Absolute Norms of Compliance and Contribution in the Global Climate Change Context' at 484.

194 Ibid. at 487.

195 Ibid.

196 AM Halvorssen, *Equality among Unequals in International Environmental Law: Differential Treatment for Developing Countries* (Westview Press 1999) at 69.

197 Pallemaerts, 'International Environmental Law from Stockholm to Rio: Back to the Future?' at 6.

198 Art 2 of the UNFCCC.

is meant by 'common but differentiated', and which state should take what action in order to fulfil its obligations. The heavy focus on economic distinctions completely ignores the severity of the threat of climate change.[199] This demotion of the environment has been made visible by the change of wording of the principle regarding a state's sovereignty over natural resources in the 1992 Rio Declaration. The added developmental domain takes account of the emerging principle of 'sustainable development'; however, this concept has yet to prove its effectiveness in international environmental law. The resulting downgrading, however, is jeopardising the protection of the global climate system, since developing countries are already outpacing the developed ones in terms of growth.

It seems like many governments are misusing the concept of CBDR to delay meaningful policies. Instead of demanding bold and timely action, negotiations focus on the various perceptions of equity and what exactly is meant by differentiated responsibilities. Hence, governments are able to play for time and hang on to their specific national interests and the derived notions of equity.[200] The absence of binding uniform obligations to reduce GHG emissions will encourage the economies of developing countries to proceed on their path of unsustainable development. Hence, the precedence of national economic development issues over (inter)national measures to tackle climate change will certainly cause the global community to miss the goal of the UNFCCC.[201] Another shortcoming of CBDR within the climate change arena is the fixing of negotiation blocs. Until the grouping of states is based on objective criteria, it will remain purely political.[202] What is the sense in treating countries as different as Mali and Brazil equally? Although bargaining as one united group, the fixing of the 'Annex I'/'non-Annex I' classification of the UNFCCC obscures the real differences between the various countries.[203] The result is that international negotiations lead to suboptimal results, and thus are more costly than necessary.

Furthermore, CBDR's notion on intergenerational equity is contradictory. The differentiation between developed and developing countries is quite questionable, since here 'late developers' are actually compensated by the forerunners for the foregone developmental opportunities.[204] Obviously, this makes

199 Weisslitz, 'Rethinking the Equitable Principle of Common but Differentiated Responsibility: Differential Versus Absolute Norms of Compliance and Contribution in the Global Climate Change Context' at 489.

200 Rajamani, *Differential Treatment in International Environmental Law* at 190.

201 Pallemaerts, 'International Environmental Law from Stockholm to Rio: Back to the Future?' at 6.

202 Shelton, 'Equity' at 655.

203 M Heyward, 'Equity and International Climate Change Negotiations: A Matter of Perspective' (2007) *Climate Policy*, 7, 518 at 519.

204 H Verbuggen, 'Commentary: In Response to the Paper by Timothy Swanson, Negotiating Effective International Environmental Agreements: Is an Objective Approach to Differential Treatment Possible?' (2001) *International Environmental Agreements: Politics, Law and Economics*, 1, 155 at 157.

sense on the basis of the equitable principle of responsibility, since industrialised states enjoyed free access to the global commons atmosphere. However, this historical responsibility is not straightforward. It is true that today developing countries have to operate in a climate-constrained world – leaving the forerunners better off indeed. However, developing countries also benefit from the achievements attained by the forerunners – e.g., the higher level of technological and scientific development. It is impossible to make an accurate comparison between the benefits of developing and industrialised countries; discussions about the extent of historical responsibilities will be endless.[205] Furthermore, if developing countries are allowed to pursue a mostly unrestricted development path, the whole reasoning of historical responsibilities would be reduced to absurdity, since today's developing countries would become tomorrow's irresponsible polluters.

An efficient long-term framework on climate change cannot be built upon differential obligations, since they are bound to be problematic in the future. Just as the global environment is by no means static, the international economic order, and thus the balance of power in international politics, is also changing. Consequently, differentiated obligations have to be renegotiated again and again once the formerly agreed framework appears unfair. The costs of such an approach will be immense.[206] Since the differentiated emission targets for developed countries were not based on a specific formula but rather on political power games, it can be assumed that negotiations among developed and developing countries on the issue of distributing the burdens of mitigating climate change risk will be even more complex.[207]

4.2.2.3 The legal status of the 'principle'

In order to be in a position to rethink the concept of CBDR, it is essential to identify its legal status, and thus its flexibility. If it can be recognised as a principle of customary international law, its further development might be much more constrained than in the case of less stringent legal implications. Principle 7 of the 1992 Rio Declaration enshrines that

> States shall cooperate in a spirit of global partnership to conserve, protect and restore the health and integrity of the Earth's ecosystem. In view of the different contributions to global environmental degradation, states have common but differentiated responsibilities. The developed countries acknowledge the responsibility that they bear in the international pursuit

205 Ibid.

206 T Swanson, 'Negotiating Effective International Environmental Agreements: Is an Objective Approach to Differential Treatment Possible?' (2001) *International Environmental Agreements: Politics, Law and Economics*, 1, 125 at 125.

207 Cazorla and Toman, 'International Equity and Climate Change Policy' at 2.

to sustainable development in view of the pressures their societies place on the global environment and of the technologies and financial resources they command.[208]

The first sentence has to be analysed separately to the rest of the provision, since it merely points to the principle of cooperation.[209] The core of Principle 7 can be found in the following two sentences. While the notion of 'common responsibilities' actually coincides with the principle of cooperation, 'differentiated responsibilities' takes into account the varying levels of contribution to the particular environmental problem and each state's ability to prevent or mitigate the threat.[210] As a result, environmental policies differ in the particular obligations of individual states. In consequence, CBDR does not qualify as a rule of international law, but rather as a principle acting as a base from which subsequent rules can emerge.[211] This is due to the fact that only rules are applicable in an 'all-or-nothing' fashion, whereas principles contain a dimension of 'weight or importance'.[212]

So, does CBDR then qualify as a legal principle? Although the notion of CBDR has been adopted in various conventions and declarations, it is difficult to argue that it has acquired the status of customary international law.[213] The reason for this is the rather ambiguous term of 'responsibility'. It can hardly be argued that it entails an unconditional obligation to take action.[214] Further, CBDR does not provide for the needed *opinio juris* to qualify as customary international law, since there exist numerous contrary definitions of its content and its legal obligations.[215]

However, the concept of CBDR still has a certain legal gravitas which can be assigned to that of 'twilight norms', i.e., it is more authoritative than soft law but also definitely less authoritative than customary international law.[216] Even soft law often has a normative quality in political and moral domains.[217] This is

208 Principle 7 of the 1992 Rio Declaration.

209 P Sands and J Peel, *Principles of International Environmental Law* (3rd edn, Cambridge University Press 2012) at 249.

210 Ibid. at 286.

211 U Beyerlin, 'Different Types of Norms in International Environmental Law: Policies, Principles, and Rules' in Bodansky D, Brunnée J and Hey E (eds), *The Oxford Handbook of International Environmental Law* (Oxford University Press 2007) at 442.

212 Ibid. at 434.

213 J Brunnée, 'Common Areas, Common Heritage, and Common Concern' in Bodansky D, Brunnée J and Hey E (eds), *The Oxford Handbook of International Environmental Law* (Oxford University Press 2007) at 567.

214 Beyerlin, 'Different Types of Norms in International Environmental Law: Policies, Principles, and Rules' at 442.

215 Stone, 'Common but Differentiated Responsibilities in International Law' at 281.

216 Rajamani, *Differential Treatment in International Environmental Law* at 253.

217 See P-M Dupuy, 'Formation of Customary International Law and General Principles' in Bodansky D, Brunnée J and Hey E (eds), *The Oxford Handbook of International Environmental Law* (Oxford University Press 2007).

why ideas like CBDR (another example would be 'sustainable development') should be evaluated in the light of their normative potential rather than focusing on their current legal status.[218] This would also allow for the critical assessment, rethinking and further development of the concept.[219]

4.3 Conclusion

This chapter has demonstrated in which ways the concept of solidarity has already been integrated into norms of international law. The disciplines of development law, international humanitarian law and refugee law represent the natural turf for the 'substantive' development of solidarity rules – even though they are, at times, far from being perfect. In the realm of international environmental law, the concept of common but differentiated responsibilities has tried to prove itself as a powerful tool towards the clarification and future development of the principle of solidarity; however, it falls short on various grounds.

The indisputably highest degree of juridification of solidarity can be found in the UN Charter, where the purpose of the United Nations is described to include the maintenance of international peace and security.[220] This, however, leaves much to be discussed regarding the actual procedures which should flow from such a high aim. In its procedural sense, solidarity focuses on secondary rules. Differentiated responsibilities can be found in both international environmental and trade law. The chapter also touched on relevant legal frameworks linking state responsibility with the concept of solidarity – such as the UN Convention Relating to the Status of Refugees, GATT and UNFCCC. Since the principle of solidarity is operating across several fields of international law and strives to protect fundamental values of the international community by penetrating both primary and secondary rules, it has even been claimed to have reached 'constitutional status'.[221]

Due to its nature, solidarity is often referred to as a value-driven principle with a strong ethical underpinning.[222] This foundation ensures that hydrosolidarity can help frame the negotiations between riparians of a transboundary watercourse and challenge inequity often witnessed in the form of abusive hydro-hegemony. However, this can only be achieved if states are willing to follow this path. Hence, if hydroegoism continues to define hydropolitics in a particular region, the idea of hydrosolidarity might be a noble one, but one without vigorous effect. The moral principle of (hydro)solidarity can only facilitate such a required change, and thus challenge the self-interests of states,

218 Ibid. at 462.

219 Rajamani, *Differential Treatment in International Environmental Law* at 245.

220 Art 1(1) of the UN Charter.

221 Wellens, 'Revisiting Solidarity as a (Re-)Emerging Constitutional Principle: Some Further Reflections' at 5.

222 Wellens, 'Solidarity as a Constitutional Principle: Its Expanding Role and Inherent Limitations' at 5.

by allowing international law to play a more prominent role. As argued above, international law contains several examples of instances where solidarity already heavily influences actions of states pursuant to a common interest. International law can induce the orderly change the international society needs to effectively address the world water crisis – and ultimately sustain peace and security. In order to do so, however, the legal regime itself needs to undergo a process of refinement. International (water) law is often being seen as counterproductive when it comes to solving transboundary problems, as it is being said to be reactive rather than setting a path towards peaceful and sustainable management of natural resources.

Together, the core legal requirements of water security – availability, access, adaptability and ambit – require reviewing established paradigms, including some of the most fundamental tenets of international law, such as state sovereignty.[223] Hence, what is desperately needed is a way out of the environment-sovereignty conundrum. At some point, international law may 'focus on preserving the collective rights of the community of states, as co-stewards of our planet'.[224] What the path into this future solidarity in international water law could look like is addressed in the following chapter.

223 See Brunnée and Toope, 'Environmental Security and Freshwater Resources: A Case for International Ecosystem Law' at 56.

224 World Future Council Councillor Marie-Claire Cordonier Segger, director of the Centre for International Sustainable Development Law, cited in World Future Council, *Future Justice Starts Today* <http://www.worldfuturecouncil.org/fileadmin/user_upload/PDF/FJposition_paper.pdf> at 13.

5 Regional common concern – the legal foundation for common water security

After having established that hydrosolidarity is a useful concept in the attempt to improve global water security, but that the lack of normativity is impeding its widespread implementation, the question arises: how can international law best support hydrosolidarity in order to strengthen water security? Detailed consideration of this question will have broad implications for other areas of international law, since it addresses a fundamental struggle of international governance – the 'clash between the idealistic ambitions of environmentalists and the harsh reality of international diplomacy'.[1] This challenge, again, sits within the wider debate of how to build a fairer world order. An ethical concept, such as the concept of hydrosolidarity, not only poses critical questions within the realm of philosophy and politics; it also constantly challenges the set system of responsibilities in the international arena. Are the frameworks governing the world order still fit for the task of maintaining international peace and security?[2] Does the new geopolitical landscape with its new emerging powers (like China and India) demand that the international legal system be upended? With its focus on legal norms and institutions, international law can provide a path for the implementation of concepts which address questions of what is right or good and shine a light on potential hurdles along the way.[3] However, international law needs to better reflect the differing cultural norms in providing this framework.

Today, the most significant challenges for states are likely to emerge from international or even global threats – like nuclear proliferation, economic instability, diseases, climate change and water security.[4] In a world which is shaped by the constantly changing forces of globalisation, the emergence of new transboundary threats and complex security challenges highlight the fact

1 R Falkner, 'Global Environmentalism and the Greening of International Society' (2012) *International Affairs*, 88, 503 at 503.

2 Art 1(1) of the UN Charter.

3 S Ratner, 'Ethics and International Law: Integrating the Global Justice Project(S)' (2013) *International Theory*, 5, 1 at 1.

4 SJ Stedman, B Jones and C Pascual, *A Plan for Action: A New Era of International Cooperation for a Changed World: 2009, 2010, and Beyond* (Center for International Security and Cooperation 2008) at 6.

that the level of interdependence between states causes nations to depend even more on the cooperation of others to protect their own national security interests.[5] This reality has long been acknowledged and brought about the conviction that none of these complex threats can be addressed by any one country alone – not even by the most powerful ones. Compared to the seriousness of the quest, however, the results in terms of international cooperation with regard to the management of natural resources are surprisingly meagre:[6]

> And certainly it will be more difficult at the international level than at national levels of decision-making. So locked are we within our tribal units, so possessive over national rights, so suspicious of any extension of international authority, that we may fail to sense the need for dedicated and committed action over the whole field of planetary necessities.[7]

It is true that we have witnessed the development of the new major fields of international environmental law and policy since the UN Conference on the Human Environment in 1972, which has triggered the development of new forms of international governance, like the various conferences of parties (COPs) to multilateral conventions. Since the early twenty-first century, the politicisation of international environmental problems has been complemented by a process of securitisation (see Chapter 2), which declared selected global challenges (e.g., climate change) as political issues of utmost priority which were deemed to require extraordinary measures – including security measures.[8] These developments gave rise to 'global environmentalism', which has had a persisting impact on international relations.[9] This is evident in the various ways solutions for environmental concerns have been woven into the normative fabric of international society.[10] Yet there are indications that, despite these efforts, we are approaching our planetary boundaries at an increasing pace, jeopardising our natural life-support systems.[11] This continuing negative trend points to the fact that the gap between political talk and cooperative action on international environmental issues is immense.[12] It becomes obvious that

5 Ibid. at 10.
6 See, e.g., the disappointing outcomes of the most recent climate change negotiations or the Rio+20 process.
7 B Ward and RJ Dubos, *Only One Earth: The Care and Maintenance of a Small Planet* (Norton 1972) at 294.
8 HG Brauch, 'Introduction: Facing Global Environmental Change and Sectorialization of Security' in Brauch HG and others (eds), *Facing Global Environmental Change: Environmental, Human, Energy, Food, Health and Water Security Concepts* (Springer 2009) at 22.
9 Falkner, 'Global Environmentalism and the Greening of International Society' at 504.
10 P Sands (ed.), *Greening International Law* (Earthscan 1993) at xv.
11 See V Galaz and others, '"Planetary Boundaries" – Exploring the Challenges for Global Environmental Governance' (2012) *Current Opinion in Environmental Sustainability*, 4, 80.
12 For a more detailed analysis of the state of the global environment, see United Nations Environment Programme, *Global Environment Outlook 5: Environment for the Future We Want* (UNEP 2012).

both scope and depth of international cooperation have to be intensified to effectively address the pressing issues of transboundary, regional and sometimes global dimensions. Given the fact that even one of the most powerful and best joined-up global institutional system – finance – is struggling to guarantee financial stability,[13] it seems as if some of the existing international institutions are unfit for the tasks of the twenty-first century. Which role can international law play in bringing about the desperately needed transformation towards cooperation which fully comprehends the complexities of the security challenges ahead?

At the heart of the criticism of the international legal order lies the concept of sovereignty. It has often been seen as a hindrance to achieving truly joint management of natural resources, rather than a way out of state-centrism. This has been particularly true for disciplines other than law.[14] However, even international lawyers have been rather critical of the concept, as some perceive it as a 'narrow, ethnocentric way to think about the relations of human beings'.[15] This makes one of the fundamental tenets of international law also one of its highly charged notions. With regard to the global water crisis, the concept of hydrosolidarity is trying to bring states together to effectively tackle their shared challenges in transboundary water resources management. In order to be successful, to overcome the self-centred approach in water cooperation (hydroegoism), the concept needs normative strength. Since state-centrism is *the* challenge to common water security, the question now arises, how international water law can help overcome the prevalent thinking – and acting – in nationalistic terms when it comes to transboundary water management? If this endeavour proves to be feasible, hydrosolidarity could be more than a mere theoretical construct, as it is often perceived – it could actually be achieved more widely in practice.

5.1 The changing landscape of international law

The orthodox understanding of international law is based on the Westphalian order, which is organised around the concept of the sovereign state as the supreme political and legal driver of international affairs.[16] Hence, the sovereignty of each state is at the core of our current perception of public international law.[17] It injects order and stability into international relations, since all

13 See, e.g., I Goldin, *Divided Nations: Why Global Governance Is Failing, and What We Can Do About It* (Oxford University Press 2013) at 81.

14 SD Krasner, 'Compromising Westphalia' (1995) 20 International Security 115; A Osiander, 'Sovereignty, International Relations, and the Westphalian Myth' (2001) *International Organization*, 55, 251.

15 M Koskenniemi, 'What Use for Sovereignty Today?' (2011) *Asian Journal of International Law*, 1, 61 at 61.

16 C Harding and CL Lim (eds), *Renegotiating Westphalia: Essays and Commentary on the European and Conceptual Foundations of Modern International Law* (Martinus Nijhoff Publishers 1999) at ix.

17 DA French, 'A Reappraisal of Sovereignty in the Light of Global Environmental Concerns' (2001) *Legal Studies*, 21, 376 at 376.

nations, regardless of their political power or size, are considered to be independent of all other nations and exercise sovereign control over their population, their diplomatic affairs and their territory. This principle is enshrined within the Charter of the UN which states that the UN is 'based on the principle of the sovereign equality of all its members',[18] and that 'All members shall refrain in their international relations from the threat or use of force against the territorial integrity or political independence of any state.'[19] Further elements describing what exactly is meant by sovereign equality were specified in the UN Declaration on Principles of International Law concerning Friendly Relations and Co-operation among States.[20] Accordingly, states are legally equal, enjoy territorial integrity and political independence, have a right to determine their own political, social, economic and cultural systems, and do not have the right to intervene, directly or indirectly, for any reason whatever, in the internal or external affairs of any other state.[21] The principle of sovereignty consists of three basic domains: (1) a state is 'nationally independent' to freely decide on its relations with other states; (2) it has the 'internal autonomy' to determine the character of its own governance, and (3) each state has the 'territorial integrity' to control activities within its own territory.[22]

The perception of sovereignty has always been in flux. In the sixteenth and seventeenth centuries, it was understood as an 'absolute and perpetual power of a state',[23] limited only by divine and natural law. After the Peace of Westphalia in 1648, the independence of states was limited by higher principles – such as the obligation to defend and protect the peace between nations – and religion. Later, sovereignty was interpreted as an absolute and unlimited supreme right. Here, war was seen as a legitimate tool for the realisation of a nation's own national interest (*ius ad bellum*) – yet with some limitations during war, such as the continuation of diplomatic means (*ius in bello*).[24] Hegel also understood sovereignty as absolute independence and freedom, and the relationship between nations as one determined by morals, rather than by law.[25] Since the

18 Art 2(1) of the UN Charter.

19 Art 2(4) of the UN Charter.

20 UN General Assembly, Declaration of Principles of International Law Concerning Friendly Relations and Co-operation Among States in Accordance with the Charter of the United Nations (24 October 1970) UNGA Res 2625, 25 UN GAOR Supp 18, UN Doc A/5217 at 121; reprinted in 65 AJIL 243 (1971); available at <http://www.un.org/ga/search/view_doc.asp?symbol=A/RES/2625(XXV)>.

21 Ibid.

22 French, 'A Reappraisal of Sovereignty in the Light of Global Environmental Concerns' at 378.

23 Jean Bodin quoted in AC Dowling, '"Un-Locke-Ing" a "Just Right" Environmental Regime: Overcoming the Three Bears of International Environmentalism – Sovereignty, Locke, and Compensation' (2002) *William & Mary Environmental Law and Policy Review*, 26, 891 at 894.

24 HG Brauch, 'Conceptual Quartet: Security and Its Linkages with Peace, Development, and Environment' in Brauch HG and others (eds), *Globalization and Environmental Challenges: Reconceptualizing Security in the 21st Century* (Springer 2008) at 70.

25 See FX Perrez, *Cooperative Sovereignty: From Independence to Interdependence in the Structure of International Environmental Law* (Kluwer Law International 2000) at 344.

establishment of the League of Nations and, later, the United Nations, the principle is being interpreted as limited independence which is the result of international law, rather than being in opposition to it. In a famous ruling from 1922, the Permanent Court of International Justice (PCIJ) stated that 'The question whether a certain matter is or is not solely within the jurisdiction of a State is an essentially relative question; it depends upon the development of international relations.'[26] Thus, it seems reasonable to believe that the principle of sovereignty as such is (and to some extent always has been) a relative matter which depends on the particular circumstances in each particular case. This development becomes apparent when analysing the historical impact of international water law on the various allocation theories.[27] Being limited from above by international law, from the side by the concept of good neighbourliness and from below by human rights, it only seems to grow in complexity as the various processes of globalisation shape the global legal and political landscape.[28]

Today, the inequalities between states and their socio-economic and ecological interdependences yield critical challenges to contemporary international cooperation.[29] In the realm of environmental cooperation, for example, this has long raised the fear among many that

> a world of states, each with its own self-serving rendering of historical experience and bolstered by deeply ingrained traditions of sovereignty, varying material circumstances, and wildly uneven perceptions of the character and seriousness of different types of environmental harm, [is] structurally incapable of meeting the ecological challenge.[30]

This view holds that sovereign states seem to be unable to address global environmental challenges, as the prevalent behaviour of states reflects the sole pursuit of their own national interests.[31] Hence, preservation of the nation state's autonomy seems to be of more value than the protection of the global environment. This is even more problematic when it comes to

26 PCIJ, Dispute between France and Great Britain as to the Nationality Decrees issued in Tunis and Morocco (French Zone) on 8 November 1921, Advisory Opinion (7 February 1922) at para 40; available at <http://www.worldcourts.com/pcij/eng/decisions/1923.02.07_morocco.htm>; see also M Koskenniemi, *From Apology to Utopia: The Structure of International Legal Argument* (Cambridge University Press 2005) at 258.

27 A Rieu-Clarke, R Moynihan and B-O Magsig, *UN Watercourses Convention : User's Guide* (IHP-HELP Centre for Water Law, Policy and Science 2012) at 101.

28 Perrez, *Cooperative Sovereignty: From Independence to Interdependence in the Structure of International Environmental Law* at 345.

29 See S Barrett, *Why Cooperate? The Incentive to Supply Global Public Goods* (Oxford University Press 2007).

30 R Falk, 'Environmental Protection in the Era of Globalization' (1995) *Yearbook of International Environmental Law*, 6, 3 at 10.

31 P Allott, *International Law and International Revolution* (Hull University Press 1989) at 8.

shared freshwater resources, since watercourses and aquifers ignore political boundaries. Therefore, the concept of absolute national sovereignty, which attempts to uphold the primacy of sovereignty without regard to the reality of the hydrological cycle, is ill-conceived and simply unworkable.[32]

Yet, while it is true that the world is still facing large-scale and detrimental environmental challenges, the international community has, at least to some extent, shown collective effort in the forms of dialogue, negotiations and legal regimes tackling the global environmental crisis.[33] What, then, is the relationship between sovereignty and cooperation on environmental issues – and how is sovereignty to be understood in order to achieve common water security? Does the model of the state system of Westphalia constitute the inescapable limit of how we design any future form of international community?

5.1.1 Sovereignty: the eroding principle of international law?

Many scholars have rehearsed a moral case against sovereignty, since, in their view, it is being used to uphold egocentric interests of only few communities against the common interests of the world at large,[34] providing vast opportunities for internal oppression – also referred to as 'organised hypocrisy'.[35] A country claiming that a particular issue is merely a matter of its domestic jurisdiction sometimes refers to the norm of non-intervention, enshrined in Article 2(7) of the UN Charter, which states that 'Nothing contained in the present Charter shall authorize the United Nations to intervene in matters which are essentially within the domestic jurisdiction of any state'.[36] This tactic is often interpreted as a strategy to hide from vocal, and sometimes well-founded, international criticism. However, there is no agreed understanding as to what actually falls under 'matters which are essentially within the domestic jurisdiction of any state'.

The limitations on how the community of states can act in situations of clear breaches of international law have long been criticised.[37] This is why a revised concept of national sovereignty has been proposed, one which gives the international community the power to act in situations of state fragility and misconduct. Arguably, the main developments with regard to trying to limit the 'non-intervention' norm can be witnessed in the area of military interventions.

32 See AT Wolf, 'Conflict and Cooperation Along International Waterways' (1998) *Water Policy*, 1, 251 at 252.

33 See L Rajamani, 'The Nature, Promise, and Limits of Differential Treatment in the Climate Regime' (2006) *Yearbook of International Environmental Law*, 16, 81 at 81.

34 See Koskenniemi, 'What Use for Sovereignty Today?' at 61.

35 SD Krasner, *Sovereignty: Organized Hypocrisy* (Princeton University Press 1999).

36 Art 2(7) of the UN Charter.

37 For a detailed discussion on the 'international community', see B Simma and AL Paulus, 'The "International Community": Facing the Challenge of Globalization' (1998) *European Journal of International Law*, 9, 266.

One group of scholars suggests that sovereignty should depend on a state's ability to prove its commitment to a set of conditions established by an outside authority.[38] This notion of 'contingent sovereignty' promotes a policy of military intervention which is based on a predetermined set of criteria – e.g., humanitarian concerns. By arguing that serious breaches of human rights justify a military intervention by foreign powers, violations of the norms of territorial integrity and non-intervention are being vindicated and the supremacy of the principle of sovereignty is being brought into question.[39] The apparent conflict between the norm of non-intervention and moral considerations still divides 'Western' nations from those of the South and East. Following the NATO intervention in Kosovo in 1999, the then UN Secretary General, Kofi Annan, argued that the international community needs to 'forge unity behind the principle that massive and systematic violations of human rights – wherever they take place – should never be allowed to stand'.[40] However, it has to be noted that the concept of contingent sovereignty is still in an embryonic state and has not been codified in international law.

The doctrine of 'responsibility to protect' (R2P) builds, to a large extent, on the ideas of contingency as it draws from the understanding that sovereignty not only constitutes a right, but also bears a responsibility.[41] In 2001, the International Commission on Intervention and State Sovereignty (ICISS) published a report on R2P, which aimed to answer the question when (and how) the international community should respond to humanitarian crises and crimes against humanity?[42] The report attracted widespread attention – mainly for the central proposition that there is indeed a duty of the international community to act in cases of serious violations of human rights. In order to stress the fact that unilateral action is not advocated, it argues that it is actually a duty of the UN to take the appropriate measures.[43] In 2005, R2P was adopted by the UN General Assembly at the World Summit, stating that

> Each individual State has the responsibility to protect its populations from genocide, war crimes, ethnic cleansing and crimes against humanity. This responsibility entails the prevention of such crimes, including their incitement, through appropriate and necessary means. We accept

38 K Claussen and T Nichol, 'Reconstructing Sovereignty: The Impact of Norms, Practices and Rhetoric' (2007) *Bologna Center Journal of International Affairs*, 10, 21 at 27.

39 Ibid. at 28.

40 Kofi Annan during the UN General Assembly session (20 September 1999); quoted in MJ Glennon, 'Why the Security Council Failed' (2003) *Foreign Affairs*, 82, 23.

41 Risk Response Network of the World Economic Forum, *From Risk to Opportunity: Building a Response to the New Reality* (World Economic Forum 2011) at 29.

42 International Commission on Intervention and State Sovereignty, *The Responsibility to Protect* (International Development Research Centre 2001).

43 Ibid. at 54.

> that responsibility and will act in accordance with it. The international community should, as appropriate, encourage and help States to exercise this responsibility and support the United Nations in establishing an early warning capability.[44]

Since then, proponents of the concept have called to apply R2P to justify various military interventions – for example, in 2008 in Burma where military force was deemed necessary by the foreign minister of France, Bernard Kouchner, to allow humanitarian aid into the country.[45] In 2011, with the United Nations Security Council Resolution 1973, the international community invoked R2P for the first time by military means.[46] This action taken by the UN Security Council has been interpreted by many proponents of the doctrine as a further step towards the demise of sovereignty.[47] Yet, the debate about the morality, legality and legitimacy of humanitarian interventions did not end with the application of R2P in Libya.[48]

Furthermore, drawing conclusions from these developments for the realm of international law governing natural resources is rather difficult, as there is reasonable doubt whether the scope of R2P extends beyond 'genocide, war crimes, ethnic cleansing and crimes against humanity'.[49] Should the international community be concerned about 'massacres perpetrated against critically endangered species',[50] for instance? Could a state be forced to halt its large-scale dam project, which it intends to build unilaterally without giving consideration to environmental and social devastation caused, on the grounds of R2P? While the legal-philosophical question of whether large-scale mismanagement of transboundary watercourses – or any other natural resources for that matter –

44 UN General Assembly Resolution 60/1, *2005 World Summit Outcome* (24 October 2005) UN Doc A/RES/60/1 (2005) at para 138; available at <http://www.unhcr.org/refworld/docid/44168a910.html>.

45 See ME O'Connell, 'Responsibility to Peace: A Critique of R2P' in Cunliffe P (ed.), *Critical Perspectives on the Responsibility to Protect : Interrogating Theory and Practice* (Routledge 2011) at 76.

46 'Reiterating the responsibility of the Libyan authorities to protect the Libyan Population . . . '; United Nations Security Council, Resolution 1973 (17 March 2011) UN Doc S/RES/1973 (2011) available at <http://www.un.org/ga/search/view_doc.asp?symbol=S/RES/1973(2011)>.

47 American Jewish Committee, 'Assessing the UN Security Council Resolution on Libya' (21 March 2011) <http://www.ajc.org/atf/cf/%7B42d75369-d582-4380-8395-d25925b85eaf%7D/ASSESSING_UNSC_RESOLUTION_ON_LIBYA_032111.PDF>.

48 See, e.g., A Hehir, 'The Responsibility to Protect and International Law' in Cunliffe P (ed.), *Critical Perspectives on the Responsibility to Protect : Interrogating Theory and Practice* (Routledge 2011); O'Connell, 'Responsibility to Peace: A Critique of R2P'; A Orford, *International Authority and the Responsibility to Protect* (Cambridge University Press 2011); R Tarnogórski, 'Libya and Syria: Responsibility to Protect at a Crossroads' (2012) PISM Strategic File 1.

49 UN General Assembly Resolution 60/1, 2005 World Summit Outcome (24 October 2005) UN Doc A/RES/60/1 (2005) at para 138.

50 R Eckersley, 'Ecological Intervention: Prospects and Limits' (2007) *Ethics & International Affairs*, 21, 293 at 293.

should be considered against terms such as 'ecocide'[51] might be an interesting one, the chances that the international community would recognise it as the fifth crime against peace, and thus address ecocide in the same way as genocide, are rather slim.[52] Thus, it is highly questionable to expect that any form of ecocide – for instance, the unilateral development of a shared watercourse which causes detrimental impact on the environment and communities downstream – will fall within the scope of R2P anytime soon.

In addition to the moral case against some aspects of sovereignty, scholars who foresee its demise argue that the notion, as it is being understood today, fails to articulate two main developments which have shaped international relations in general and transboundary water management in particular: (1) the increasingly complex interdependencies between states, and (2) the increasingly important role of non-state actors. With an orthodox understanding of sovereignty, these shifts of power – mainly brought about by globalisation – cannot be grasped. Thus, the Westphalian model has been deemed obsolete, as it is based on the independence of states. Given that the orthodox interpretation of sovereignty is still widespread, we see many scholars declaring the principle to be 'threatened by the increase in global flows, growing economic and political interdependence, and the rise of supranational political entities that make delineation of sovereignty more problematic'.[53]

This seems to be the case as well with regard to the management of the world's freshwater resources. While the particular complex interdependences between states (e.g., through the concept of virtual water) have already been addressed in previous chapters, a very important question linked to the sovereignty debate is rarely being asked: who are the actual drivers of (international) water law and policy today? Despite the fact that transboundary water regimes are largely silent on this, the answer is more and more the non-state actors. Globally, we can witness the phenomenon of relocation of authority both downwards (to local groups) and upwards (to supranational, international organisations).[54] The previous chapter discussed the diversity of the water community, which showed how varied are the actors, as well as their respective approaches. In many transboundary basins around the world, bilateral donors (e.g., German Society for International Cooperation), regional and

51 Ecocide has been defined as 'the extensive damage to, destruction of or loss of ecosystem(s) of a given territory, whether by human agency or by other causes, to such an extent that peaceful enjoyment by the inhabitants of that territory has been severely diminished'; P Higgins, D Short and N South, 'Protecting the Planet after Rio – the Need for a Crime of Ecocide' (2012) *Criminal Justice Matters*, 90, 4 at 4.

52 For a discussion, see ED Richter and others, 'Malthusian Pressures, Genocide, and Ecocide' (2007) *International Journal of Occupational and Environmental Health*, 13, 331.

53 C Rudolph, 'Sovereignty and Territorial Borders in a Global Age' (2005) *International Studies Review*, 7, 1 at 3.

54 KT Litfin, 'Sovereignty in World Ecopolitics' (1997) *Mershon International Studies Review*, 41, 167 at 175.

multilateral development banks (e.g., Asian Development Bank, World Bank), non-governmental organisations (e.g., World Wide Fund for Nature), business (e.g., Veolia Environnement, PepsiCo, Nestlé) and epistemic communities are growing more and more vocal in their respective views of how the global water crisis should be addressed – sometimes with huge implications for both soft and hard law.[55] The International Law Association (ILA), for instance, played a very prominent role in the development of international water law with the 1966 Helsinki Rules[56] and the 2004 Berlin Rules[57] on the management of freshwater resources.[58] Furthermore, NGOs have successfully pushed for the entry into force of the UN Watercourses Convention by drafting policy briefs, engaging in workshops and providing publications which make international law more accessible for practitioners.[59] In addition, multinational companies, like Nestlé, play an increasing role in lobbying for water laws and policies through networks like the World Economic Forum[60] and the 2030 Water Resources Group.[61]

While these developments are not necessarily negative, since they can provide valuable input from a wide range of stakeholders, and thus stir debate, they may point towards a slow demise of the state in the arena of international freshwater governance. The concept of sovereignty, so it seems, moulders into a merely rhetorical device employed by politicians to maximise their national interests.[62] Even if states continue to be the central players in international law, the role of non-state actors is obviously growing in importance. The part non-state actors play in legal processes, however, raises pressing questions of legitimacy, which have to be researched in more depth. Furthermore, when following the line of argument that state sovereignty is in demise, one has to raise the question of which guiding principle could or should come in its place?

55 See, e.g., R Costanza and others, *Planning Approaches for Water Resources Development in the Lower Mekong Basin* (Institute for Sustainable Solutions, Portland State University 2011) at 5.

56 The Helsinki Rules on the Uses of the Waters of International Rivers, adopted by the International Law Association at the 52nd conference, held at Helsinki in August 1966; available at <http://www.mpil.de/shared/data/pdf/pdf/8helsinki_rules_on_the_waters_of_international_rivers_ila.pdf>.

57 Berlin Rules on Water Resources, approved by the International Law Association's Water Resources Law Committee at the 71st conference, held at Berlin in 2004; available at <http://www.internationalwaterlaw.org/documents/intldocs/ILA_Berlin_Rules-2004.pdf>.

58 O McIntyre, *Environmental Protection of International Watercourses under International Law* (Ashgate 2007) at 67.

59 See Rieu-Clarke, Moynihan and Magsig, *UN Watercourses Convention: User's Guide*. For more information on the UN Watercourses Convention Global Initiative, see <http://www.dundee.ac.uk/water/research/unwcglobalinitiative/>.

60 See, e.g., the recent publication by the World Economic Forum Water Initiative: D Waughray (ed.), *Water Security: The Water-Food-Energy-Climate Nexus* (Island Press 2011).

61 2030 Water Resources Group, *Charting Our Water Future – Economic Frameworks to Inform Decision-Making* (2009).

62 J Linarelli, 'The Economics of Sovereignty' in Harding C and Lim CL (eds), *Renegotiating Westphalia: Essays and Commentary on the European and Conceptual Foundations of Modern International Law* (Martinus Nijhoff Publishers 1999) at 351.

The lack of answers implies that sovereignty is still an integral tenet of international law – even if it 'degenerates more and more into an empty shell'.[63] However, this supposed erosion of sovereignty, which is said to gain speed as the impacts of globalisation spread, has not triggered a rethinking of the international legal system. International legal scholars seem to unwaveringly resume the 'worship [of] sovereignty without reflecting on its continued sense'.[64]

5.1.2 The nation state reborn?

The reason for this might be that there are others who do not believe that the principle of sovereignty is eroding. On the contrary, some scholars argue that we can actually witness the 'rebirth' of the nation state.[65] Instead of a borderless world, they see a future which will bring a reinvigorated concept of state sovereignty.

Several recent developments seem to support such a claim. Employing again the example of humanitarian intervention: while various commentators saw the further demise of sovereignty with Resolution 1973 on Libya,[66] the fact that in 2014 the UN Security Council took a very different stance with regard to a comparable situation (at least to some extent) in Syria calls this reasoning into question. In contrast to the decisive and unified action on Libya, 'the [Security] Council's activities with respect to Syria have been faltering and divisive'.[67] This challenges the claim that Libya was indeed a turning point for R2P – and thus for how the international society perceives state sovereignty.[68] While some individual states may still be guided by the belief in their responsibility towards suppressed and ostracised populations, the limits of the doctrine have been revealed quite dramatically, as its status is still tenuous in the UN Security Council. Another event which, supposedly, brought back a more nationalistic view of sovereignty was the financial crisis which began in 2007 and at present (2014) had continued unabated; it is said to have slowed down global and regional integration processes considerably. Even within the European Union, where the institutional framework is comparatively strong, national interests dominated policy making during the 'Euro Crisis'.[69] A repercussion from the

63 K Zemanek, 'International Law Needs Development. But Where To?' in Fastenrath U and others (eds), *From Bilateralism to Community Interest : Essays in Honour of Bruno Simma* (Oxford University Press 2011) 802.

64 Ibid. at 802.

65 R Scruton for the American Spectator, 'The Rebirth of Nations' (23 June 2011) <http://spectator.org/archives/2011/06/23/the-rebirth-of-nations>.

66 United Nations Security Council, Resolution 1973 (17 March 2011) UN Doc S/RES/1973 (2011) available at <http://www.un.org/ga/search/view_doc.asp?symbol=S/RES/1973(2011)>.

67 S Mohamed, 'The U.N. Security Council and the Crisis in Syria' (2012) *ASIL Insights*, 16, 1 at 1.

68 L Bellodi, 'Libya's Assets and the Question of Sovereignty' (2012) *Survival*, 54, 39; MN Schmitt, 'Wings over Libya: The No-Fly Zone in Legal Perspective' (2011) *Yale Journal of International Law Online*, 36, 45.

69 D Rodrik for Project Syndicate, 'The Nation-State Reborn' (13 February 2012) <http://www.project-syndicate.org/commentary/the-nation-state-reborn>.

global financial crisis was the populist move by Denmark, party to the Schengen Agreement which had abolished passport and immigration controls at the common borders,[70] to reintroduce permanent border controls – and thus challenge the principle of freedom of movement within the Schengen area by prioritising its own national sovereignty.[71] David Cameron, the current Prime Minister of the United Kingdom, went a step further when he promised a referendum on whether the UK should remain in the European Union, which has long been seen as a success story of regionalism,[72] as he feared a decline in control over national economic policies.[73] With regard to transboundary and global environmental challenges, we also witness an increased reluctance of states to enter into meaningful and effective multilateral environmental agreements (MEAs). The withdrawal of governments such as Canada from the Kyoto Protocol[74] and the UN Convention to Combat Desertification[75] point towards a more state-centred future of international environmental governance – one where sovereignty, again, is based on independence rather than interdependence.

The assumption that states – at least the most powerful amongst them – are 'free to do as they wish' is shared by many scholars.[76] This view has, to some extent, been confirmed by the Permanent Court of International Justice, which states that

> International law governs relations between independent States. The rules of law binding upon States therefore emanate from their own free will as expressed in conventions or by usages generally accepted as expressing principles of law and established in order to regulate the relations between these co-existing independent communities or with a view to the achievement of common aims.[77]

70 Agreement between the Governments of the States of the Benelux Economic Union, the Federal Republic of Germany and the French Republic on the gradual abolition of checks at their common borders (14 June 1985; entered into force 15 June 1985) available at <http://eur-lex.europa.eu/LexUriServ/LexUriServ.do?uri=CELEX:42000A0922%2801%29:EN:NOT>.

71 BBC News, 'Schengen State Denmark to Re-impose Border Control' (11 May 2011) <http://www.bbc.co.uk/news/world-europe-13366047>.

72 See, e.g., CH Lin, 'ASEAN Charter: Deeper Regional Integration under International Law?' (2010) *Chinese Journal of International Law*, 9, 821 at 823.

73 BBC News, 'David Cameron Promises in/out Referendum on EU' (23 January 2013) <http://www.bbc.co.uk/news/uk-politics-21148282>; David Cameron's speech on Europe (23 January 2013) is available at <http://www.number10.gov.uk/news/eu-speech-at-bloomberg/>.

74 E Assadourian, 'The Path to Degrowth in Overdeveloped Countries' in Worldwatch Institute (ed.), *State of the World 2012 : Moving toward Sustainable Prosperity* (W.W. Norton & Company 2012) at 23.

75 The Canadian Press, 'Canada Quietly Pulls out of UN Anti-droughts Convention' (27 March 2013) <http://www.cbc.ca/news/canada/story/2013/03/27/un-droughts-deserts-convention-canada.html>.

76 CL Lim, 'Authority and Personality: Non-State Entities as Law-Makers?' in Harding C and Lim CL (eds), *Renegotiating Westphalia : Essays and Commentary on the European and Conceptual Foundations of Modern International Law* (Martinus Nijhoff Publishers 1999) at 54.

77 Judgment of the Permanent Court of International Justice, *The Case of the S.S. Lotus (France v Turkey)*, 1927 PCIJ (Ser A) No 10 (7 September 1927) at 18.

The basis of international legal obligation, then, is the original liberty of states which demands treatment recognising them as being free and equal.[78] Hence, one could argue, there is evidence which indicates that the principle of sovereignty is far from being in decline. On the contrary, the nation state actually seems to have (re)gained importance in the global arena.

5.1.3 The need for cooperative sovereignty

The previous sections gave a brief overview of the opposing views as to how the cornerstone of international law and international relations, i.e., the sovereignty of states, should be interpreted in this day and age – or if it still has a role to play at all. What became obvious is that none of the extreme positions offered an adequate proposal as to how future challenges – like tackling the global water crisis – can be effectively addressed. As Bartelson stated, 'The attempt to throw the state concept out was futile as this concept was invariably replaced with others that were semantically equivalent.'[79] What the often heated debate shows, however, is that state sovereignty can no longer be perceived as a clear-cut principle – if it ever could be. According to Dahrendorf, 'Nation states are welcome; they are important elements of a liberal world order. But they have to be open to cooperation and coordination with others.'[80] Yet, this cooperation and coordination is often lacking; in many cases, this lack of will is being blamed on an orthodox understanding of state sovereignty. Hence, the way we interpret sovereignty does not merely determine our managerial vocabulary; it defines the future path of international cooperation – and thus the future of international law itself.

Instead of attempting to determine the exact extent of sovereignty, which is an impossible endeavour given the complexity of the concept and the often nebulous perceptions it triggers, it is useful to recall that one of the main goals of international law is to strengthen international peace and security.[81] With the global water crisis in mind, the goal should be to overcome state-centrism of international water law (see previous chapters) in order to achieve common water security. The various discourses revolving around sovereignty show that the problematique is much more complex and the issues and interests of states much more dynamic than a static understanding of sovereignty – or international law in general – allows. While often seen as a hindrance to effective international governance (environmental governance, in particular), it is obvious that the principle of sovereignty will not vanish. Hence, in order to move the debate forward, the principle as such has to be defended – though certainly not the orthodox interpretation of it. If we manage to lead the

78 Lim, 'Authority and Personality: Non-State Entities as Law-Makers?' at 54.

79 J Bartelson, *The Critique of the State* (Cambridge University Press 2001) at 124.

80 R Dahrendorf for Project Syndicate, 'The Nation State Revisited' (14 April 2006) <http://www.project-syndicate.org/commentary/the-nation-state-revisited>.

81 See Art 1(1) UN Charter which defines the purpose of the United Nations.

discussion in a more open way, we might be able to ensure that it remains a 'morally sound response to persistent and profound disagreement within the international community'.[82] So, if we don't witness the demise of sovereignty; how should we interpret the bedrock foundation for conducting international relations? As Javier Solana, in his capacity as Secretary General of NATO, stated: 'The Westphalian system had its limits. For one, the principle of sovereignty it relied on also produced the basis for rivalry, not community of states; exclusion, not integration.'[83] Yet, many scholars still equate sovereignty with independence, and many governments still use this perception to avoid meaningful international cooperation.[84]

What is needed instead, is a rediscovery of the ethical foundations of public international law and a closer look at the obligation to cooperate. The reason for this being that 'even the sanctity of contract may be challenged by claims of "unjust enrichment" and that of treaties (*pacta sunt servanda* [agreements must be kept]) by claims of justice based on "impossibility of performance" or "fundamental change of circumstance."'[85] International politics is in a state of flux – and international law has to provide the tools for maintaining the manoeuvrability of the international community. We have to remind ourselves that one of the principal functions of international law is 'to serve as a mechanism by which the domestic politics of different states can be linked, in order to construct a formal mechanism of international politics'.[86] Yet, some nations still seem to be able to use the concept of state sovereignty as a cover in order to maximise their own national gains. International law is often only applied by states when they consider its implementation to be advantageous to their national interests.[87] This misuse is being encouraged by a purely instrumentalised view of international law. By reducing international law to a mechanism for the advancement of functional objectives, it becomes more 'vulnerable to the criticisms raised against thinking about it as an instrument for state policy'.[88] Thus, instead of trying to overcome state-centrism by pronouncing the (slow) death of sovereignty, injecting ethics into the international arena seems to be a much more promising way forward.

82 BR Roth, *Sovereign Equality and Moral Disagreement: Premises of a Pluralist International Legal Order* (Oxford University Press 2011) at 3.

83 Speech by Javier Solana, former Secretary General of NATO, 'Securing Peace in Europe' (Münster, Germany on 12 November 1998) available at <http://www.nato.int/docu/speech/1998/s981112a.htm>.

84 See L Henkin, 'The Mythodology of Sovereignty' (1993) ASIL Newsletter 1.

85 TM Franck, *Fairness in International Law and Institutions* (Clarendon Press; Oxford University Press 1995) at 24.

86 JP Trachtman, *The Future of International Law : Global Government* (Cambridge University Press 2013) at 2.

87 J Klabbers, 'The Idea(S) of International Law' in Muller S and others (eds), *The Law of the Future and the Future of Law* (Torkel Opsahl Academic EPublisher 2011) at 71.

88 M Koskenniemi, 'The Fate of Public International Law: Between Technique and Politics' (2007) *The Modern Law Review*, 70, 1 at 1.

What does this suggest for international environmental governance in general – and for transboundary water cooperation in particular? It implies the need for a move beyond the either/or debate on sovereignty and the joint management of natural resources. While states, in theory, have now accepted a more nuanced interpretation of sovereignty, the debate about how sovereignty over freshwater resources should be interpreted today is still of highest significance. After all and critically, the notion of sovereignty carries a responsibility to cooperate with it. Article 1 of the UN Charter reads:

> The purposes of the United Nations are: . . . (3) To achieve international co-operation in solving international problems of an economic, social, cultural, or humanitarian character, and in promoting and encouraging respect for human rights and for fundamental freedoms for all without distinction as to race, sex, language, or religion . . . .[89]

While the provisions on the duty to cooperate are rather brief, the need for amplifying one of the key principles of international law was met with the 1970 Declaration on Principles of International Law concerning Friendly Relations and Co-operation among States in accordance with the Charter of the United Nations.[90] The section of this Declaration which is dedicated to international cooperation stipulates that

> States have the duty to co-operate with one another, irrespective of the differences in their political, economic and social systems, in the various spheres of international relations, in order to maintain international peace and security and to promote international economic stability and progress, the general welfare of nations and international co-operation free from discrimination based on such differences.[91]

While the Declaration does not constitute binding international law, its universal recognition as a standard of conduct and its perception as an elaboration of 'principles of international law' gives it considerable legal weight. The general obligation to cooperate is also at the heart of the MOX case before the International Tribunal for the Law of the Sea (ITLOS). Here, Ireland claimed that the UK failed to cooperate as demanded by the rules of the United Nations Convention on the Law of the Sea (UNCLOS)[92] with regard to matters of

89 Art 1(3) of the UN Charter.

90 UN General Assembly, Declaration of Principles of International Law Concerning Friendly Relations and Co-operation Among States in Accordance with the Charter of the United Nations (24 October 1970) UNGA Res 2625, 25 UN GAOR Supp 18, UN Doc A/5217 at 121; reprinted in 65 AJIL 243 (1971).

91 Ibid.

92 United Nations Convention on the Law of the Sea (10 December 1982; entered into force 16 November 1994) 1833 UNTS 3; reprinted in 21 ILM 1261 (1982) [hereinafter UNCLOS] available at <http://www.un.org/Depts/los/convention_agreements/texts/unclos/unclos_e.pdf>.

communication and the exchange of information.[93] In its order, the Tribunal endorsed the cooperation between states as a general principle of international law.[94] According to Judge Wolfrum, the duty to cooperate

> balances the principle of sovereignty of States and thus ensures that community of interests are taken into account vis-à-vis individualistic State interests. It is the matter of prudence and caution as well in keeping with the overriding nature of the obligation to cooperate that the parties should engage therein as prescribed in paragraph 89 of the Order.[95]

Against this background, the Tribunal ordered Ireland and the UK to cooperate and enter into consultations.[96]

It follows from the foregoing that ultimately, there is a need to arrive at a stage where the concept of state sovereignty is understood as one of 'cooperative sovereignty'.[97] Implementing the general obligation to cooperate, however, is not a straightforward task. This task is easier when the benefits for cooperation are quantifiable and the positive impact can already be seen in the short term – like, e.g., in global trade.[98] Here, a very detailed body of international law has evolved over the last decades, which brought forth the World Trade Organization and its highly sophisticated system of dispute resolution.[99] How far away are we from a perception of cooperative sovereignty in international environmental law? The UN Conference on the Human Environment in 1972 is widely regarded as the first global environmental conference. Here, the delegations from 144 states agreed on the 'Stockholm Declaration',[100] which contains 26 principles, several of which have been incorporated into subsequent

93 See P Sands, *Principles of International Environmental Law* (2nd edn, Cambridge University Press 2003) at 251.

94 According to the Tribunal, 'the duty to cooperate is a fundamental principle in the prevention of pollution of the marine environment under Part XII of the [1982 UNCLOS] Convention and general international law.' The MOX Plant Case (Ireland v. United Kingdom), Provisional Measures, Order of 3 December 2001, ITLOS, at Para 82; available at <http://www.itlos.org/fileadmin/itlos/documents/cases/case_no_10/Order.03.12.01.E.pdf>.

95 The MOX Plant Case (Ireland v. United Kingdom), Provisional Measures, Order of 3 December 2001, ITLOS, Separate Opinion of Judge Wolfrum; available at <http://www.itlos.org/fileadmin/itlos/documents/cases/case_no_10/sep.op.Wolfrum.E.orig.pdf>.

96 The MOX Plant Case (Ireland v. United Kingdom), Provisional Measures, Order of 3 December 2001, ITLOS, at Para 83.

97 See Perrez, *Cooperative Sovereignty: From Independence to Interdependence in the Structure of International Environmental Law.*

98 For a detailed discussion on this topic, see JH Jackson, *Sovereignty, the WTO and Changing Fundamentals of International Law* (Cambridge University Press 2006).

99 Annex 2 of the Marrakesh Agreement Establishing the World Trade Organization (15th April 1994) is entitled 'Understanding on Rules and Procedures Governing the Settlement of Disputes', available at <http://www.wtopunjab.gov.pk/wto_agreement/dispute_settlement_understanding.pdf>.

100 Declaration of the United Nations Conference on the Human Environment (16 June 1972) UN Doc A/Conf.48/14/Rev. 1(1973); reprinted in 11 ILM 1416 (1972).

international environmental agreements. Of particular importance for the discussion at hand is Principle 21, which affirms that

> States have, in accordance with the Charter of the United Nations and the principles of international law, the sovereign right to exploit their own resources pursuant to their own environmental policies, and the responsibility to ensure that activities within their jurisdiction or control do not cause damage to the environment of other States or of areas beyond the limits of national jurisdiction.[101]

The attempt to strike a balance between national sovereignty and the responsibility to prevent transboundary damage is obvious here. As already mentioned earlier, this 'delicate balance' suffered a loss in 1992 at the UN Conference on Environment and Development in Rio de Janeiro. Here, Principle 2 reads:

> States have, in accordance with the Charter of the United Nations and the principles of international law, the sovereign right to exploit their own resources pursuant to their own environmental *and developmental* policies, and the responsibility to ensure that activities within their jurisdiction or control do not cause damage to the environment of other States or of areas beyond the limits of national jurisdiction'.[102]

While it is almost an exact copy of Principle 21 of the Stockholm Declaration, the two additional words make it clear that the emphasis is, again, on national development, rather than on cooperation to prevent transboundary harm. Hence, after a period of 'greening' the principle of sovereignty over natural resources, which had originally been established within an economic setting, we witnessed one which subordinated environmental concerns under national economic ones.[103]

This constant push and pull of environmental cooperation and state sovereignty at the political level also brought a certain level of uncertainty amongst international legal scholars as to whether the duty to cooperate is indeed a binding legal obligation, rather than a mere goal or a guideline for conduct.[104] The main question arising here is: can one assert that states must (rather than merely should) cooperate; and if so, can this obligation actually be imposed on states and legally enforced?[105] It is this debate which renders the precise status of

101 Principle 21 of the 1972 Stockholm Declaration.

102 Principle 2 of the 1992 Rio Declaration (emphasis added).

103 M Pallemaerts, 'International Environmental Law from Stockholm to Rio: Back to the Future?' in Sands P (ed.), *Greening International Law* (Earthscan 1993) at 6.

104 See J Delbrück, 'The International Obligation to Cooperate: An Empty Shell or a Hard Law Principle of International Law? A Critical Look at a Much Debated Paradigm of Modern International Law' in Hestermeyer HP and others (eds), *Coexistence, Cooperation and Solidarity*, vol. 1 (Martinus Nijhoff Publishers 2012).

105 P Wouters and others, *Sharing Transboundary Waters: An Integrated Assessment of Equitable Entitlement: The Legal Assessment Model* (UNESCO 2005) at 23.

the duty to cooperate under international law uncertain. While it succeeds in balancing the principle of 'sovereignty over natural resources' and the 'no significant harm' rule, cooperation is too broad to qualify as a rule.[106] Its status as a general principle of international law, rather than a customary rule, however, does not diminish its pivotal role in international law and politics; especially as more and more states now realise that cooperating with their neighbours on transboundary issues is ultimately in their self-interest. Interestingly, state practice shows that in specific contexts,[107] nations do not interpret international cooperation as an undue burden on their respective state sovereignty.[108]

In the area of international water law, both global instruments – the 1997 UN Watercourses Convention and the 2008 Draft Articles on the Law of Transboundary Aquifers[109] – promote the general obligation to cooperate. Furthermore, regional treaty regimes, such as the UNECE Helsinki Convention,[110] follow the same approach. With regard to the UN Watercourses Convention, Article 8(1) provides that 'Watercourse states shall cooperate on the basis of sovereign equality, territorial integrity, mutual benefit and good faith in order to attain optimal utilisation and adequate protection of an international watercourse.' This general obligation to cooperate contains the procedural duties of prior information and of prior consultation,[111] which aim to 'operationalise' the rather vague principle.[112] While the provisions on cooperation in the UN Watercourses Convention surely have a positive impact on the implementation of the general principle within the realm of transboundary water cooperation,[113] it still leaves a lot to be desired when it comes to

106 Rieu-Clarke, Moynihan and Magsig, *UN Watercourses Convention: User's Guide* at 123.

107 E.g., with regard to the protection of human rights (traditionally been seen as a purely national matter), see the Preamble of the Universal Declaration of Human Rights, which states that 'Member States have pledged themselves to achieve, in co-operation with the United Nations, the promotion of universal respect for and observance of human rights and fundamental freedoms . . . '; UN General Assembly, Universal Declaration of Human Rights, Resolution 217 A (III) (10 December 1948) available at <http://www.un.org/en/documents/udhr/index.shtml>.

108 Delbrück, 'The International Obligation to Cooperate : An Empty Shell or a Hard Law Principle of International Law? A Critical Look at a Much Debated Paradigm of Modern International Law' at 4.

109 Art 7(1) of the Draft Articles on the Law of Transboundary Aquifers: 'Aquifer States shall cooperate on the basis of sovereign equality, territorial integrity, sustainable development, mutual benefit and good faith in order to attain equitable and reasonable utilization and appropriate protection of their transboundary aquifers or aquifer systems.'

110 Art 2 (6) of the UNECE Helsinki Convention: 'The Riparian Parties shall cooperate on the basis of equality and reciprocity, in particular through bilateral and multilateral agreements, in order to develop harmonized policies, programmes and strategies covering the relevant catchment areas, or parts thereof, aimed at the prevention, control and reduction of transboundary impact and aimed at the protection of the environment of transboundary waters or the environment influenced by such waters, including the marine environment.' Interestingly, the parties to the UNECE Helsinki Convention have now opened up the Convention to states outside of UNECE.

111 Arts 11–19 of the UN Watercourses Convention.

112 Rieu-Clarke, Moynihan and Magsig, *UN Watercourses Convention: User's Guide* at 125.

113 See C Leb, 'The UN Watercourses Convention: The Éminence Grise Behind Cooperation on Transboundary Water Resources' (2013) *Water International*, 38, 146.

fundamentally changing the way states perceive their national sovereignty over freshwater resources. One shortcoming of the UN Watercourses Convention is that states still have a good deal of discretion with regard to the particular means of cooperation. The setting-up of joint institutions, for instance, is not explicitly compulsory,[114] even though their immense benefit for transboundary freshwater management has long been proven.[115] Merely recommending the establishment of joint river-basin organisations was probably as far as the Convention could go in order and still receive widespread political support. Yet, a high price was paid for this approach when it comes to strengthening the legal basis of the obligation to cooperate, as it does not change the perception of state sovereignty. The UN Watercourses Convention missed an opportunity to trigger widespread implementation of the concept of cooperative sovereignty.

This shortcoming, however, is not limited to the area of international water law. As a general observation, the international system still encourages powerful states to act unilaterally, since they have the liberty to argue on the basis of an orthodox understanding of sovereignty.[116] The international community seems to be stuck in a system which interprets international law as a law of coexistence, rather than one of cooperation, despite the general obligation to cooperate. While the phenomenon of sovereignty seems to impede the emergence of stronger relations of solidarity, there is little doubt that many states understand more and more clearly the necessity to cooperate at the international level to put an end to an array of problems whose solution simply cannot be found domestically.[117] However, what is still missing is the urgency to act jointly on more issues which bar unilateral action – like the cooperation over transboundary freshwater resources. In order to be able to move closer to a perception of cooperative sovereignty, the international legal frameworks governing common challenges of transboundary resources management have to be developed further; based on the idea of 'responsible sovereignty'.[118] Only then

114 Art 8(2) of the UN Watercourses Convention reads: 'In determining the manner of such cooperation, watercourse States may consider the establishment of joint mechanisms or commissions, as deemed necessary by them, to facilitate cooperation on relevant measures and procedures in the light of experience gained through cooperation in existing joint mechanisms and commissions in various regions.'

115 See R Berardo and AK Gerlak, 'Conflict and Cooperation Along International Rivers: Crafting a Model of Institutional Effectiveness' (2012) *Global Environmental Politics*, 12, 101; J Lautze and others, 'International River Basin Organizations: Variation, Options and Insights' (2013) *Water International*, 38, 30; S Schmeier, *Governing International Watercourses: River Basin Organizations and the Sustainable Governance of Internationally Shared Rivers and Lakes* (Routledge 2013); S Schmeier, 'Navigating Cooperation Beyond the Absence of Conflict: Mapping Determinants for the Effectiveness of River Basin Organisations' (2012) *International Journal of Sustainable Society*, 4, 11.

116 C Schreuer, 'State Sovereignty and the Duty to Cooperate – Two Incompatible Notions?' in Delbrück J (ed.), *International Law of Cooperation and State Sovereignty: Proceedings of an International Symposium of the Kiel Walther Schücking-Institute of International Law, May 23–26, 2001* (Duncker & Humblot 2002) at 177.

117 P Cullet, 'Differential Treatment in International Law: Towards a New Paradigm of Inter-State Relations' (1999) *European Journal of International Law*, 10, 549 at 550.

118 On this concept see SD Krasner, 'Verantwortliche Souveränität' (2010) *Internationale Politik*, 65, 10.

can the international community arrive at a stage where cooperation is being interpreted as what it actually is – 'the most important manifestation of sovereignty'.[119] Until then, cooperative sovereignty remains an aspiration limited to certain areas of international (treaty) law, rather than being a widespread reality in world politics based on customary international law.

The bottom line of the discourse around state sovereignty is that the principle is far from eroding. It is an ever-evolving concept which serves as the basis of international relations; and will do so in the future. Hence, we should not fight sovereignty as the evil standing between 'us' and achieving common water security. We should rather focus on how to best make use of the concept, push the debate forward and come up with legal frameworks that fully comprehend the constantly changing political, societal and environmental settings sovereignty is exposed to. This in turn requires sovereignty to be understood and treated as the flexible concept it actually is, rather than a static given, through which states can address the increasingly interdependent challenges they are facing today. This is why the environment/sovereignty debate is not only about 'greening' international relations. Instead, it illustrates the core issue of international law in addressing contemporary challenges of world politics.[120] Sovereignty will remain an invaluable principle of international law and international relations if it is interpreted and applied as comprising the responsibility to cooperate. Only then will it cease to be the often blamed roadblock for joint management of freshwater resources; and ultimately able to truly promote international peace and security. This would also support the development of the concept of water security towards one which addresses the common challenges rather than solely the narrow self-interests of states. For this to materialise, new legal frameworks for addressing common water security on the basis of the progressive development of international law and a renewed understanding of cooperative sovereignty have to be developed which are more responsive to contemporary challenges than the orthodox ones.

5.2 Natural resources and the concept of communality in international law

Acknowledging the fact that the only meaningful way forward in addressing the global water crisis is taking a perspective of common water security, the notion ultimately challenges the supremacy of absolute national sovereignty.[121] The proposed methodology of the 4As (namely availability, access, adaptability and ambit, as introduced in Chapter 3) supports this development by recognising

119 Schreuer, 'State Sovereignty and the Duty to Cooperate – Two Incompatible Notions?' at 179.

120 See KT Litfin, 'The Greening of Sovereignty: An Introduction' in Litfin KT (ed.), *The Greening of Sovereignty in World Politics* (MIT Press 1998).

121 See R Falk, 'The Coming Global Civilisation: Neo-Liberal or Humanist?' in Anghie A and Sturgess G (eds), *Legal Visions of the 21st Century – Essays in Honour of Judge Christopher Weeramantry* (Kluwer Law International 1998).

that only a truly common strategy can ensure the peaceful management of transboundary freshwater resources. Considering the main shortcoming of the current legal regime – the state-centred take on the water crisis based on an orthodox understanding of sovereignty – the question arises: what should serve as the normative basis for the needed refinement of international water law? How can we arrive at an understanding of 'cooperative sovereignty' which supports attaining common water security? Communality has been addressed by international law in different ways. In general, its role is to facilitate both the coordination of states' individual actions regarding a common concern, and the institutionalisation of 'normative communities'.[122] The following section will outline the various conceptual paths international law has taken on this course, with the aim to find the most appropriate one for the future development of international water law.

5.2.1 Common areas

The concept of 'common areas' is limited to areas or resources which are perceived as being common while all states have, at least in theory, open access to them. Since not many places fall into that category of being beyond the limits of national jurisdiction, the notion is only being applied with regards to the high seas[123] and outer space.[124] Since access to common areas or resources is in principle open to anybody, it has to be regulated in order to avoid a tragedy of the commons; where states are locked into a system which compels them to increase their respective national benefits without limit – 'in a world that is limited'.[125]

Except for the general duty to cooperate placed upon states (see above), the only universally applicable substantive obligation in international environmental law limiting these freedoms is the no significant harm rule. This encompasses the protection of areas beyond national jurisdiction, and thus, at least this dimension of the no significant harm rule can be interpreted as an obligation owed *erga omnes*.[126] However, despite its international legal standing, the

122 J Brunnée, 'Common Areas, Common Heritage, and Common Concern' in Bodansky D, Brunnée J and Hey E (eds), *The Oxford Handbook of International Environmental Law* (Oxford University Press 2007) at 555.

123 Part VII of the United Nations Convention on the Law of the Sea (10 December 1982; entered into force 16 November 1994) 1833 UNTS 3; reprinted in 21 ILM 1261 (1982) [hereinafter UNCLOS].

124 Treaty on Principles Governing the Activities of States in the Exploration and Use of Outer Space, including the Moon and Other Celestial Bodies (27 January 1967; entered into force 10 October 1967) 610 UNTS 205; reprinted in 6 ILM 386 (1967) [hereinafter Outer Space Treaty].

125 See G Hardin, 'The Tragedy of the Commons' (1968) *Science*, 162, 1243 at 1244.

126 See ICJ, The Legality of the Threat or Use of Nuclear Weapons, Advisory Opinion (8 July 1996), ICJ Reports 1996, 226; available at <http://www.icj-cij.org/docket/files/95/7495.pdf>; at para 29: 'The existence of the general obligation of States to ensure that activities within their jurisdiction and control respect the environment of other States or of areas beyond national control is now part of the corpus of international law relating to the environment.'

enforcement of the protection of common areas solely on the basis of customary law remains questionable.[127] While the Draft Articles on State Responsibility distinguish between injured states (Article 42) and states that have not been injured (Article 48);[128] in practice, the options available to any state would still be limited to demanding a cessation of the internationally wrongful act or omission. However, even these meagre options are not that certain, as state practice does not support the argument that this right has reached the status of customary international law. One example demonstrating the dilemma is the Nuclear Tests Case (New Zealand v. France) of 1973, in which New Zealand, demanded France to stop its nuclear testing activities in the South Pacific, arguing, inter alia, that France violated the rights of the international community to be free from nuclear contamination of the high seas and atmosphere.[129] While the ICJ – in consideration of France's declaration that it would terminate testing – never decided the merits of this case, nor of Australia's parallel case, various opinions, both separate and dissenting, revealed the strong division of the judges on this important issue. On the one hand, several judges remarked that while 'the existence of a so-called *actio popularis* in international law is a matter of controversy . . . the question is one that may be considered as capable of rational legal argument and a proper subject of litigation before this Court'.[130] On the other hand, judges noted that the applicants had 'no legal title . . . to act as spokesman for the international community and ask the Court to condemn France's conduct'.[131]

Hence, it was deemed necessary to develop frameworks for the protection of areas and resources beyond national jurisdictions. Regarding the marine environment, one approach was to simply 'shrink the areas that lie completely beyond individual states' jurisdiction'[132] through the gradual extension of states' sovereign rights to the 200-nautical-mile Exclusive Economic Zone (EEZ), which gives countries control over the exploitation and protection

127 Brunnée, 'Common Areas, Common Heritage, and Common Concern' at 557.

128 ILC Draft Articles on Responsibility of States for Internationally Wrongful Acts (3 August 2001) 53 UN GAOR Supp. (No. 10) at 43, UN Doc A/56/10 (2001); available at <http://untreaty.un.org/ilc/texts/instruments/english/draft%20articles/9_6_2001.pdf>. Art. 48 reads: '1. Any State other than an injured State is entitled to invoke the responsibility of another State in accordance with paragraph 2 if: (a) the obligation breached is owed to a group of States including that State, and is established for the protection of a collective interest of the group; or (b) the obligation breached is owed to the international community as a whole.'

129 ICJ, Nuclear Tests Case (New Zealand v. France), Interim Measures (22 June 1973), ICJ Reports 1973, 135 at 139; available at <http://www.icj-cij.org/docket/files/59/6115.pdf>.

130 ICJ, Nuclear Tests Case (Australia v. France), Joint Dissenting Opinion of Judges Onyeama, Dillard, Jiménez de Aréchaga and Sir Humphrey Waldock, (20 December 1974) ICJ Reports 1974, 312 at 370; available at <http://www.icj-cij.org/docket/files/58/6109.pdf>.

131 ICJ, Nuclear Tests Case (Australia v. France), Dissenting Opinion of Judge de Castro, (20 December 1974) ICJ Reports 1974, 372 at 390; available at <http://www.icj-cij.org/docket/files/58/6111.pdf>.

132 Brunnée, 'Common Areas, Common Heritage, and Common Concern' at 558.

of natural resources.[133] For the remaining (common) areas, i.e., the high seas, UNCLOS provides an important regulatory framework which is based upon the general rule to avoid transboundary environmental harm. This led to a significant change of the classical freedom of the high seas, since the area now falls under several environmental protection requirements of which many have their roots in the general provisions of UNCLOS.[134] Very similar to the high seas, outer space is being handled as common property,[135] which no country can appropriate and to which all states have, at least in theory, equal access.[136]

While the concept of common areas has provided an important legal basis for the protection of such territories and the resources located therein, the fact that it solely focuses on geographical locations beyond national jurisdictions means that its application to international water law is impracticable.

5.2.2 Common heritage

Closely linked to the notion of common area is the concept of 'common heritage'. It is focused on the equitable sharing of benefits from the exploitation of resources beyond the limits of national jurisdiction and demands economically powerful states to renounce unilateral development for their own national advantage.[137] This concept has found recognition in the UN Convention on the Law of the Sea (UNCLOS),[138] the Moon Treaty[139] and, to a much lesser degree, in the framework for the protection of the Antarctic environment.[140]

133 Art 55 of UNCLOS, Specific legal regime of the exclusive economic zone, states that 'The exclusive economic zone is an area beyond and adjacent to the territorial sea, subject to the specific legal regime established in this Part, under which the rights and jurisdiction of the coastal State and the rights and freedoms of other States are governed by the relevant provisions of this Convention.'

134 See, e.g., the UN Agreement for the Implementation of the Provisions of the United Nations Convention on the Law of the Sea of 10 December 1982 relating to the Conservation and Management of Straddling Fish Stocks and Highly Migratory Fish Stocks (4 August 1995; entered into force 11 December 2001) 2167 UNTS 88; available at <http://www.un.org/Depts/los/convention_agreements/convention_overview_fish_stocks.htm>.

135 Art I of the Outer Space Treaty refers to the exploration and use of outer space as 'the province of all mankind'.

136 For a more detailed analysis of the regime, see V Leister, 'Economic Governance and Space Law: Emerging Foundations for Development of "Common Pool Resources" in Outer Space' (2010) *Indian Journal of International Economic Law*, 3, 64; IH Rowlands, 'Atmosphere and Outer Space' in Bodansky D, Brunnée J and Hey E (eds), *The Oxford Handbook of International Environmental Law* (Oxford University Press 2007).

137 P Hilpold, 'Solidarität Als Rechtsprinzip : Völkerrechtliche, Europarechtliche und Staatsrechtliche Betrachtungen' (2007) 55 Jahrbuch des öffentlichen Rechts 195 at 202.

138 Art 136 of UNCLOS reads: 'The Area and its resources are the common heritage of mankind.'

139 Agreement Governing the Activities of States on the Moon and Other Celestial Bodies (18 December 1979; entered into force 11 July 1984) 1363 UNTS 21; reprinted in 18 ILM 1434 (1979) [hereinafter Moon Treaty].

140 See Recommendation ATCM IX-1 of the Antarctic Consultative Parties on the future regime on Antarctic mineral resources (London, 1977); available at <http://www.ats.aq/devAS/info_measures_listitem.aspx?lang=e&id=117>; 'They endorse the following principles: . . . (iv) the Consultative Parties, in dealing with the question of mineral resources in Antarctica, should not prejudice the interests of all mankind in Antarctica.'

The common heritage principle has been applied whenever the distribution of resources outside the boundaries of national jurisdiction has been debated. Hence, it is, again, only relevant with regard to areas which are open to the exploitation of all nations.[141] However, the concept of common heritage adds another dimension to the international legal debate, by looking at how to regulate the access – which in theory is supposed to be equal, but in practice is determined by each state's technological and financial abilities.[142]

As early as 1966, the Economic and Social Council of the United Nations (ECOSOC) had requested the UN Secretary-General

> to make a survey of the present state of knowledge of these resources of the sea, beyond the continental shelf, and of the techniques for exploiting these resources . . . [and] to attempt to identify those resources now considered to be capable of economic exploitation, especially for the benefit of developing countries.[143]

As a result, the UN Secretary-General declared that the underprivileged status of the developing countries demanded a revision of the legal framework governing the law of the sea.[144] Furthermore, the concept of common heritage was included in Resolution 15 of the Geneva World Peace through Law Conference in 1967, which reads:

> Whereas new technology and oceanography have revealed the possibility of exploitation of untold resources of the high seas, and the bed thereof beyond the continental shelf; and, more than half of mankind find itself underprivileged, underfed and underdeveloped; and, that the high seas are the common heritage of all mankind. Resolved, that the World Peace Through Law Center: (1) Recommend to the General Assembly of the United Nations the issuance of a proclamation declaring that the non-fishery resources of the high seas, outside the territorial waters of any State, and the bed of the sea beyond the continental shelf, appertain to the United Nations and are subject to its jurisdiction and control.[145]

Thus, the emergence of the concept of common heritage must be seen against the background of the effort by the newly independent states in the 1960s

141 R Wolfrum, 'The Principle of the Common Heritage of Mankind' (1983) *Zeitschrift für ausländisches öffentliches Recht und Völkerrecht*, 43, 312 at 313.

142 Brunnée, 'Common Areas, Common Heritage, and Common Concern' at 562.

143 United Nations Economic and Social Council, Resolution on non-agricultural resources (7 March 1966) ESCOR, 40th session, 1417th plenary meeting, E/Res.1112 (XL); available at <http://daccess-dds-ny.un.org/doc/UNDOC/GEN/NR0/761/29/IMG/NR076129.pdf?OpenElement>.

144 Note by the Secretary-General (31 October 1967) UN Doc A/C. 1/952.

145 Resolution adopted by the Geneva World Peace Through Law Conference (13 July 1967), GAOR, 22nd Session, Annexes, agenda item 92, UN Doc A/6695; available at <http://archive.org/stream/interimreportonu00unit/interimreportonu00unit_djvu.txt>.

and 1970s to influence the development of international law to better reflect their own priorities and concerns.[146] This explains that developed nations were initially not in favour of the proposal by Ambassador Arvid Pardo of Malta to declare the seabed the common heritage of mankind.[147] In 1970, the UN General Assembly declared the seabed to be common heritage – with 108 (developing) countries voting in favour, and 16 (developed) countries abstaining.[148] The concept did eventually become the foundation for Part XI, Section 2 of UNCLOS on the principles governing the 'Area',[149] where Article 136 reads: 'The Area and its resources are the common heritage of mankind.' Subsequent articles elaborate on what constitutes the key elements of it: (1) the Area, as a commons, is not subject to appropriation by individual states;[150] (2) the Area must be used exclusively for peaceful purposes and activities must be carried out 'for the benefit of mankind as a whole', which must be equitably shared among all states,[151] and (3) the Area's non-living resources have to be managed by an international authority which regulates their exploitation, ensures the equitable distribution of the benefits, and takes measures for environmental protection.[152] A comparable approach can be found in the Moon Treaty, which states that

> (1) The moon and its natural resources are the common heritage of mankind . . . . (2) The moon is not subject to national appropriation by any claim of sovereignty, by means of use or occupation, or by any other means. (3) Neither the surface nor the subsurface of the moon, nor any part thereof or natural resources in place, shall become property of any State, international intergovernmental or non-governmental organization, national organization or non-governmental entity or of any natural person . . . .[153]

With regard to the significance of the common heritage principle for the management of seabed activities, it is worth mentioning that attempts were made to even classify it as a *jus cogens* norm.[154] However, except for UNCLOS and

146 Brunnée, 'Common Areas, Common Heritage, and Common Concern' at 562.

147 Note Verbale of 17 August 1967 from Malta to UN Secretary-General, UN Doc A/6695.

148 UN General Assembly Resolution 2749, Declaration of Principles Governing the Seabed and Ocean Floor (12 December 1970) UN Doc A/RES/25/2749; available at <http://www.un-documents.net/a25r2749.htm>.

149 According to Art 1(1) of UNCLOS, '"Area" means the seabed and ocean floor and subsoil thereof, beyond the limits of national jurisdiction.'

150 Art 137 of UNCLOS.

151 Art 140 and 146 of UNCLOS.

152 Arts 137 and 145 of UNCLOS.

153 Art 11 of the Moon Treaty.

154 Letter from the representatives of Chile, Colombia, Ecuador and Peru to the President of the 3rd United Nations Conference on the Law of the Sea, UN Doc A/CONF.62/101 (28 July 1980); available at <http://untreaty.un.org/cod/diplomaticconferences/lawofthesea-1982/docs/vol_XIV/a_conf-62_101.pdf>.

the Moon Treaty, the concept never gained much traction. The main reason for the lack of application beyond those two legal regimes might be its underlying motivation – states' appetite for natural resources rather than the general interest of the international community in their protection. As Brunnée puts it, 'Its focus on access to resources and benefits gets the concept entangled in and, it appears, sidelined by the competition that these preoccupations entail.'[155] Since the concept does little in overcoming the environment vs. development conundrum, it has been called 'a political and rhetorical tool of convenience used by both the industrialized and the industrializing worlds whenever it suits their respective interests'.[156] As a result, this deems it unsuitable for the application in the area of common water security, as the theme of common heritage is limited to issues of (re)distribution – neglecting other management challenges, such as environmental protection and conservation.[157]

5.2.3 Community of interest

Another interesting take on communality is the concept of 'community of interest', which has actually been applied in international water law. This supranational approach takes away all national sovereignty from the basin states with regard to the governance of a shared watercourse, while calling for the management of the watercourse as a unit.[158] Here, the cooperation between states is supposed to reach the maximum level, preventing water disputes and guaranteeing the optimal utilisation of the resource – for the benefit of all basin states.

The origins of the community of interest as a legal notion can be found in the River Oder Case decided by the Permanent Court of International Justice (PCIJ).[159] Here, the PCIJ stated that the community of interest of riparian states

> becomes the basis of a common legal right, the essential features of which are perfect equality of all riparian states in the use of the whole course of the river and the exclusion of the preferential privilege of any riparian state in relation to the others is relevant to the non-navigational uses.[160]

155 Brunnée, 'Common Areas, Common Heritage, and Common Concern' at 563.

156 I Mgbeoji, 'Beyond Rhetoric: State Sovereignty, Common Concern, and the Inapplicability of the Common Heritage Concept to Plant Genetic Resources' (2003) *Leiden Journal of International Law*, 16, 821 at 826.

157 LD Guruswamy and others, *International Environmental Law and World Order* (2nd edn, West Group 1999) at 986.

158 SC McCaffrey, *The Law of International Watercourses* (2nd edn, Oxford University Press 2007) at 147.

159 Case Relating to the Territorial Jurisdiction of the International Commission of the River Oder (United Kingdom, Czechoslovakia, Denmark, France, Germany, Sweden v. Poland), Judgment of 10 September 1929, PCIJ (ser A) No. 23 (1929).

160 M Fitzmaurice, 'Water Management in the 21st Century' in Anghie A and Sturgess G (eds), *Legal Visions of the 21st Century – Essays in Honour of Judge Christopher Weeramantry* (Kluwer Law International 1998) at 429.

However, since the term 'community' only implies that riparians *should* work together on the management of the watercourse, they are not automatically *required* to actually do so.[161] This is why, for now, the approach of a community of interest is of little use for the pragmatic management of international watercourses, as its legal implications are not clear.[162] According to Fitzmaurice and Elias:

> The theory of community of interest should be distinguished from the so-called theory of common management. The latter is supported by some state practice, but the narrowness of this practice puts in doubt the possibility that the theory of community of interest or common management has entered the body of customary law.[163]

One of the few cases where the concept was actually implemented is the management of Lake Titicaca.[164] In 1957, Bolivia and Peru signed a treaty declaring that 'the two countries have joint, indivisible and exclusive ownership over the waters of Lake Titicaca'.[165] The step of attributing joint ownership over the freshwater resource explains why the concept of community of interest has not found wider acceptance amongst the international community. For many states, it is simply too sovereignty intrusive. The reason why Bolivia and Peru chose to follow this path might have been their relatively good relations and thus the absence of the typical upstream vs downstream conflicts of interests between states we usually find in freshwater hot spots around the world.[166] Hence, even though it can be considered a legal approach which has been applied in a few cases,[167] the future development of the notion of a community of interest with regard to a water security has to be regarded as a cul-de-sac, since widespread support of the concept is questionable. Rather than achieving stronger cooperation between countries sharing freshwater resources, it might cause the basin states to turn away, as the concept aims too high by stripping the basin states of all national sovereignty concerning the management of the watercourse.

161 McCaffrey, *The Law of International Watercourses* at 167.

162 Ibid. at 165.

163 M Fitzmaurice and O Elias, *Watercourse Co-Operation in Northern Europe: A Model for the Future* (TMC Asser Press 2004) at 14.

164 For a brief case study on the Lake Titicaca Basin, see United Nations World Water Assessment Programme, *The United Nations World Water Development Report 2: Water: A Shared Responsibility* (UNESCO 2006) at 488.

165 Art 1 of the Agreement between Bolivia and Peru concerning a Preliminary Economic Study of the Joint Utilization of the Waters of Lake Titicaca (19 February 1957).

166 J Rieckermann and others, *Assessing the Performance of International Water Management at Lake Titicaca* (Center for Comparative and International Studies 2006) at 19.

167 Case Relating to the Territorial Jurisdiction of the International Commission of the River Oder (United Kingdom, Czechoslovakia, Denmark, France, Germany, Sweden v. Poland), Judgment of 10 September 1929, PCIJ (ser A) No. 23 (1929).

5.2.4 Common concern

The UN Conference on Environment and Development in Rio de Janeiro in 1992 marked a milestone in the development of international environmental law. Here, for the first time, a global framework for environmental responsibilities was designed – based on a 'common concern' – which constitutes a considerable leap forward when compared to the (still) prevalent merely transboundary responsibilities based on the concept of good neighbourliness.[168] The common concern is based on the understanding that harm to the environment (e.g., depletion of the ozone layer resources, or the changing climate) has the potential to adversely affect humanity as a whole; thus, cooperation on those issues can only be effective if it is being concerted at a global level. This in turn implies both a right and an obligation of the international community as a whole to have concern for the global environment.[169] While the Rio Declaration itself does not mention the term 'common concern',[170] both of the treaties which were negotiated in Rio – the UN Framework Convention on Climate Change (UNFCCC)[171] and the Convention on Biological Diversity (CBD)[172] – follow this approach.

The Convention on Biological Diversity clearly states that 'the conservation of biological diversity is a common concern of humankind'.[173] While this affirmation was initially ranked as a fundamental principle during the drafting process, it ultimately was downgraded to the Preamble.[174] Interestingly, the parties dropped the concept of common heritage rather early in the negotiating process. In contrast to UNCLOS and the Moon Treaty, which both include reference to the notion of common heritage, the developing countries would not have benefited from such an approach in CBD. Here, developing countries are dealing with the management of resources within their own jurisdictions – rather than resources outside any national jurisdiction. Hence, the developing countries were reluctant to relinquish their respective sovereign rights over

168 PW Birnie, AE Boyle and C Redgwell, *International Law and the Environment* (3rd edn, Oxford University Press 2009) at 128.

169 IUCN Commission on Environmental Law and International Council of Environmental Law, *Draft International Covenant on Environment and Development* (4th edn, IUCN 2010) at 39.

170 1992 Rio Declaration on Environment and Development (14 June 1992) UN Doc A/CONF.151/26 (Vol. I); available at <http://www.un.org/documents/ga/conf151/aconf15126-1annex1.htm>.

171 United Nations Framework Convention on Climate Change (9 May 1992; entered into force 21 March 1994) 1771 UNTS 107; UN Doc A/AC.237/18 (Part II)/Add.1; reprinted in 31 ILM 849 (1992).

172 Convention on Biological Diversity (5 June 1992; entered into force 29 December 1993) 1760 UNTS 79; reprinted in 31 ILM 818 (1992).

173 Preamble of the Convention on Biological Diversity.

174 Art 1(3) of the Fifth Revised Draft Convention on Biological Diversity (20 February 1992) UNEP/Bio.Div/N7-INC.5/2; available at <http://www.cbd.int/doc/meetings/iccbd/bdn-07-inc-05/official/bdn-07-inc-05-02-en.pdf> reads: 'The conservation of biological diversity is a [matter of] common concern of all humankind and requires cooperation by all Contracting Parties.'

those resources covered by CBD.[175] Still, even without strong procedural support, the inclusion of common concern does ensure that the loss of biodiversity is being acknowledged as a major issue which the international community has to address on a common basis.

However, this cannot make up for the shortcomings of the Convention. For a start, the provisions on in-situ and ex-situ conservation and sustainable use in Articles 8–10 of the Convention are considerably weakened by the caveat 'as far as possible and appropriate'.[176] Another major flaw of CBD is that it does not extend state responsibility for extra-territorial harm to damage caused to the global commons.[177] Thus, the Convention remains deeply flawed, as it fails to provide a balancing tool for the clash between the protection of biological diversity and the national sovereignty to exploit natural resources. This is evident in the fact that the target agreed by the members to the Convention in 2002 'to achieve by 2010 a significant reduction of the current rate of biodiversity loss at the global, regional and national level as a contribution to poverty alleviation and to the benefit of all life on Earth',[178] has been missed considerably.[179] The Convention simply does not manage to challenge the orthodox perception of sovereignty.

To a large extent, the UN Framework Convention on Climate Change has to be regarded as a failure as well. Here, just like in CBD, the concept of common concern can be found in the Preamble, which acknowledges that 'change in the Earth's climate and its adverse effects are a common concern of humankind'.[180] While it kick-started a process of legal and political engagement around the globe, the Convention failed to overcome the state-centrism of the climate change negotiations. Ultimately, this led to watered-down obligations in weak agreements which were 'designed to mask the political failure of the international community to create a global climate treaty'.[181]

In this regard, the Draft International Covenant on Environment and Development, a collaborative effort by the IUCN Commission on Environmental Law and the International Council of Environmental Law, tried to reanimate the concept of common concern. The Draft Covenant

175 LD Guruswamy, *International Environmental Law* (2nd edn, Thomson West 2003) at 137.

176 Arts 8–10 of the Convention on Biological Diversity.

177 LD Guruswamy, 'The Convention on Biological Diversity: Exposing the Fawed Foundations' (1999) *Environmental Conservation*, 26, 79 at 79.

178 6th Conference of the Parties to the Convention on Biological Diversity, Strategic Plan for the Convention on Biological Diversity, COP 6 Decision VI/26; available at <https://www.cbd.int/decision/cop/default.shtml?id=7200>.

179 Secretariat of the Convention on Biological Diversity, *Global Biodiversity Outlook 3* (Secretariat of the Convention on Biological Diversity 2010) at 9.

180 Preamble of the UNFCCC.

181 RS Dimitrov, 'Inside UN Climate Change Negotiations: The Copenhagen Conference' (2010) *Review of Policy Research*, 27, 795 at 795.

was designed as a 'living blueprint' for an international framework agreement which consolidates and further develops already existing legal principles related to environment and development. It was first presented at the United Nations Congress on Public International Law in 1995 and has subsequently been revised. In its Article 3, the Covenant states that 'The global environment is a common concern of humanity and under the protection of the principles of international law, the dictates of the public conscience and the fundamental values of humanity.'[182] The commentary to this article illustrates that the concept should to be interpreted as 'the basis upon which the international community at all levels can and must take joint and separate action to protect the environment'.[183] It aims to clarify that not only single issues, such as global climatic changes or the loss of biodiversity, should be regarded as being of common concern to the international community, but the environment as a whole. This closes the circle with the 1992 Rio Declaration which tried to establish a common responsibility to the global environment, resting upon the scientific reality that harm to the environment in one region of the world can have a considerable impact on humanity as a whole. Hence, the international community has to accept both the right and the obligation to 'have concern for the global environment'.[184] The basic idea here is that the notion of common concern entails both spatial and temporal components. While the Draft Covenant considers the Earth's biosphere as a whole, due to the various interdependencies, it also extends the temporal element by recognising long-term impacts of environmental harm and the responsibility of the international community owed to future generations.[185] However, due to the lack of legitimacy, the Draft Covenant has attracted only little attention amongst international legal scholars. This is deeply regrettable, as the document offers a new take on the continual struggle to reconcile the need for environmental protection with the need for development.

Despite not enjoying enormous popularity at its embryonic stage, the concept of common concern is of particular interest to the further development of international water law. Although the attention is again on (common) benefits, it regards the benefits from common action, rather than those derived from the mere exploitation of a resource.[186] Furthermore, instead of targeting one area or resource, this concept focuses on what renders a concern as being common. In so doing, it avoids discussions about common property and territorial sovereignty.

182 IUCN Commission on Environmental Law and International Council of Environmental Law, *Draft International Covenant on Environment and Development* at 3.

183 Ibid. at 39.

184 Ibid.

185 Art 5 of the Draft Covenant reads: 'Equity and justice shall guide all decisions affecting the environment and shall oblige each generation to qualify its environmental conduct by anticipating the needs of future generations.'

186 Brunnée, 'Common Areas, Common Heritage, and Common Concern' at 564.

5.3 Regional common concern as the legal foundation of water security

While the approaches of common area and common heritage are limited to a certain geographical area and its resources, and the concept of community of interest seems to be too sovereignty-intrusive, the notion of common concern appears to be more promising. This becomes apparent when recalling the definition of water security, which benefits from a wider concept:

> A community is water secure when it has sustainable access to freshwater of sufficient quantity and quality, or to the benefits derived therefrom; and the ability to minimise water-related risk and its various repercussions to an acceptable level – without compromising the supporting ecosystems.

The main advantage of the notion of common concern is that it does not automatically connote specific rules and obligations, but rather establishes the fundamental basis for the international community to act. This distinguishes it from the concepts of common area and common heritage, both of which provide an inadequate legal basis for achieving common water security. Furthermore, the notion was developed with the weaknesses of the concept of common heritage in mind. The conclusion that some particular challenge is being perceived as a matter of common concern results in the appreciation that it can no longer be considered as a mere national issue. It also triggers a shift from the orthodox reciprocity and material benefit sharing we often find in treaties to joint action in the long-term interest of community.[187] This is evident in the inclusion of the principle of inter-generational responsibility.[188]

However, both the UNFCCC and CBD face difficulties in achieving strong legal force with regard to the common concern at the level upon which they are intended to have an impact: the global one. First and foremost, this is due to the fact that it is impossible to phrase a global set of values and interests which is independent of the interests of individual states.[189] While it is relatively easy to agree on including a reference to a common concern in the preamble of a framework agreement, as was the case for UNFCCC and CBD, actually implementing the desired change of thought, by providing it with the necessary political and legal clout, is a completely different challenge. Are there any lessons to be learned for international water law when it comes to global governance? Would it be politically feasible to agree, at a global level, on a definition of water security as a common concern of humankind? Given the sheer

187 IUCN Commission on Environmental Law and International Council of Environmental Law, *Draft International Covenant on Environment and Development* at 40.

188 MK Tolba, 'The Implications of the "Common Concern of Mankind" Concept on Global Environmental Issues' (1991) *Revista IIDH*, 13, 237 at 238.

189 Arguing the opposite; D Shelton, 'Common Concern of Humanity' (2009) *Iustum Aequum Salutare*, 5, 33 at 34.

scope of the global water crisis, and recalling the detrimental impacts water disputes have on communities all over the world, it should not be impossible to construct an analogous mindset to the loss of biodiversity or global climate change for transboundary freshwater management. Yet, it is still difficult to sufficiently prove international consensus on whether water security is indeed of common concern.[190] However, scaling one level down by looking at the regional layer could be a fruitful middle road, which can sufficiently accommodate the national interests and the global challenge. The strategy has to be to seize the idea of common concern while keeping it at the more workable – regional – level.[191]

Not only are the common concerns relating to freshwater cooperation more obvious and easier to spell out in the regional than in the global arena, it is also this level which acts as the connecting link between the global water cycle and local water management.[192] The global level seems to be too removed to have an actual impact on the ground; while, at the same time, it often provokes comparisons with imperialism. The regional level, by contrast, can utilise the political and economic power and influence of regional bodies to push for change – change which is home-grown, since (in general) regional bodies are not too far removed from issues on the ground. Furthermore, the security dimension as such, which (so far) managed to hide behind the orthodox perception of state sovereignty, would also become regional – rather than remaining solely national.[193] Finally, framing water security as a regional common concern opens up the enormous potential of including actors and interests beyond the basin. This is due to the fact that a region is not a narrowly defined geographical area – contrary to a basin – but instead can be interpreted in exactly the way a particular community of states deems appropriate in order to manage their water challenges in the most effective and peaceful manner. This in turn may add a new dimension to international freshwater cooperation, which is commonly being perceived as a zero-sum game where competing interests of riparians regarding their desired uses are being negotiated.[194] Instead, the inclusion of non-riparian interests in the design and performance of international water agreements can play a key role in addressing the common security interests of all involved.[195] On these grounds, the notion of a regional

190 On the idea of a global water law, see JW Dellapenna and J Gupta, 'The Evolution of Global Water Law' in Dellapenna JW and Gupta J (eds), *The Evolution of the Law and Politics of Water* (Springer 2009).

191 See J Brunnée and SJ Toope, 'Environmental Security and Freshwater Resources: A Case for International Ecosystem Law' (1994) *Yearbook of International Environmental Law*, 5, 41 at 74.

192 B-O Magsig, 'Rising to the Challenge of Water Security: International (Water) Law in Need of Refinement' (2012) *International Journal of Sustainable Society*, 4, 28 at 30.

193 Brunnée and Toope, 'Environmental Security and Freshwater Resources: A Case for International Ecosystem Law' at 46.

194 See, e.g., the 1992 UNECE Helsinki Convention.

195 Brunnée and Toope, 'Environmental Security and Freshwater Resources: A Case for International Ecosystem Law' at 75.

common concern is the most suitable conceptual vehicle for the endeavour to achieve common water security.

Considering water security as a 'regional common concern' would certainly strengthen international law in this area and equip it with the needed basis for overcoming state-centrism.[196] Fully embracing the notion of ambit, which acknowledges the fact that security can no longer be considered as a zero-sum game between states, will permit a perspective on water security which endorses the argument that ultimate – common and sustainable – security can only be achieved with a truly joint strategy for the benefit of all riparians. However, simply proclaiming a new paradigm will not accomplish these goals alone. It has to be supported by substantive rules and underlaid with procedural obligations which help addressing the 4As of the water security methodology: availability, access, adaptability and ambit.[197] This does not necessary involve re-inventing the wheel of transboundary freshwater cooperation. Instead, it requires states to subscribe to certain basic principles and minimum managing standards as cornerstones for their transboundary water relations, and thus triggers a process of rethinking focused on the respective regional approach – based on a new understanding of water security as a regional common concern. Widely accepted rules of customary international law, such as equitable and reasonable utilisation, will not become redundant. To the contrary, their implementation will be strengthened by the new conceptual underpinning; and thus their contribution towards a more fair and peaceful management of transboundary freshwater resources will be significantly improved.

The obvious way of implementing the concept of regional common concern seems to be through regional treaty regimes, as their role in the development of international water law has been of paramount importance in the past.[198] Regional framework agreements in particular provide for the needed flexibility in order to effectively address water security challenges. Here, common visions and guiding principles can serve to establish the appropriate institutional settings, while at the same time restricting the freedom of the member states to disregard the regional common concern by developing their waters unilaterally.[199] A framework agreement at this level of governance can be customised to a high degree; and thus cater for the regional differences in water challenges, political circumstances and legal traditions. Hence, the regional focus, accompanied by a growing number of protocols implementing the notion, could pave the way for the development of customary international law by helping

196 B-O Magsig, 'Overcoming State-Centrism in International Water Law: "Regional Common Concern" as the Normative Foundation of Water Security' (2011) *Göttingen Journal of International Law*, 3, 317 at 334.

197 See analysis in Chapter 3.

198 See A Rieu-Clarke, 'The Role of Treaties in Building International Watercourse Regimes: A Legal Perspective on Existing Knowledge' (2010) *Water Policy*, 12, 822.

199 On the advantages of framework agreements, see N Matz-Lück, 'Framework Conventions as a Regulatory Tool' (2009) *Göttingen Journal of International Law*, 1, 439.

to shape the concept and settle its legal consequences.[200] This is vital, since until treaties specify the regional common concern as *erga omnes partes*, issues of state responsibility will still come up.[201] International agreements would also help constitute the relevant community which shares the regional common concern.

5.4 How to materialise regional common concern

While the preceding discussion has proposed the fundamental alterations needed in order to reorient international law so as to address common water security concerns more effectively, the following section will point towards avenues which may be useful for transposing the notion of water security as regional common concern into one which carries legal clout. How can the notion of regional common concern evolve in response to the needed change in perception of state sovereignty – a bedrock norm of international relations?

5.4.1 The disregarded vigour of customary international law

The question of what constitutes customary international law has always intrigued legal scholars – while at the same time, it has consistently frustrated governments trying to determine whether its planned conduct is in line with its international legal obligations.[202] Clearly, it is one of the three main sources of international law – together with treaties and 'general principles of law recognized by civilized nations'.[203] Customary rules are state practices which have been recognised by the international community as determining legally binding patterns of conduct.[204] Thus, contrary to the legal codification process; the emergence of new customary rules does not depend on the expressed consent of each individual state. Due to the fact that both their nature and importance are controversial, the demise of customary international rules has long been predicted.[205] However, codification processes, the discussions within the epistemic community and ICJ case law have contributed to a 'contemporary resurrection of custom'.[206] Much of this has not been derived from a particularly Western tradition, but rather springs from the mere necessities of regulating the inter-dependencies between states.[207]

200 On the question of when a specific rule actually becomes customary international law, see BD Lepard, *Customary International Law: A New Theory with Practical Applications* (Cambridge University Press 2010).

201 Brunnée, 'Common Areas, Common Heritage, and Common Concern' at 566.

202 Lepard, *Customary International Law: A New Theory with Practical Applications* at 25.

203 Art 38(1) of the ICJ Statute.

204 MN Shaw, *International Law* (6th edn, Cambridge University Press 2008) at 6.

205 See JP Kelly, 'The Twilight of Customary International Law' (2000) *Virginia Journal of International Law*, 40, 449.

206 AE Roberts, 'Traditional and Modern Approaches to Customary International Law: A Reconciliation' (2001) *American Journal of International Law*, 95, 757 at 757.

207 SM Schwebel, *Justice in International Law* (Cambridge University Press 1994) at 517.

Against the backdrop of the rapidly exacerbating global water crisis, is there a way to tap this source of law in order to achieve common water security? International water lawyers patiently wait until the ICJ declares that some rule has reached the status of customary international law.[208] Given the small number of cases brought before the ICJ which deal primarily with freshwater resources, and the slow speed in which those cases are being decided, the attempt to accelerate the formation of customary international law is alluring. The following example will show how quickly it can develop.

After the terror attacks in September 2001, the UN Security Council was presented with a moment of 'simultaneous opportunity and peril'.[209] It was this painful event which brought forth an international consensus on the necessity for collective action against the (perceived) global threat of terrorism. It only took a couple of days until the Security Council had unanimously adopted a resolution condemning the attacks by referring to them as a 'threat to international peace and security' and reaffirming the 'inherent right of individual or collective self-defence in accordance with the Charter'.[210] Shortly afterwards, the Security Council adopted another resolution which was targeted at combating terrorists and states which 'support, harbor, provide safe haven to, finance, supply weapons to, help recruit, or aid terrorists', and required wide-ranging cooperation of all member states'.[211] What followed was the rapid establishment of a comprehensive legal framework, backed by its enforcement power under Chapter VII of the UN Charter, for states to effectively tackle international terrorism by mutually cooperating and coordinating their respective criminal justice systems.[212]

Only one month later, the United States had started its initiative against the training camps of Al-Qaida as well as military facilities of the Taliban in Afghanistan – all under the cover of its 'inherent right of individual or collective self-defence'.[213] This so-called 'Bush Doctrine' reflected the perception that a state has the right to use military force in its 'self-defence' against any state which has not implemented Resolution 1373.[214] This assertion had far-reaching consequences – not only for the collective security system of the UN,

208 See, e.g., the recent determination by the ICJ that the obligation to conduct a transboundary environmental impact assessment (EIA) has now reached the status of customary international law: ICJ, Case Concerning Pulp Mills on the River Uruguay (Argentina v. Uruguay), Judgment of 20 April 2010, ICJ Reports 2010, 14, at paras 119–121; available at <http://www.icj-cij.org/docket/files/135/15877.pdf>. See also on this matter: O McIntyre, 'The World Court's Ongoing Contribution to International Water Law: The Pulp Mills Case between Argentina and Uruguay' (2011) *Water Alternatives*, 4, 124.

209 PG Danchin and H Fischer, 'Introduction: The New Collective Security' in Danchin PG and Fischer H (eds), *United Nations Reform and the New Collective Security* (Cambridge University Press 2010) at 3.

210 UN Security Council Resolution 1368 (12 September 2001).

211 UN Security Council Resolution 1373 (28 September 2001).

212 Danchin and Fischer, 'Introduction: The New Collective Security' at 3.

213 Art 51 of the UN Charter.

214 Danchin and Fischer, 'Introduction: The New Collective Security' at 4.

but also for international law in general. While the 'Bush Doctrine' obviously encouraged the use of force rather than diplomatic or legal measures, it also brought about a new category of states' preventive anti-terror activities into the traditional laws of war.[215]

Without going into detail about the moral grounds on which the 'coalition of the willing' tried to justify the invasion of Iraq in 2003, the war that followed challenged nothing less than the idea of international order and collective security, since it 'split the Security Council, divided the North Atlantic Treaty Organisation (NATO), and prompted the creation of a high-level panel to rethink the very idea of collective security'.[216] While it caused a long-overdue debate about the necessity to reform the United Nations and triggered a discourse about how to 'vanquish war and power politics through international law',[217] the case of the Bush Doctrine also shows how quickly customary law can develop. While this development has met with some resistance, less controversial insights with regard to the formation of customary law can be drawn from the North Sea Continental Shelf cases.[218] Here, the ICJ rejected the principle of equidistance, but upheld the idea of 'equitable principles', which refers to several cooperative factors. Furthermore, the ICJ also upheld the principle of customary international law by using the text of the Geneva Convention and its purpose to exclude the mechanism of equidistance.[219]

Thus, one might ask whether the time has come to grant a legal concept which aims to address an even more severe challenge – one which already has a grave impact on billions of people around the world – a shortcut for reaching the status of customary international law? As noble as this idea might seem, it is rather unrealistic to expect a sudden willingness of states to declare water security as a common concern of mankind and thus provoke a fundamental change of international (water) law. Most nations might be wary of opening Pandora's box with regard to the concept of state sovereignty and the management of other natural resources. However, the possibility of regional forces in changing the understanding of international water law should not be discounted, as it is generally accepted that subgroups of states can develop their own customary law.[220] Eventually, when the time is ripe, one might see the slow formation of a

215 Ibid.

216 S Chesterman, 'Reforming the United Nations: Legitimacy, Effectiveness, and Power after Iraq' (2006) *Singapore Year Book of International Law*, 10, 59 at 60.

217 Danchin and Fischer, 'Introduction: The New Collective Security' at 6.

218 Cases concerning the North Sea Continental Shelf (Federal Republic of Germany v. Denmark; Federal Republic of Germany v. Netherlands), Judgment of 20 February 1969, ICJ Reports 1969, 3 at para 37; available at <http://www.icj-cij.org/docket/files/52/5561.pdf>.

219 Ibid. at para 60.

220 Lepard, *Customary International Law : A New Theory with Practical Applications* at 33. For instance, the ICJ found that customary law could exist even between just two states; concluded in 2009 that 'fishing by the inhabitants of the Costa Rican bank of the San Juan River for subsistence purposes from that bank is to be respected by Nicaragua as a customary right.' ICJ, *Dispute regarding Navigational and Related Rights Case (Costa Rica v Nicaragua)*, Judgment (13 July 2009) ICJ Reports 2009, 213 at paras 141 and 144; available at <http://www.icj-cij.org/docket/files/133/15321.pdf>.

customary principle concerning water security as a common concern – maybe even at the global level.

5.4.2 The overlooked strength of soft law

There has long been a rift between two camps of international legal scholars regarding the issue of 'soft law'. While some perceive it as a threat to 'international law proper' or the 'normative continuum',[221] others acknowledge the legal potential it entails.[222] While there is no generally accepted definition of soft law, it usually refers to any written instrument, other than a treaty, which contains general principles, specific norms, or any other provisions determining expected behaviour.[223] Its goal is the achievement of functional cooperation between states in order to reach common international goals. The concept of soft law is closely linked to the international relations theory of 'soft power'[224] and thus puts forward a structure of normative constraints on actors which does not depend on the coercive characteristics of hard law. Hence, in general, soft law does not have the objective of creating rights and obligations under international law.[225]

The sheer amount of non-legal instruments in the area of transboundary water management which intend to shape states' behaviour seems to justify a (renewed) reflection on the possibilities soft law can have in promoting the concept of regional common concern.[226] Due to the fact that many non-binding instruments are drafted like binding international law – providing a basis for legal arguments and disputes – and are having a significant impact on the issues they address, it has been argued that soft law does not really differ from binding international law – except for the fact that it is officially non-binding.[227] One cannot limit the concept of soft law to those instruments that

221 J D'Aspremont and T Aalberts, 'Which Future for the Scholarly Concept of Soft International Law? Editors' Introductory Remarks' (2012) *Leiden Journal of International Law*, 25, 309 at 309.

222 See, e.g., the role soft law played with regard to the rights of indigenous peoples; M Barelli, 'The Role of Soft Law in the International Legal System: The Case of the United Nations Declaration on the Rights of Indigenous Peoples' (2009) *International and Comparative Law Quarterly*, 58, 957.

223 D Shelton, 'Soft Law' in Armstrong D (ed.), *Routledge Handbook of International Law* (Routledge 2009) at 69.

224 M Zeitoun, N Mirumachi and JF Warner, 'Transboundary Water Interaction II: The Influence of "Soft" Power' (2011) *International Environmental Agreements: Politics, Law and Economics*, 11, 159 at 177.

225 See, e.g., J Ellis, 'Shades of Grey: Soft Law and the Validity of Public International Law' (2012) *Leiden Journal of International Law*, 25, 313; D Bodansky, 'Prologue to a Theory of Non-Treaty Norms' in Arsanjani MH and others (eds), *Looking to the Future : Essays on International Law in Honor of W Michael Reisman* (Martinus Nijhoff Publishers 2010); J D'Aspremont, 'Softness in International Law: A Self-Serving Quest for New Legal Materials' (2008) *European Journal of International Law*, 19, 1075.

226 For a discussion on the various approaches within the global water community, see Chapter 4.

227 M Goldmann, 'We Need to Cut Off the Head of the King: Past, Present, and Future Approaches to International Soft Law' (2012) *Leiden Journal of International Law*, 25, 335 at 346.

interact with binding legal norms.[228] Rather, the dynamic character of many soft law instruments has to be acknowledged. While some of its instruments represent a first step in a process which may lead from soft to hard law; some soft law instruments are actually drafted with the intention to remain soft, and thus more easily amendable. Understanding this requires recognising soft law as a 'functional equivalent' to binding international law.[229]

There are several reasons for states to enter into non-treaty arrangements – such as the need for mutual confidence-building; the desire to create a preliminary, rather flexible regime; concern that potential failure of a hard treaty could burden international relations; usually speedier finalisation, and parties which do not have the legal standing to conclude treaties under international law – such as non-state actors (NSAs) – can be included in the process.[230] Yet, legal positivism still does not consider soft law as international law proper: 'Just as physicists view dark matter only through its interplay with visible matter, modern legal positivists grasp soft law purely through its interplay with hard law.'[231] In merely treating soft law as an indicator for the emergence or development of customary law, some of its important functions are being missed out.

While the role of NSAs on the creation and implementation of (soft) law is increasing, there are several examples where non-basin states' engagement in hydro-diplomacy has made real impacts on the ground. While this is nothing new, the efforts of NSAs have recently gained momentum, as water security is being seen as an important issue of world politics. Two recent examples are the US Water Partnership[232] and Scotland's 'Hydro Nation Programme'. The Scottish initiative is of particular interest, as it not only involves demonstrating 'leadership in meeting the challenges and opportunities that the water industry presents across the world',[233] but it may also provide a channel of (hydro)diplomacy for the nation which is (as yet) part of the United Kingdom; as such, the UK Parliament retains power over certain 'reserved' matters – including international relations.[234] Other examples of states engaged in active

228 See, however, T Meyer, 'Soft Law as Delegation' (2009) *Fordham International Law Journal*, 32, 888 at 889.

229 Goldmann, 'We Need to Cut Off the Head of the King: Past, Present, and Future Approaches to International Soft Law' at 346.

230 H Hillgenberg, 'A Fresh Look at Soft Law' (1999) *European Journal of International Law*, 10, 499 at 501.

231 Goldmann, 'We Need to Cut Off the Head of the King: Past, Present, and Future Approaches to International Soft Law' at 345.

232 'Announced in March 2012 by U.S. Secretary of State Hillary Rodham Clinton, the U.S. Water Partnership (USWP) unites and mobilizes U.S. expertise, resources and ingenuity to address water challenges around the globe, particularly in the developing world. A joint effort of both public and private sectors in the U.S., the partnership is supported by government agencies, academic organizations, water coalitions, NGOs and the private sector.' <http://uswaterpartnership.org/>.

233 The Scottish Government, 'Making Scotland a World Leading Hydro Nation' (28 June 2012) <http://www.scotland.gov.uk/News/Releases/2012/06/scotland-water28062012>.

234 Schedule 5, Part I of the Scotland Act 1998 (19 November 1998) available at <http://www.legislation.gov.uk/ukpga/1998/46>.

hydro-diplomacy around the world are France,[235] Germany,[236] Japan,[237] the Netherlands[238] and Sweden.[239]

It follows from the discussion above that legal scholars should not shy away from including soft law in their research, as it has already played an important role in both norm creation and norm formation within international water law and more broadly. If anything, more emphasis should be given to the analysis of the potential of this legal avenue in changing the current legal system governing the world's transboundary freshwater resources. The fact that international (hard) law does not operate detached from (soft) political and societal processes has to be reflected in future international legal research.

5.5 Conclusion

International water law does not merely constitute a niche product of the international system. Due to the unique characteristics of the global water crisis and the conglomerate challenges they pose to the international community, international water law can – and should – affect the very substance of general international law.[240] Not only is international water law a rather new field of international law, it can also introduce new methods and new ways of thinking into the wider sphere of legal research. The challenges we are facing regarding the peaceful management of our shared freshwater resources are bigger than states – indeed, bigger than basins. In an increasingly water-insecure world, a 'react-and-correct' approach is no longer adequate. What is needed instead is one of 'foresee-and-prevent'.[241] This, however, can only be possible if we overcome the prevailing state-centrism in international water law. Doing so requires fundamental changes to the interpretation of the established paradigms of international law – above all, the principle of state sovereignty.

The community of states has manoeuvred itself to the tipping point of global water insecurity, by ignoring the growing inter-dependences with regard to their shared water resources and clinging to the orthodox state-centred approach in

235 Through the World Water Council and the biannual World Water Forum <http://www.worldwatercouncil.org/>.

236 E.g., with the Deutsche Gesellschaft für internationale Zusammenarbeit (GIZ) <http://www.giz.de/Themen/en/28146.htm>.

237 Through the Japan Water Forum (JWF) <http://www.waterforum.jp/en/home/pages/index.php>.

238 E.g., with the Bank-Netherlands Water Partnership (BNWP) <http://water.worldbank.org/water/wpp>.

239 Mainly through the Stockholm International Water Institute (SIWI) and its yearly World Water Week <http://www.siwi.org/>.

240 For a discussion on how global environmental concerns affect international law, see French, 'A Reappraisal of Sovereignty in the Light of Global Environmental Concerns' at 377.

241 AS Timoshenko, 'Ecological Security: Response to Global Challenges' in Weiss EB (ed.), *Environmental Change and International Law: New Challenges and Dimensions* (United Nations University Press 1992).

fear of losing sovereignty. Recalling the obligation of the global community 'to maintain international peace and security',[242] the lack of collective political will to address the widespread water insecurity with the utmost effort seems astonishing. The looming water crisis, together with the recognition that the fair sharing of transboundary water resources is gaining significance, sets the course for future transboundary freshwater cooperation. Applying the 4A operational methodology as a template for analysing the key issues related to water security can serve as a point of departure for the refinement of international (water) law. It is our responsibility to make the case that as long as states keep focusing on their own respective interests, pursuing their own benefits; the international community will fail in achieving ultimate security. While the notion of common water security is still in its infancy, it nevertheless provides a novel mindset – one which may, if backed by the normative concept of regional common concern, ultimately be capable of overcoming state-centrism. Joint efforts of governments, the epistemic community and the public are of key importance for pushing the concept forward beyond a vague political ideal.[243] Only when based on such combined efforts can the new mindset acquire necessary legal validity. The previous sections have shown how this normative foundation can be guided out of its embryonic stage, materialise in international law and ultimately base international freshwater cooperation on a more common ground. Following in the next chapter is an analysis as to how likely this change of course is in the region of the Himalayas, and how far along the road are the Asian hydro-hegemons, China and India, in overcoming state-centrism.

242 Art 1(1) of the UN Charter.

243 Tolba, 'The Implications of the "Common Concern of Mankind" Concept on Global Environmental Issues' at 246.

6 Water security in Himalayan Asia

The previous chapters have proposed a working definition of water security and how this evolving concept should be underpinned ethically (through hydrosolidarity) and legally (through regional common concern). The following sections examine the current state of affairs in Himalayan Asia and how the novel understanding of common water security and its legal foundations could help achieve hydrosolidarity. The region serves as a useful area of study, since several of the global challenges which put pressure on transboundary water management can be found here – such as climate change, population growth, urbanisation and economic development. In addition, political tensions between several of the states depending on the runoff of the 'Third Pole' hamper regional cooperation – e.g., the conflicts in the volatile parts of Kashmir and Tibet. Contrary to other studies that investigate the water issues of Himalayan Asia,[1] this chapter will maintain an objective focus by basing the analysis on the 4A operational methodology of water security (see Chapter 3). It is true that this problem-oriented approach in choosing a region is not without its shortcomings. Analysing a region which already applies an institutional framework based on a well-advanced environment of mutual trust and cooperation, like the European Union, might have shown more obvious links to an understanding of water security developed in this book. However, the further development of the concept, as well as international water law, will benefit more by studying a challenging environment which highlights some hurdles regarding its implementation. If it can be demonstrated that even in such a complex and volatile region, looking at international water law through the lens of common water security could help to break with the prevalence of zero-sum games, and thus lead towards hydrosolidarity, it may serve as an inspiring model for other regions.

6.1 The particularities of the region

Himalayan Asia is especially interesting for studies on water security. This is mainly due to the water challenges it faces, but also because of its political setting. While some of these challenges are very particular to the region, others are being observed all around the world; although with different intensities. Since

1 See, e.g., B Chellaney, *Water : Asia's New Battleground* (Georgetown University Press 2011).

'Himalayan Asia' is a variously defined area, it is important to point out that this chapter looks at the transboundary freshwater interaction between Afghanistan, Bangladesh, Bhutan, Burma, Cambodia, China, India, Laos, Nepal, Pakistan, Thailand and Vietnam – who are all, at least to some extent, dependent on transboundary river systems that originate in the Himalayas (see Figure 6.1).[2]

The speed of economic development in the region is remarkable. Looking at China and India, the average growth in GDP over the last five years was 9.3 per cent and 7.2 per cent respectively – in a time of global economic crisis.[3] Not only the speed, but also the nature of economic development throughout the region triggers difficult environmental and social challenges. In Cambodia and Laos, for example, the aftermath of conflict and the transition from centrally planned towards (more) market-oriented economies has resulted in increased foreign investment in resource extraction.[4] One of the results is an increase in large-scale commercial logging which threatens the unique biodiversity of the region as well as sustainable water management, since it damages wetlands, including those protected under the Ramsar Convention,[5] and thus compromises the vital ecosystem services they provide.[6] In some countries, the major source of direct foreign investment is in hydropower developments – for instance, along the Mekong River – trying to quench the nations' increasing thirst for energy.[7] Already, the region is home to around 45 per cent of the world's population,[8] while more than 1.5 billion people (22 per cent of the global population) are directly dependent on the rivers originating in the Himalayas.[9] Although the birth rate in some countries of the region is rather

2 This geographic scope leaves out five countries in Central Asia – Kazakhstan, Kyrgyzstan, Tajikistan, Turkmenistan and Uzbekistan – which lie in catchment areas of two rivers also originating in the Himalayas: Amu Darya and Syr Darya. The reason behind excluding Central Asia lies in the particularities of this sub-region which is being covered extensively by other authors. See, e.g., D Ziganshina, *Promoting Transboundary Water Security in the Aral Sea Basin through International Law* (Brill Nijhoff 2014); MM Rahaman, 'Principles of Transboundary Water Resources Management and Water-Related Agreements in Central Asia: An Analysis' (2012) *International Journal of Water Resources Development*, 28, 475.

3 See ADB, 'Asian Development Bank and People's Republic of China' (April 2014) <http://www.adb.org/sites/default/files/pub/2014/PRC.pdf>; ADB, 'Asian Development Bank and India' (April 2014) <http://www.adb.org/sites/default/files/pub/2014/IND.pdf>.

4 J Barnett, 'Environmental Security in the Asia-Pacific Region: Contrasting Problems, Places, and Prospects' in Brauch HG and others (eds), *Facing Global Environmental Change : Environmental, Human, Energy, Food, Health and Water Security Concepts* (Springer 2009) at 942.

5 Convention on Wetlands of International Importance especially as Waterfowl Habitat (2 February 1971; entered into force 21 December 1975) 996 UNTS 245; reprinted in 11 ILM 963 (1972) [hereinafter Ramsar Convention].

6 E Lorraine, 'ASEAN and Environmental Governance: Strategies of Regionalism in Southeast Asia' (2012) *Global Environmental Politics*, 12, 38 at 39.

7 See K Bakker, 'The Politics of Hydropower: Developing the Mekong' (1999) *Political Geography*, 18, 209.

8 See Population Division of the United Nations Department of Economic and Social Affairs, *2010 Revision of the World Population Prospects* (2010) available at <http://esa.un.org/unpd/wpp/index.htm>.

9 D Grey and G Connors, *The Water Security Imperative: We Must and Can Do More* (World Water Council 2009) at 60.

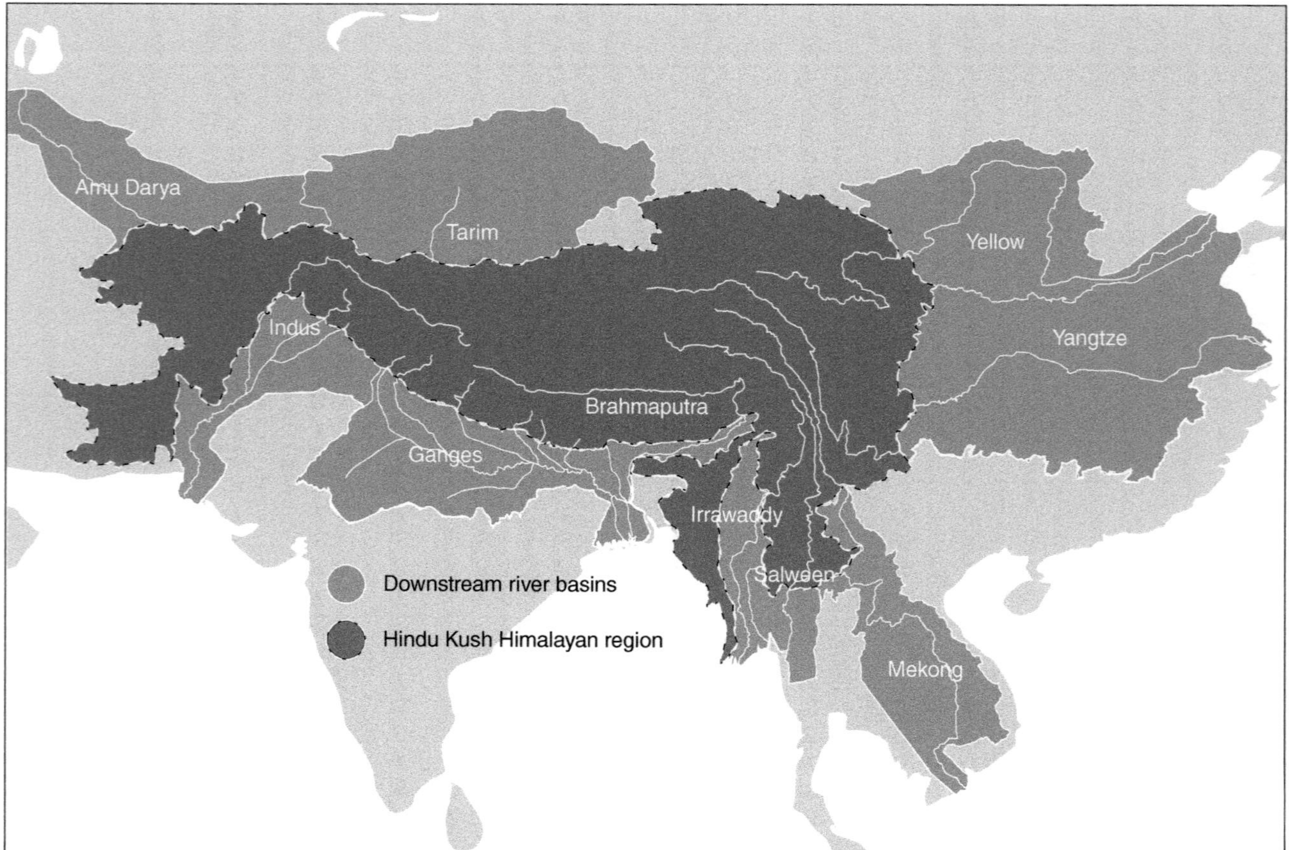

Figure 6.1 ICIMOD – Hindu Kush Himalayan region, courtesy of the International Centre for Integrated Mountain Development (ICIMOD)

stable (e.g., in China with 0.5 per cent per year),[10] other nations will grow rapidly. The population of Afghanistan, for example, is projected to more than double by the middle of the century – increasing from today's 32 million to around 76 million.[11] Due to the aforementioned factors, most countries in the region have seen their renewable freshwater resources and water availability drop continuously over the last decades.[12]

Climate change is acting as a constantly intensifying threat multiplier around the world, since it 'poses a major conceptual challenge to water managers, water resource users (e.g., agriculture, industry), as well as to policy makers in general, as it is no longer appropriate to assume that past climatic and hydrological conditions will continue into the future'.[13] In Himalayan Asia, the challenges posed by global warming are of particular severity and complexity. The increased rainfall variability will adversely affect both surface and groundwater reliability and quality by making floods, droughts and other extreme events more likely; and rising sea levels will cause a degradation of coastal aquifers through salinity intrusion.[14] Furthermore, the rise in global mean temperatures has already resulted in the acceleration of glacier melt. While the exact speed of this process is still being debated,[15] the noticeable decline in Asian mountain glacial cover is widely acknowledged.[16] However, due to diverse hydrological characteristics of the Himalayas, the impact of the melting glaciers is being felt very differently in the various river basins. The basins highly dependent on the glacial meltwater are the Indus (44.8 per cent),[17] the Ganges (29 per cent)

10 ADB, 'Asian Development Bank and People's Republic of China' (31 December 2012) <http://www.adb.org/sites/default/files/pub/2013/PRC.pdf>.

11 Pakistan is expected to grow as well – from 173,593,000 in 2010 to 274,875,000 in 2050; see Population Division of the United Nations Department of Economic and Social Affairs, *2010 Revision of the World Population Prospects* (2010) available at <http://esa.un.org/unpd/wpp/index.htm>.

12 Asian Development Bank, *Asian Water Development Outlook 2013 : Measuring Water Security in Asia and the Pacific* (Asian Development Bank 2013) at 29. For a up-to-date country-by-country data see, World Bank, 'Renewable Internal Freshwater Resources per Capita', available at <http://data.worldbank.org/indicator/ER.H2O.INTR.PC>.

13 BC Bates and others, Climate Change and Water: Technical Paper of the Intergovernmental Panel on Climate Change (Intergovernmental Panel on Climate Change 2008) at 127.

14 Asian Development Bank, *Meeting the Water and Climate Change Challenges* (Asian Development Bank 2009) at 2.

15 In 1999, a report by the Working Group on Himalayan Glaciology (WGHG) of the International Commission for Snow and Ice (ICSI) stated that 'glaciers in the Himalayas are receding faster than in any other part of the world and, if the present rate continues, the likelihood . . . of them disappearing by the year 2035 is very high'; WWF Nepal Program, *An Overview of Glaciers, Glacier Retreat, and Subsequent Impacts in Nepal, India and China* (WWF Nepal Program 2005) at 29. WWF has apologised for having used this erroneous statement in their reports; which caused a stir as it was used to claim that Himalayan glaciers will 'vanish within 40 years'.

16 Leadership Group on Water Security in Asia, *Asia's Next Challenge: Securing the Region's Water Future* (Asia Society 2009) at 33.

17 J Xu and others, 'The Melting Himalayas: Cascading Effects of Climate Change on Water, Biodiversity, and Livelihoods' (2009) *Conservation Biology*, 23, 520 at 524.

and the Yangtze (19 per cent); while others, e.g., the Yellow (1.3 per cent), are much less reliant on this source.[18] When looking at seasonal variations, the complexity of the link between glaciers and river basin becomes even more apparent. While snow and ice pack melt contribute to 29 per cent of the annual flow of the Ganges, in summer the river runoff is said to be 70 per cent dependent on glacier melt.[19] Furthermore, a significant amount of freshwater reserves are being stored in the ground as permafrost.[20] The projected decline in areas covered by permafrost could have a significant impact on groundwater storage and recharge patterns in the region.[21] However, the glaciers of the Himalayas have not yet been extensively mapped – and thus, a lot more research needs to be done in order to better understand the different rates of glacial retreat and the consequential effects on the various river basins. None the less, even if the downstream impact of reduced snow and ice cover cannot be determined precisely, the general trend of a temporary increase and a long-term decrease in river runoff holds true.[22]

Another consequence of global climate change is the shift in monsoon patterns. This development is of serious concern for various river basins in the region, as it causes freshwater supplies to be less predictable, and thus makes water management less reliable.[23] Due to the fact that the Himalayan region as a whole is highly sensitive to global climatic changes, these impacts will have a detrimental effect on the socio-economic development of states in Himalayan Asia. The repercussions of global warming for Pakistan, for instance, will cost its national economy around US$14 billion (almost 5 per cent of its GDP) each year.[24]

Yet, while Asia is hit hard by global environmental change, migration patterns seem to make things even worse. Against common belief, people are as likely to move towards areas of environmental risk (e.g., floodplains or

18 Strategic Foresight Group, *The Himalayan Challenge: Water Security in Emerging Asia* (Strategic Foresight Group 2010) at 10. See also, SP Singh, V Singh and M Skutsch, 'Rapid Warming in the Himalayas: Ecosystem Responses and Development Options' (2010) *Climate and Development*, 2, 221 at 224.

19 Strategic Foresight Group, The Himalayan Challenge: Water Security in Emerging Asia at 10.

20 X Li and others, 'Distribution and Changes of Glacier, Snow and Permafrost in China' in Braun LN and others (eds), *Assessment of Snow, Glacier and Water Resources in Asia*, vol. 8 (International Hydrological Programme of UNESCO; German IHP/HWRP National Committee 2009) at 122.

21 C Andermann and others, 'Impact of Transient Groundwater Storage on the Discharge of Himalayan Rivers' (2012) *Nature Geoscience*, 5, 127; B Bookhagen, 'Hydrology: Himalayan Groundwater' (2012) *Nature Geoscience*, 5, 97.

22 Humanitarian Futures Programme, The Waters of the Third Pole: Sources of Threat, Sources of Survival (2010) at 9.

23 F Biermann, '"Earth System Governance" as a Crosscutting Theme of Global Change Research' (2007) 17 Global Environmental Change 326 at 330; BP Kaltenborn, C Nellemann and II Vistnes (eds), *High Mountain Glaciers and Climate Change : Challenges to Human Livelihoods and Adaptation* (UNEP, GRID-Arendal 2010) at 20.

24 The News International, 'Climate Change to Cost Pakistan $14 Billion Annually' (24 March 2012) <http://www.thenews.com.pk/Todays-News-2-99268-Climate-change-to-cost-Pakistan-$14-billion-annually>.

low-lying coastal zones) as they are to move away from them. This phenomenon might cause the number of people living in floodplains of urban areas in South East Asia to rise from around 7 million in 2000 to 30–49 million by 2060.[25] Another significant population group is simply too poor to be able to migrate, despite increasing environmental hardship. This shows that the profound changes in environmental conditions (such as too much or too little freshwater) will affect human migration patterns in a very complex way. While previous studies have mainly focused on groups leaving vulnerable areas, future research has to analyse how to address the issues of migrating towards environmental risk and how to better help the millions of people that will be 'trapped' in vulnerable regions.[26]

These pressures not only affect the states in their national development and policies. It is the feature of water to transform these domestic challenges into regional ones. The glaciers of the Tibetan Plateau, also referred to as the 'Third Pole', feed the headwaters of the mighty rivers Yellow, Yangtze, Mekong, Salween, Irrawaddy, Ganges-Brahmaputra and Indus. Around 1.5 billion people downstream directly depend upon these waters – not to mention the (hidden) global implications of the 'virtual water' trade. Since the outlook for this region is especially worrisome, one can expect that governments will increasingly look beyond their borders to secure freshwater resources – leading to even more geopolitical tensions.[27] In light of the predicted freshwater shortages in the long run, glacial waters are only gaining in value, which in turn adds political significance to the regions in which these waters are stored. While this is true for various regions of the world (e.g., in the Andes),[28] this applies especially to the geopolitical relevance of the Tibetan Plateau.[29] In few other places has the prospect of conflicts over water resources been more seriously anticipated than in Himalayan Asia, where some of the world's greatest river systems crisscross international boundaries of several of the world's most densely populated and hostile nations – including Bangladesh, China, India and Pakistan.[30] While the two dominant powers in the region – China and India – try to maintain an understanding of water security as being of supreme national importance, their downstream neighbours are pushing more and more for a new understanding of common water security.

The recently published Asian Water Development Outlook provides a first comprehensive analysis of water security on a country-by-country basis

25 Foresight, Migration and Global Environmental Change: Future Challenges and Opportunities (The Government Office for Science 2011) at 13.

26 Ibid.

27 See, e.g., Strategic Foresight Group, The Himalayan Challenge: Water Security in Emerging Asia.

28 J Painter, 'Deglaciation in the Andean Region' (2007) 55 Human Development Report Office Occasional Paper.

29 Circle of Blue, 'China, Tibet, and the Strategic Power of Water' (8 May 2008) <http://www.circleofblue.org/waternews/2008/world/china-tibet-and-the-strategic-power-of-water/>.

30 See, e.g., Chellaney, *Water: Asia's New Battleground*.

in Asia.[31] While, as is so often the case, the study does not move beyond a state-centred perception of water security,[32] the national results are none the less very important in understanding the pressing water issues in the region. The overall conclusion of the exercise is that the 37 of the 49 states which had been assessed are either facing a 'hazardous' level of water security (e.g., India) or have barely begun to engage in tackling water security issues (e.g., China).[33] While the study acknowledges the fact that 'water security impacts often transcend national boundaries',[34] it remains largely silent on how to improve transboundary freshwater management.[35] However, it highlights two realities which also have a heavy impact on international hydropolitics: (1) rapidly increasing inequality in access to water and sanitation, and (2) the deteriorating environmental state of the river basins.[36] Furthermore, the fact that the region's great hydropower potential, particularly in Bhutan, Burma, China, India, Laos and Thailand, is still mainly untapped has not gone unnoticed.[37] Against the backdrop of an energy-hungry Asia, the development of this source of electricity will have far-reaching implications way beyond the countries' respective national boundaries.

This brief overview of water security issues in Himalayan Asia shows quite blatantly that the cumulative effects of the various challenges are already reshaping the region's international relations. Asia's freshwater resource challenge is exceptionally complex – encompassing a blend of political, economic, social and environmental dimensions. The increasingly water-focused rivalries between nations, some of which are nuclear armed (China, India and Pakistan) has caused great anxiety amongst international security experts.[38] This disquiet

31 Asian Development Bank, *Asian Water Development Outlook 2013: Measuring Water Security in Asia and the Pacific*.

32 Instead, it remains on the national level and understands national water security to be achieved when societies can 'successfully manage their water resources and services to (1) satisfy household water and sanitation needs in all communities; (2) support productive economies in agriculture, industry, and energy; (3) develop vibrant, livable cities and towns; (4) restore healthy rivers and ecosystems; and (5) build resilient communities that can adapt to change'. See ibid. at 5.

33 The following countries have achieved the two lowest National Water Security Index (NWSI) values: 'hazardous': Afghanistan, Bangladesh, Cambodia, India, Kiribati, Nauru, Pakistan, and Tuvalu; 'engaged': Azerbaijan, Bhutan, Burma, China, Cook Islands, Federated States of Micronesia, Fiji, Georgia, Indonesia, Kyrgyz Republic, Laos, Maldives, Marshall Islands, Mongolia, Nepal, Niue, Palau, Papua New Guinea, Philippines, Samoa, Solomon Islands, Sri Lanka, Thailand, Timor-Leste, Tonga, Turkmenistan, Uzbekistan, Vanuatu, and Vietnam. Ibid. at 8.

34 Ibid. at 88.

35 The report does merely suggest to 'support the creation and implementation of transboundary institutional frameworks for water resource management' as a means to increase economic water security; ibid. at 40.

36 Ibid.

37 Asian Development Bank, Asian Development Outlook 2012: Confronting Rising Inequality in Asia (Asian Development Bank 2012) at 164; Leadership Group on Water Security in Asia, Asia's Next Challenge: Securing the Region's Water Future at 17.

38 See, e.g., JF Brennan, 'The China-India-Pakistan Water Crisis: Prospects for Interstate Conflict' (MA Dissertation in Security Studies, Naval Postgraduate School, 2008).

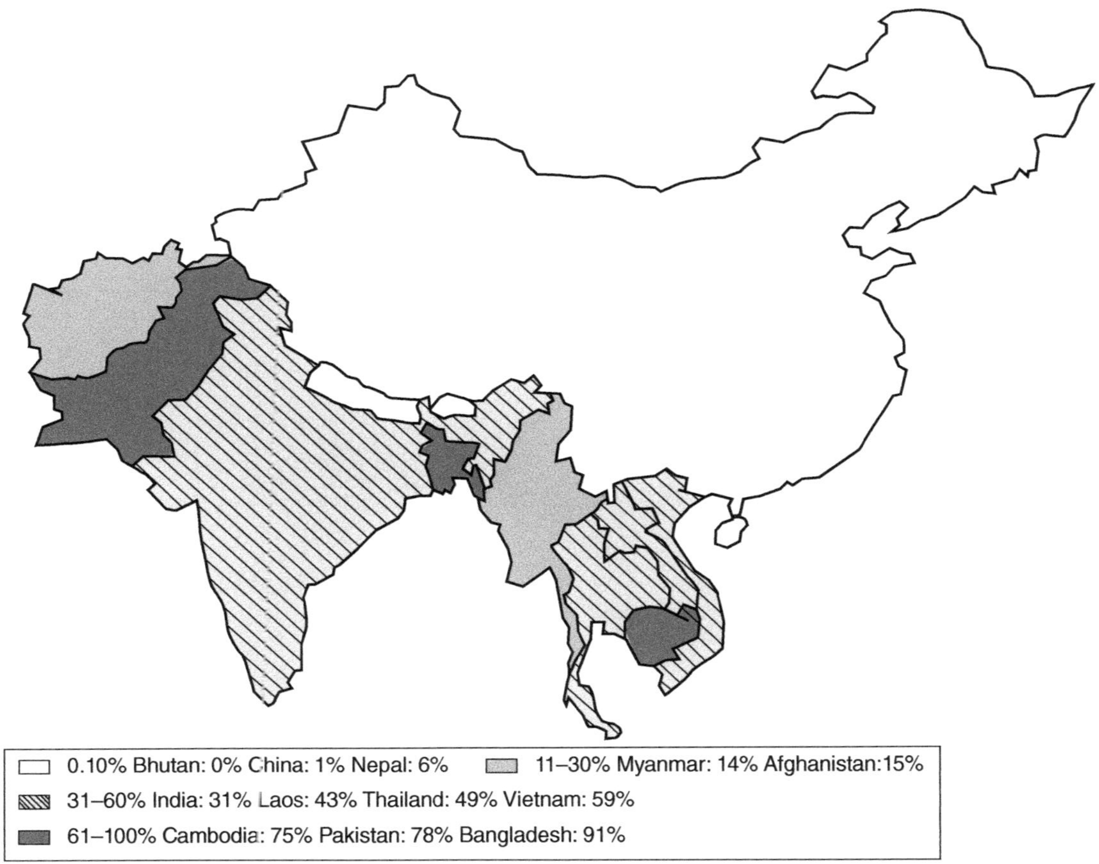

Figure 6.2 Dependencies on transboundary water resources. Data: AQUASTAT, Food and Agriculture Organization of the United Nations (FAO)

is mainly due to the fact that states still tend to voice their water needs in terms of national interests.[39] Here, a new understanding of common water security could help changing the path the nations pursue in their cooperation over transboundary freshwater – from independence to inter-dependence.

6.2 The rise of two global powerhouses

What China does regarding its water management affects ten countries downstream: Bangladesh, Bhutan, Burma, Cambodia, India, Laos, Nepal, Pakistan, Thailand and Vietnam; while India's riparian policies heavily affect four countries: Bangladesh, Bhutan, Nepal and Pakistan.[40] The importance of China is stressed even more when one realises that the headwaters of all the transboundary rivers flowing through these countries, except the main Ganges River, rise in the Tibetan Plateau. Thus, all of the aforementioned mighty basins depend – at least to some degree – on China, which explains the crucial geopolitical feature of Tibet (see Figure 6.3).[41] All those social and environmental pressures

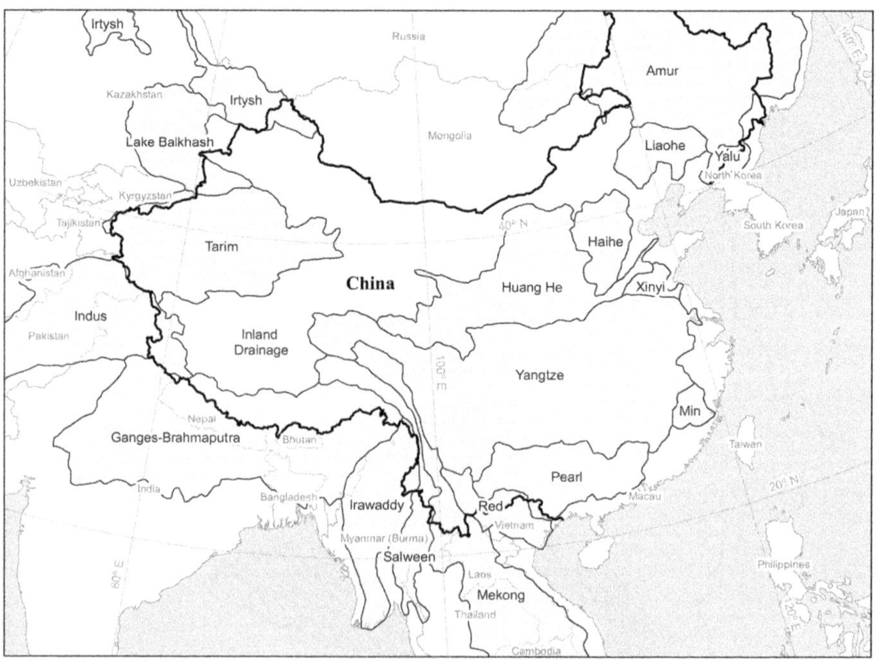

Figure 6.3 Major river basins of China. Cartographer: Matthew Heberger.

39 RG Wirsing, DC Stoll and C Jasparro, *International Conflict over Water Resources in Himalayan Asia* (Palgrave Macmillan 2013) at 8.

40 G Siwakoti, Trans-Boundary River Basins in South Asia: Options for Conflict Resolution (International Rivers 2011).

41 For an interesting discussion on the statehood of Tibet, see B Sautman, 'Tibet's Putative Statehood and International Law' (2010) *Chinese Journal of International Law*, 9, 127.

seem even more daunting, when looking at them in light of the political setting of the region.

China's and India's emerging role in a new world order is more evident than ever. One example is the fact that some politicians in Europe are now looking to China for a way out of the European debt crisis.[42] Both states are also trying to manifest their positions with the traditional approach of military security. While this is of course highly significant for the security and stability of South and South East Asia, the repercussions of the power struggles within the highly critical region can be felt far beyond its boundaries. A recent study showed that while India was the world's largest importer of arms in the period between 2007 and 2011 (accounting for 10 per cent of global imports), Pakistan was the third largest (with 5 per cent of global imports).[43] The only reason why China fell 'behind' from being the largest to the fourth largest importer is due to its dramatic increase in production back home, making it less dependent on imports.[44] These worrisome developments within the three nuclear-armed countries, coupled with their economic rise and environmental degradation, have accorded the region renewed international attention.

For the elite leaders of the two regional powerhouses, sustaining economic growth seems to take precedence over all other social and environmental challenges they face. Some scholars argue that setting the priority on the economy is the only way for the Chinese Communist Party to secure its legitimacy,[45] and that India's only chance to not let its regional position of power diminish is to not allow China to romp away in the race for economic growth. The demand for various natural resources (including water, minerals and fossil fuels) in the two economies is already outstripping domestic supplies.[46] China in particular has now changed its foreign policy in order to be able to quench its resource thirst. It is more and more willing to go abroad, forging relationships with countries in Africa, the Middle East and South America it would prefer not to (i.e., states which are considered unreliable, unsavoury, or ruled by dictatorships). While this is nothing new in the international arena – most Western nations have gone through this development – it shows that China, which has always been trying to portray itself as a developing country rather than an imperial power, is now also trapped in the 'reverse resource curse' of major importing countries.[47] This means that China is ensnared in inconvenient relationships in order to keep its economy growing and its own citizens tame.

42 P Kuhn for Deutsche Welle, 'Debate on China's Role Regarding the Euro Crisis Rages on' (5 April 2012) <http://www.dw.de/dw/article/0,,15861225,00.html>.

43 P Holtom and others, *Trends in International Arms Transfers, 2011* (Stockholm International Peace Research Institute 2012) at 6.

44 Ibid. at 5.

45 Listen to M Klare's interview with Le Monde Diplomatique on China's resource hunger at <http://mondediplo.com/2012/09/06podcast>.

46 UBS, The Rush for Resources Challenges Emerging Markets (UBS 2010) at 28.

47 M Klare for Le Monde Diplomatique, 'China's Imperial Predicament' (September 2012) <http://mondediplo.com/2012/09/06imperial>.

The ventures to secure precious resources far from home have even pushed China to engage in the already heated race over the natural wealth of the Arctic Sea by defining itself as a 'near-arctic state'.[48]

The rapid economic expansion of China and India also results in an increased use of water and hydropower. Both countries have plans to step up inter-basin water transfers and have accelerated their dam construction programmes, in order to meet their ever-growing freshwater demands.[49] In addition to this obvious link to their own transboundary freshwater management at home, both China and India are among the top 'land grabbers', engaged in foreign investment in farmland in order to feed their citizens at home. These large-scale leases or purchases of agricultural areas are not only likely to have a huge impact on the environment, but also on the livelihoods of communities in the target countries, as they often meddle with local water management.[50] Together with Brazil, China and India are involved with around 24 per cent of the total number of hectares leased or sold worldwide.[51] The World Bank released a report in 2010 which, while highlighting the undeniable need for more yield output in Africa, raises concerns about the potential these investments have in undermining land rights and marginalising small-scale producers in the host states.[52]

These developments show that the two powerhouses do not shy away from a more aggressive path of satisfying their resource needs – be it for minerals, food, or water. The undeniable fact that China and India overshadow their smaller downstream riparians, both economically and politically, poses some serious questions on how the future of transboundary freshwater cooperation in the region will look like. How do China and India perceive their emerging roles in a new world order? Does power really breed responsibility?[53] And more importantly for this study: how can international water law help prevent confrontations from escalating and instead foster international cooperation? Before analysing the legal framework for water security in the region, the following sections highlight the two (hydro)hegemons' water issues and demonstrate the current legal response based on applying the 4A methodology to the regimes governing the Indus and the Mekong.

48 L Jakobson, *China Prepares for an Ice-Free Arctic* (Stockholm International Peace Research Institute, 2010).

49 Siwakoti, Trans-Boundary River Basins in South Asia: Options for Conflict Resolution.

50 For a more detailed analysis see A Rice, 'Investing in Africa's Land: Crisis and Opportunity' in Worldwatch Institute (ed.), *State of the World 2011 : Innovations That Nourish the Planet* (W.W. Norton & Company 2011).

51 C Scherer for Worldwatch Institute, 'Foreign Investment in Agricultural Land Down from 2009 Peak' (21 June 2012) <http://vitalsigns.worldwatch.org/vs-trend/foreign-investment-agricultural-land-down-2009-peak>.

52 World Bank, Rising Global Interest in Farmland: Can It Yield Sustainable and Equitable Benefits? (World Bank 2010).

53 A Nollkaemper, 'Power and Responsibility' (2014) 42 SHARES Research Paper 1.

6.2.1 China

6.2.1.1 The water challenge

While some commentators are in animated discussions about whether China's power has already peaked,[54] the impact of its rapid rise already left a mark on its environment which will have a long-term impact for society – even if its economic growth will slow down in the future. Protecting its environment during times of rapid change has finally been identified as a serious dilemma by its officials. In 2011, Minister of the Environment, Zhou Shengxian, stated in an essay published in his ministry's official newspaper that 'In China's thousands of years of civilization, the conflict between humanity and nature has never been as serious as it is today.'[55] Water plays a key role in this struggle, as its diminishing supplies are putting an enormous amount of pressure on the Chinese people and on the country's ability to continue its global economic rise.[56] While some of the impacts are solely felt at the local level inside China, many of the countermeasures prove to have far-reaching spillover effects.

This conflict is most visible in the many mega-cities which mushroomed in recent decades. In the period 1990–2005, China's urban population more than doubled, from 254 million people to 572 million people.[57] By 2025, China's 15 largest cities could well have a combined population greater than the entire United States.[58] While rapid urbanisation will contribute to China's economic growth, it carries social and environmental challenges with it which urgently need to be addressed – water management in particular, as two-thirds of China's 660 largest cities are affected by water scarcity.[59] Despite this rapid urbanisation, more than 700 million people are still living in rural areas. The tension caused by the increasing wealth gap between urban regions and the countryside has, so far, caused the government to accelerate the urbanisation process even more, in order to create more jobs for the unemployed rural population.[60] At the national average, per capita natural freshwater resources amounted to 2,156 cubic metres in 2007, and are expected to decrease to 1,875 cubic metres when China's population is projected to peak around 2033.[61] In the north of

54 See P Minxin for The Diplomat, 'Superpower Denied? Why China's 'Rise' May Have Already Peaked' (9 August 2012) <http://thediplomat.com/2012/08/09/superpower-denied-why-chinas-rise-may-have-already-peaked/?all=true>.

55 Quoted in: C Buckley for Reuters, 'China Minister Warns Pollution, Waste Imperil Growth' (28 February 2011) <http://www.reuters.com/article/2011/02/28/us-china-environment-idUSTRE71R21020110228>.

56 E Economy for World Politics Review, 'China's Water Crisis' (9 August 2011) <http://www.worldpoliticsreview.com/articles/9684/chinas-growing-water-crisis>.

57 Dow Water & Process Solutions, *China's Thirst for Water* (Dow Water & Process Solutions 2011) at 1.

58 J Woetzel and others, *Preparing for China's Urban Billion* (McKinsey Global Institute 2009) at 112.

59 L Carmody, *Water in China: Issues for Responsible Investors* (Responsible Research 2010) at 11.

60 Asian Development Bank, Asian Development Outlook 2012: Confronting Rising Inequality in Asia at 84.

61 J Xie and others, Addressing China's Water Scarcity: Recommendations for Selected Water Resource Management Issues (World Bank 2009) at 1.

China, the situation is already a lot more serious. The Hai River basin, for example – with 120 million inhabitants, including the cities of Beijing and Tianjin – can only provide for around 300 cubic metres of freshwater per person.[62] Based on the standard definitions, North China is already a water-scarce region; while China as a whole will soon be a water-stressed country.[63] The challenge grows more complex when considering that many of the driest areas of the country are not only densely populated, but also industrial centres, such as the provinces of Hebei, Shandong and Shanxi.[64]

Already, the grave concerns about China's water supply have called into question the country's energy ambitions. By 2030, China plans to produce an additional 1.2 TWh (terawatt-hours) of power; which is almost six times the total installed capacity of India.[65] While this amount seems incredibly high, it will merely bring its installed per capita capacity in line with the current Group of 20 (G20) average.[66] According to its 12th Five-Year Plan (5YP) for 2011–15, China wants to achieve this goal mainly by building new thermal power plants fired by coal and nuclear, as well as by increasing its hydropower capacity.[67] All of these new sources need huge amounts of water – for driving the steam turbines and cooling purposes, as well as in the process of extracting the fossil fuels. Considering the available water resources, it also seems highly unlikely that China will achieve its goal to become a global player in the production of shale gas. While the development of this source seems to be an important part of China's strategy to quench its thirst for energy,[68] the unconventional process of drilling for shale gas faces its own challenges, as it uses large amounts of water

62 Ibid.

63 See ibid. at 11. A region faces absolute water scarcity if renewable water resources are below 500 cubic metres/person, chronic water shortage if renewable water resources are between 500 and 1,000 cubic metres/person, and regular water stress between 1,000 and 1,700 cubic metres/person; see FAO Land and Water Division, *Coping with Water Scarcity : An Action Framework for Agriculture and Food Security* (FAO 2012) at 7.

64 See J Yardley for the New York Times, 'Beneath Booming Cities, China's Future Is Drying Up' (28 September 2007) <http://www.nytimes.com/2007/09/28/world/asia/28water.html>.

65 W-S Chan, N Robins and Z Knight, No Water, No Power: Is There Enough Water to Fuel China's Power Expansion? (HSBC 2012) at 9.

66 D Tan for China Water Risk, 'China: No Water, No Power' (10 October 2012) <http://chinawater-risk.org/resources/analysis-reviews/china-no-water-no-power/>.

67 An English translation of China's 12th Five-Year Plan (2011-2015) by the Delegation of the European Union in China is available at <http://www.britishchamber.cn/sites/default/files/full-translation-5-yr-plan-2011-2015.doc>.

68 China's shale and other unconventional gas strategy 'establishes four ambitious milestones, including completion of a nationwide shale gas survey and appraisal; production output to reach 6.5 billion cubic metres by 2015, reaching an annual production of 60 billion to 100 billion cubic meters by the end of 2020; development of suitable methods, technologies and equipment for China's shale gas survey, appraisal, exploration and production; establishment of technical standards, rules and policies regulating China's shale gas development, including reserve survey, appraisal and certification, test and analysis, exploration and production, and environmental measurements.' L Genasci for China Water Risk, 'Is Fracking the Answer for Water Scarce China' (10 October 2012) <http://chinawaterrisk.org/resources/analysis-reviews/is-fracking-the-answer-for-water-scarce-china/>.

to extract natural gas (shale gas) from the ground – with a high potential for contamination of linked freshwater systems.[69] In addition, some of China's largest untapped deposits of shale gas are, as with coal, in parched regions of the country, setting the stage for conflict over use scenarios among different water users. Thus, hydraulic fracturing will certainly not be able to fill the gap in energy supply – even without considering its environmental drawbacks.[70] According to a recent study, 97 per cent of power generated in China is reliant on water.[71] Even with a change in fuel mix through China's big renewables drive, it will only manage to reduce this number to 87 per cent by 2030.[72] Hence, China's leadership is facing a difficult dilemma. With 45 per cent of its GDP being produced in water-scarce provinces which highly depend on electricity produced by coal (80 per cent), it ultimately has to decouple economic development from water consumption without leaving its path of economic growth.[73] Since it is running far behind in terms of water efficiency – requiring about four times the amount of water per USD of GDP created, when compared to the other members of the G20 – it is obvious that this challenge is of epic dimensions.[74] Conservative lower-bound figures estimate that China's water crisis is already costing the country 2.3 per cent of its GDP – 1.3 per cent can be attributed to water scarcity and 1.0 per cent to direct impacts of the widespread water pollution.[75] These numbers, however, do not include ecological impacts linked to eutrophication and the drying-up of wetlands, rivers and lakes; making the real cost of the crisis considerably higher.[76]

Over the last three years, the Chinese Ministry of Water Resources conducted the first National Water Census. The outcome was, even for Chinese standards, rather surprising, as the number of rivers with a catchment area larger than 100 km^2 has dropped by more than 50 per cent compared to the 1950s.[77] While officials blamed the 'disappearance' of around 28,000 rivers largely on inaccurate previous estimates and climate change, others fear that prioritising rapid economic development over the sustainable management of the environment is having even graver consequences on China's freshwater resources than initially imagined.[78] Not only does the nation face serious water scarcity issues, it is also

69 See, e.g., R Wood and others, Shale Gas: A Provisional Assessment of Climate Change and Environmental Impacts (Tyndall Centre 2011).

70 L Hook for the Financial Times, 'China: Running Short of Water' (19 September 2012) <http://blogs.ft.com/beyond-brics/2012/09/19/china-running-short-of-water/#ixzz291VDh29H>.

71 Chan, Robins and Knight, No Water, No Power: Is There Enough Water to Fuel China's Power Expansion? at 1.

72 Ibid.

73 Ibid. at 2.

74 Carmody, Water in China: Issues for Responsible Investors at 11.

75 World Bank, Cost of Pollution in China: Economic Estimates of Physical Damages (World Bank 2007) at xvi.

76 Xie and others, Addressing China's Water Scarcity: Recommendations for Selected Water Resource Management Issues at xxi.

77 Chinese Ministry of Water Resources, *Bulletin of First National Census for Water* (2013) available at <http://www.mwr.gov.cn/2013pcgb/merge1.pdf>.

78 A Hsu and W Miao for The Atlantic, '28,000 Rivers Disappeared in China: What Happened? ' (29 April 2013) <http://www.theatlantic.com/china/archive/2013/04/what-happened-to-chinas-rivers/275365/>.

exposed to a freshwater quality crisis of massive scale – which, of course, is being intensified by existing water shortages. It has been estimated that almost 90 per cent of Chinese cities suffers from water pollution and more than 500 million of the rural population do not have access to safe drinking water.[79] The onslaught of bad news reached a climax recently when 16,000 pig carcasses were found in tributaries of the Huangpu River which supplies the city of Shanghai's drinking water.[80] Issues of groundwater quality are being mainly ignored, as the dumping of untreated or only partially treated wastewater is a widespread practice.[81] Official figures show that more than half of the major watercourses and around one-third of China's groundwater resources are unfit for human consumption.[82] The widespread water pollution is affecting the health of 190 million people along all China's major rivers annually, with cases of diarrhoeal diseases and cancer increasing at a dramatic rate.[83]

China's water crisis, together with the decline of arable land (mainly due to pressures of population growth, urbanisation and rapid economic development),[84] is also heavily affecting the nation's food security. Groundwater levels in the North China Plains – one of the world's breadbaskets – have been declining dramatically recently.[85] While China experienced a grain deficit of 27 million tons in 2000, this gap could grow to 88 million tons in the year 2030 – under medium scenarios for population growth and irrigation area development.[86]

6.2.1.2 Domestic responses

China has long recognised its particular water management challenge. Since the crisis has worsened in recent decades – and is now threatening to slow down economic growth, weaken political stability and drive up costs of public health care – there is growing internal dissent over issues of water quality and its (re) allocation, adding pressure on both the central and regional governments to

79 RG Wirsing, 'Rivers in Contention: Is There a Water War in South Asia's Future?' (2008) *Heidelberg Papers in South Asian and Comparative Politics*, 41, at 17.

80 N Davison for The Guardian, 'Rivers of Blood: The Dead Pigs Rotting in China's Water Supply' (29 March 2013) <http://www.guardian.co.uk/world/2013/mar/29/dead-pigs-china-water-supply>.

81 PH Gleick, 'China and Water' in Gleick PH and others (eds), *The World's Water 2008-2009* (Island Press 2009) at 81.

82 J McBeath and J McBeath, 'Environmental Degradation and Food Security Policies in China' in Kassiola JJ and Guo S (eds), *China's Environmental Crisis : Domestic and Global Political Impacts and Responses* (Palgrave Macmillan 2010) at 100.

83 EC Economy, 'The Great Leap Backward? The Costs of China's Environmental Crisis' (2007) *Foreign Affairs*, 86, 38 at 47.

84 J McBeath and J McBeath, 'Environmental Stressors and Food Security in China' (2009) *Journal of Chinese Political Science*, 14, 49 at 74.

85 B Eline, C Thomas and K Elizabeth (eds), *An Ecosystem Services Approach to Water and Food Security* (United Nations Environment Programme 2011) at 11.

86 J Mu and S Khan, 'The Effect of Climate Change on the Water and Food Nexus in China' (2009) *Food Security*, 1, 413 at 413.

address China's water problems more effectively.[87] In his report to the National Congress of the Communist Party of China in 2007, former President Hu Jintao pushed for more 'scientific development' that should focus on major water issues including 'securing more clean drinking water, improving water conservation, water pollution prevention, restricting excessive water resources exploitation and cutting water waste'.[88] This is why, over the next ten years, the Central Committee of the Communist Party plans to invest 4 trillion Yuan (almost US$650 billion) in the water sector; half of which will be spent during the current Five-Year-Plan period.[89] Last year, China set performance targets for industry, irrigation and water quality, supported by measures which are supposed to promote 'water security' as a key feature for a sustainable economy.[90] Closely linked to water management issues are various other policy responses, like the restriction on arable land conversion and the program to convert marginal agricultural lands to forests and grasslands.[91] While many of these initiatives are laudable steps, their implementation leaves a lot to be desired, as they seem to have only little impact on China's food and water security.[92] One prime example here is the project to protect the Miyun reservoir and watershed, Beijing's most important source of freshwater.[93] The Chinese government introduced stricter rules on land and forest management (including a ban on logging) and, over decades, invested heavily in ambitious reforestation efforts.[94] However, much of this exercise was a waste of resources, since the newly planted young trees only have a minimal positive effect on soil and water quality, as they have not been managed appropriately.[95] The laudable first steps of reforestation could have had a much bigger impact on the capital's water quality, had they been supported by truly integrated management of the entire catchment area.[96]

Furthermore, China's water problems are hampered by the race for the rapid economic growth between the provinces and local governments – all trying to protect local industries and jobs – which is heavily affected by corruption and

87 Gleick, 'China and Water' at 79.

88 C Xie for China Daily, 'Warming Takes Toll on Water Resources' (5 November 2007) <http://www.chinadaily.com.cn/china/2007-11/05/content_6229698.htm>.

89 Y Jian for Shanghai Daily, 'China's River Pollution 'a Threat to People's Lives" (17 February 2012) <http://english.peopledaily.com.cn/90882/7732438.html>.

90 Asian Development Bank, *Asian Water Development Outlook 2013: Measuring Water Security in Asia and the Pacific* at 3.

91 McBeath and McBeath, 'Environmental Stressors and Food Security in China' at 49.

92 Ibid. at 69.

93 C Peisert and E Sternfeld, 'Quenching Beijing's Thirst: The Need for Integrated Management for the Endangered Miyun Reservoir' (2005) 7 China Environment Series 33 at 33.

94 IUCN, 'Restoring China's Water Supplies' (9 May 2011) <http://www.iucn.org/about/union/secretariat/offices/asia/asia_news/?7435/Restoring-Chinas-water-supplies>.

95 Ibid.

96 Peisert and Sternfeld, 'Quenching Beijing's Thirst: The Need for Integrated Management for the Endangered Miyun Reservoir' at 43.

the 'crippling weakness' of the State Environmental Protection Administration (SEPA).[97] At the same time, the challenges associated with the political system in China have boosted public concern and attempts to induce change. Grass-roots environmental initiatives have grown in China and become more and more successful at raising awareness and demanding action, although NGOs remain under strict surveillance by officials.[98] Adding to the challenges are water laws which are either outdated, weak, or both. Many of the rules addressing water quality were put in place several decades ago and lack necessary enforcement mechanisms, as minimal fines and 'vague civil liabilities' do not effectively change actors' behaviour.[99] Traditionally, the regulatory frameworks in China have also limited the power of national environmental agencies – e.g., SEPA – to the benefit of local control, leading to a whole range of differing standards for industries and various degrees of enforcement.[100] Interestingly, while China is often perceived to be dominated by a strong centralised single-party system, the country manages its water resources with a complex set of agencies at all levels of government, from national down to the local. Hence, competing and conflicting competences among a multitude of institutions are adding more pressure to the water woes.[101]

In order to overcome these governance-related struggles, China is investing heavily in large infrastructure projects in the form of dams, reservoirs and diversion schemes. The north-western province of Xinjiang alone is building 59 reservoirs to store the meltwater from the shrinking glaciers of the Himalayas.[102] Considering the costs for this project alone, in a rather poor part of China, of US$30 million per year over the next ten years, it becomes obvious that the economic implications of adapting to the future water challenges are immense.[103] By far the grandest scheme in recent history of freshwater management, first proposed by Mao Zedong in 1952, is the South-North Water Transfer Project (SNWTP) which is due to be completed in 2050 (see Figure 6.4).

Aimed at ensuring continuous economic growth in the dry north, around 45 billion cubic meters of freshwater will eventually be diverted annually from the south of the country, where it is available in relative abundance.[104]

97 See JL Turner, 'New Ripples and Responses to China's Water Woes' (2006) 6 China Brief.

98 See, e.g., BBC News, 'China Waste Water Pipeline Scrapped after Protest' (28 July 2012) <http://www.bbc.co.uk/news/world-asia-china-19026464>. For an in depth analysis on environmental NGOs in China, see J Schwartz, 'Environmental NGOs in China: Roles and Limits' (2004) *Pacific Affairs*, 77, 28.

99 China Daily, 'Action on Water Crisis' (6 July 2007) <http://www.chinadaily.com.cn/cndy/2007-07/06/content_911251.htm>.

100 Gleick, 'China and Water' at 88.

101 Ibid. at 89.

102 J Watts for the Guardian, 'China Plans 59 Reservoirs to Collect Meltwater from its Shrinking Glaciers' (2 March 2009) <http://www.guardian.co.uk/environment/2009/mar/02/china-glacier-reservoir-water>.

103 See S Moore, 'Climate Change, Water and China's National Interest' (2009) *China Security*, 5, 25 at 33.

104 World Bank, China Water Quality Management: Policy and Institutional Considerations (World Bank 2006) at 14.

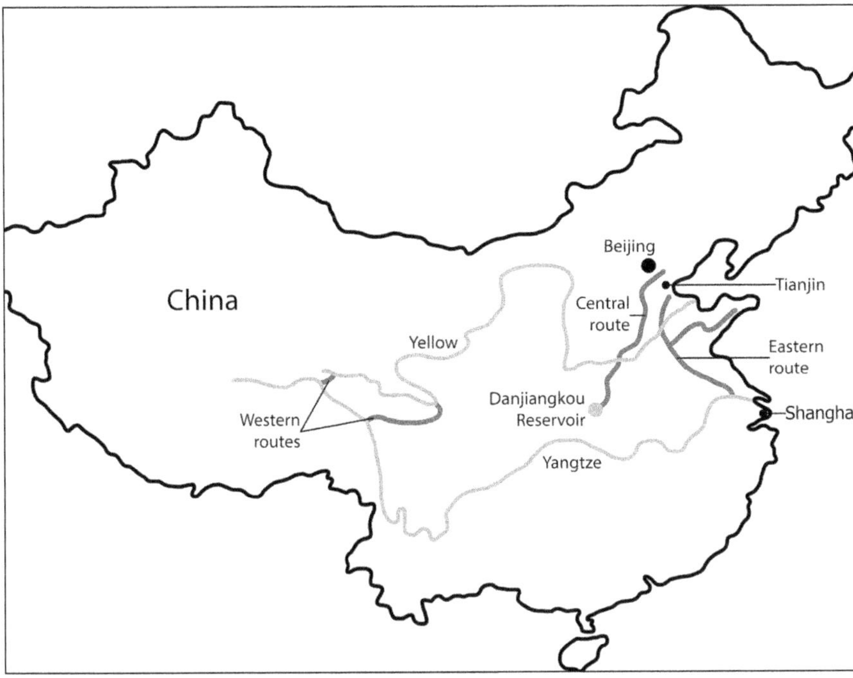

Figure 6.4 The South-North Water Transfer Project. Source: China Institute of Water Resources and Hydropower Research

This mammoth undertaking is separated into three segments.[105] (1) The Western Route diverts water from upper Yangtze tributaries in the Sichuan and Qinghai mountains by taking water from a reservoir on the Yalong River via a 170-km tunnel to the upper Yellow River. (2) The Central Route, which starts at the Danjiangkou reservoir on the Han River, a tributary of the Yangtze, will eventually – after 1,230 km – end in Beijing and include a 7.2-km tunnel underneath the Yellow River. (3) The Eastern Route, which, again, diverts water from the Yangtze includes an upgrade of the Grand Canal (originally built for navigational purposes) and supply reservoirs near the city of Tianjin.

China's bet on solving its water crises by 'replumbing' the country has been met with fierce criticism.[106] By building dams and canals which alter the

105 J Berkoff, 'China: The South-North Water Transfer Project : Is It Justified?' (2003) *Water Policy*, 5, 1 at 5.

106 S Wong for International Rivers, 'China Bets on Massive Water Transfers to Solve Crisis' (15 December 2007) <http://www.internationalrivers.org/resources/china-bets-on-massive-water-transfers-to-solve-crisis-1899>.

hydrology and natural landscape at an unprecedented scale, the water is said to bypass farmers and mainly benefit the industrial and urban centres in the north. As a result, the farmers, who are supposed to help achieve China's goal of food self-sufficiency, are forced to dig deeper and deeper groundwater wells to grow their wheat.[107] This again highlights the government's focus on economic growth – leaving little room for environmental or social concerns. It has been argued that water quality in the Yangtze is already at such a poor stage that the amount of treatment plants needed to clean the diverted water will add costs to the already expensive project, which could make it uneconomical.[108] During the National People's Congress in 2006, former Premier Wen Jiabao tried to reassure the public by stating that the government attaches great importance to 'the prevention and treatment of pollution at the sources and along the routes of the South-to-North Water Diversion Project'.[109] This promise, however, did little to silence the critics. The Central Route of the SNWTP alone will require the resettlement of more than 300,000 people, adding the risks of cultural and economic conflicts to the externalities of the project.[110]

Resettlement is also an important issue for the numerous other dam projects in China. The most prominent case might be the Three Gorges Dam, where not only around 2 million people had to leave their homes as more than a hundred towns submerged in the process of filling up the reservoir,[111] but also cultural heritage was lost.[112] The massive project, at a cost of US$41.3 billion, has been plagued by silting, pollution and ecological deterioration; even China's cabinet, the State Council, was forced to admit that the dam had 'urgent problems'.[113] However, the Three Gorges Dam is no isolated case when it comes to the disregard of social and environmental risks. It has been estimated that in all Chinese dam building projects combined, more than 23 million people have been resettled, often with long-term social impacts for these displaced communities.[114] Already the world's largest producer of hydropower, the Chinese government plans to triple its capacity by the year 2020.[115] One part of the

107 Ibid.

108 See B Crow for State of the Planet, 'China's South-North Water Transfer Project: A Means to a Political End' (3 March 2012) <http://blogs.ei.columbia.edu/2012/03/05/china%E2%80%99s-south-north-water-transfer-project-a-means-to-a-political-end/>.

109 Xinhuanet, 'Major Water Diversion Project Faces Pollution Threats' (9 March 2006) <http://news.xinhuanet.com/english/2006-03/09/content_4282100.htm>.

110 C Vörösmarty, C Lévêque and C Revenga, 'Fresh Water' in Hassan R, Scholes R and Ash N (eds), *Ecosystems and Human Well-Being: Current State and Trends* (Island Press 2005) at 185.

111 Gleick, 'Three Gorges Dam Project, Yangtze River, China' at 145.

112 World Commission on Dams, Dams and Development: A New Framework for Decision-Making (Earthscan 2000) at 118.

113 J Watts for the Guardian, 'China Warns of 'Urgent Problems' Facing Three Gorges Dam' (20 May 2011) <http://www.guardian.co.uk/world/2011/may/20/three-gorges-dam-china-warning>.

114 J Yardley for the New York Times, 'Chinese Dam Projects Criticized for Their Human Costs' (19 November 2007) <http://www.nytimes.com/2007/11/19/world/asia/19dam.html?pagewanted=all>.

115 L Zhi, Hydropower in Sichuan Province: Investigative Report (Transition Institute 2012) at 1.

reason for this ambitious goal is the announcement of the Chinese government at the climate summit in Copenhagen in 2009 to reduce its carbon emissions by at least 40 per cent by 2020.[116] Most of the increased production of hydropower will come from conventional large-scale dams at a rate which is equivalent to building one Three Gorges Dam each year for five years.[117] However, this dam-building spree not only carries socio-economic and environmental risks;[118] it may also be ill-suited for the actual aims of mitigating and adapting to climate change. First, traditional dam planning has been based on the assumption of constant stream-flow patterns in the future; which, due to climate change, is no longer valid. According to an official climate change assessment published in 2012, the concentration of rain during summer and autumn will increase, overwhelming rivers in the south, while long dry winters will increase and be especially crippling for those living in parched north-western provinces.[119] Second, the notion that hydropower dams are a source of clean (i.e., low-carbon) energy has come under scrutiny, since almost all resulting reservoirs emit one of the most potent greenhouse gases – methane.[120] Third, healthy and free-flowing river systems play an important role in trapping carbon, with scientists predicting that damming high-flow rivers in regions with warm ocean temperatures will reduce the ability to mitigate global climate change.[121] Furthermore, many of the proposed dams, canals and tunnels are located in areas of high natural seismicity, adding a whole new layer of security concerns.[122] Recent research even suggests that reservoirs are not only exposed to seismic activity, they can also trigger it – a phenomenon known as 'Reservoir-Induced Seismicity'.[123] For instance, the national tragedy of the 2008 earthquake in Sichuan, which killed an estimated 90,000 people, is said to have been at least hastened, if not caused, by the Zipingpu Dam.[124] Driven

116 J Watts for the Guardian, 'China Sets First Targets to Curb World's Largest Carbon Footprint' (26 November 2009) <http://www.guardian.co.uk/environment/2009/nov/26/china-targets-cut-carbon-footprint>.

117 K Yan for China Water Risk, 'Climate Change & Hydro: Mutually Damming' (10 October 2012) <http://chinawaterrisk.org/opinions/climate-change-and-hydro-mutually-damming/>.

118 Dams are adding to the already high risk of massive loss of China's freshwater biodiversity as the migration routes of aquatic species are being blocked and their ecosystems destroyed. See, e.g., L Zhi, M Totten and P Chou, 'Spurring Innovations for Clean Energy and Water Protection in China: An Opportunity to Advance Security and Harmonious Development' (2006) *China Environment Series*, 8, 61 at 73.

119 China Briefing, 'Climate Change Could Hamper China's Rise' (20 January 2012) <http://www.china-briefing.com/news/2012/01/20/report-climate-change-could-hamper-chinas-rise.html>.

120 J Qiu for Nature, 'Chinese Dam May be a Methane Menace' (29 September 2009) <http://www.nature.com/news/2009/090929/full/news.2009.962.html>.

121 See KB Showers, 'Congo River's Grand Inga Hydroelectricity Scheme: Linking Environmental History, Policy and Impact' (2009) *Water History*, 1, 31.

122 J Jackson, Earthquake Hazards and Large Dams in Western China (Probe International 2012) at 10.

123 Gleick, 'Three Gorges Dam Project, Yangtze River, China' at 144.

124 S LaFraniere for The New York Times, 'Possible Link Between Dam and China Quake' (5 February 2009) <http://www.nytimes.com/2009/02/06/world/asia/06quake.html>; S Ge and others, 'Did the Zipingpu Reservoir Trigger the 2008 Wenchuan Earthquake?' (2009) 36 Geophysical Research Letters 1.

by the pressure to reduce carbon emissions, China may therefore be expanding its hydropower capacity at the expense of large parts of its society and the environment. In order to reduce risks and increase its resilience, it has to better adapt its hydropower design to be able to deal with future climate variability and the impacts of dams on critical ecosystem services, while also adjusting hydropower tariffs to reflect the true social and environmental costs of dams.[125]

Given its focus on big infrastructure projects, it is evident that China is trying to build itself out of the water crisis. It is highly questionable that this will be a sustainable approach for a country which is already hit hard by other environmental pressures. While some Chinese researchers believe that the followed path is the only way out of a future restricted by climate change and population growth,[126] it has to be questioned whether it will be enough to effectively alleviate the water crisis in the long run. What use, other than short-term economic growth, is an initiative to build thousands of new wastewater treatment plants, when half of them are operating improperly or not at all?[127] The trends in surface water quality indicate a worsening in the main river systems in the north, while southern China is only experiencing slight improvements.[128] This is why more and more experts, even inside the country, are proposing alternatives to the large infrastructure solutions. In the face of these challenges, new ideas of improving the supply-and-demand side of water resource management are being developed, among them market-based tools of environmental policy under the umbrella of 'smart economics'.[129] One example here is the relatively new field of 'eco-compensation', which not only comprises payments for ecosystem services, but also includes fiscal transfer schemes between provincial governments in order to reallocate funding for environmental tasks and clarify responsibilities regarding the watershed services.[130] Another promising initiative is increasing the amount of rainwater being harvested in Beijing. Not only can urban rainwater utilisation save a huge amount of freshwater, it also minimises the risk of urban flooding, groundwater depletion and the pollution of stormwater runoff.[131] While these are important moves away from an approach solely reliant on large-scale infrastructure projects towards management practices focused on conservation and small-scale management of water resources,

125 K Yan for China Water Risk, 'Climate Change & Hydro: Mutually Damming' (10 October 2012) <http://chinawaterrisk.org/opinions/climate-change-and-hydro-mutually-damming/>.

126 S Li, 'China's Huge Investment on Water Facilities : An Effective Adaptation to Climate Change, Natural Disasters, and Food Security' (2012) *Natural Hazards*, 61, 1473.

127 CE Boyle, *Water-Borne Illness in China* (Woodrow Wilson Center 2007) at 2.

128 World Bank, Cost of Pollution in China : Economic Estimates of Physical Damages at xii.

129 Gleick, 'China and Water' at 95.

130 See Q Zhang and MT Bennett, Eco-Compensation for Watershed Services in the People's Republic of China (Asian Development Bank 2011) at viii.

131 Center for Policy and Human Development, *Afghanistan Human Development Report 2011. The Forgotten Front: Water Security and the Crisis in the Sanitation* (Center for Policy and Human Development, 2011) at 84; World Bank, Deep Wells and Prudence: Towards Pragmatic Action for Addressing Groundwater Overexploitation in India (World Bank 2010) at 24.

they are in their early stages and need to be supported by a greater effort of inter-agency collaboration and genuine participation and monitoring by civil society in order to provide long-term sustainable solutions.

Even though China has acknowledged its water crisis, its policy responses have so far fallen short, as they fail to bring about the radical changes needed. Furthermore, the lack of access to comprehensive data and information on water quality and quantity make it difficult to assess the effectiveness of the various initiatives. This situation will cause domestic pressures to increase even further; and concerns of its downstream neighbours to grow even more.

6.2.2 India

6.2.2.1 The water challenge

As in the case of China, the rapid economic development of India has heavily affected its environment and transformed its society. Freshwater management is one of the key tasks for the government if it wants to achieve a more sustainable path of development; however, this paramount challenge seems to be insurmountable, given the sheer size of the country and the diversity of natural resource-related issues surfacing. India is highly dependent on the monsoon system, with around 50 per cent of its yearly rainfall occurring in just half a month.[132] As the country's mostly rain-fed agriculture contributes to 15 per cent of India's GDP and hundreds of millions of Indians are highly dependent on it, the importance of the monsoon season becomes blatantly clear. Compared to the basins of the Colorado (US) and Murray-Darling (Australia) with about 900 days of storage capacity, India is lagging far behind with around 30 days of storage capacity in most of its basins.[133] While the average annual precipitation is about 1,200 mm, it varies widely across the country – from 150 mm in the desert of Rajasthan to more than 10 meters in the Khasi Hills.[134] This erratic distribution of rainfall often leads to floods and droughts in various areas. These hydrological circumstances do not make it easier to provide for an effective system of sanitation, which, with economic losses estimated at 6.4 per cent of India's GDP in 2006, is one of the biggest social challenges India faces.[135]

While water resources vary widely by region and season, per capita freshwater availability in India has fallen by almost 70 per cent since 1950 – now

132 J Briscoe and RPS Malik, *India's Water Economy: Bracing for a Turbulent Future* (Oxford University Press 2006) at 1.

133 IDSA Task Force, *Water Security for India: The External Dynamics* (Institute for Defence Studies and Analyses 2010) at 21.

134 Food and Agriculture Organization of the United Nations, *Review of World Water Resources by Country* (FAO 2003) at 63.

135 Water and Sanitation Program, *The Economic Impacts of Inadequate Sanitation in India* (World Bank 2010) at 1.

just slightly above the threshold of 1,700 cubic metres which indicates water stress and very likely to decline even further to around 1,100 cubic metres by 2050.[136] This is mainly due to increased demand driven by economic and population growth.[137] In addition to the inefficiency in water usage, the widespread water scarcity has triggered unregulated groundwater extraction in many regions of India. People are able to ignore the poorly operating public systems and become self-sufficient in terms of their water supplies.[138] Being the largest groundwater user in the world, India uses more than a quarter of the global total. With 65 per cent of irrigated agriculture and 85 per cent of drinking water supplies dependent on it, groundwater is a vital resource for rural areas in India.[139] By subsidising farmers' electricity costs of pumping, the government set a process in motion which is very difficult to change. The problem is that the perceived endless supply of groundwater is now approaching its limit as a large number of aquifers across the country have reached the status of peak water. If current practices continue, 60 per cent of groundwater sources in India will be in a critical state within the next twenty years.[140] Given the reliance on this source of freshwater for a huge part of society, the potential social and economic consequences are serious.

The generally poor water quality is another concern for India's water managers, as pollution has reached alarming levels and affects human, environmental and economic security. While agriculture still ranks the highest in terms of overall impact on water quality, 43 out of 88 industrial clusters in India are already 'critically polluted'.[141] The poor state of India's water quality is also putting enormous pressure on the health system, since water and sanitation-related diseases are responsible for 60 per cent of the environmental health burden.[142] Another serious issue for India is the loss of arable land and its ramifications on the country's food security, as it severely decreases agricultural productivity.[143] Large tracts of land along the Brahmaputra are prone to soil erosion, which is being aggravated by frequent floods.[144] This often has a direct socio-economic impact of national significance, as the important tea-growing areas in the Assam region are hit the hardest.

136 M Renner, Water and Energy Dynamics in the Greater Himalayan Region: Opportunities for Environmental Peacebuilding (Norwegian Peacebuilding Resource Centre 2011) at 3.

137 D Taenzler and others, *Water, Crisis and Climate Change in India: A Policy Brief* (adelphi 2011) at 10.

138 Briscoe and Malik, India's Water Economy: Bracing for a Turbulent Future at xvii.

139 P Wyrwoll, *India's Groundwater Crisis* (Global Water Forum 2012) at 2.

140 World Bank, Deep Wells and Prudence: Towards Pragmatic Action for Addressing Groundwater Overexploitation in India at 3.

141 UNICEF, FAO and SaciWATERs, *Water in India: Situation and Prospects* (UNICEF 2013) at 39.

142 Ibid.

143 KW Jaggard, A Qi and ES Ober, 'Possible Changes to Arable Crop Yields by 2050' (2010) *Philosophical Transactions of the Royal Society B: Biological Sciences*, 365, 2835 at 2846.

144 Strategic Foresight Group, The Himalayan Challenge: Water Security in Emerging Asia at 63.

All these challenges and struggles in the management of its water resources have led to an intensification of internal water disputes on various levels – i.e., between municipalities, between districts and between states. One example is the Mahbubnagar–Kurnool water conflict, which started as a disagreement between the two cities in Andhra Pradesh about utilisation of the Tungabhadra River and now involves the upstream state Karnataka, as politicians from Mahabubnagar claimed that Karnataka has to release more water in order to avoid a drinking-water crisis in the downstream state.[145] In another conflict between Karnataka and its downstream neighbour on the Cauvery River, in Tamil Nadu, protests turned violent after India's Supreme Court ruled in favour of the latter.[146] This quarrel over freshwater allocation from the Cauvery River smouldered for decades until it intensified last year during times of drought. Thousands of protesters, mainly farmers, tried to assume control over two dams and stop the demanded releases of freshwater downstream.[147] The ruling of the Supreme Court, that Karnataka would have to comply with water delivery obligations to its riparian despite the fact that Karnataka was struggling with one of the most severe droughts in decades, affirmed a previous decision on the matter by the Cauvery River Authority. Even though the Supreme Court hereby strengthened the position of the basin organisation, its decision infuriated many farmers, as they perceived it to be unfair. This example shows that despite having a democratic system in place which, in principle, guarantees the implementation of the rule of law, issues of adaptability driven by changing demands and climatic changes aggravate the sustainable and peaceful management of freshwater in India.

6.2.2.2 Domestic responses

Surprisingly, in spite of the high socio-economic costs of droughts and floods, India has (so far) failed to adequately react with improvements of its water infrastructure, in order to ensure reliable and climate-proof water supplies.[148] In order to address this challenge, large-scale dams have been built for the production of hydropower and for irrigation, and yet water storage infrastructure in India remains extremely low.[149] The Narmada Dam Project, one of the world's largest water infrastructure projects, consists of 165 medium to large-size dams

145 BV Shiv Shankar for The Times of India, 'Mahbubnagar-Kurnool Water War Hots Up' (5 April 2012) <http://timesofindia.indiatimes.com/city/hyderabad/Mahbubnagar-Kurnool-water-war-hots-up/articleshow/12538356.cms>.

146 B Walton for Circle of Blue, 'Protests Break Out After India's Supreme Court Rules in Favor of Downstream State in Cauvery River Dispute' (3 October 2012) <http://www.circleofblue.org/waternews/2012/world/protests-break-out-after-indias-supreme-court-rules-in-favor-of-downstream-state-in-cauvery-river-dispute/>.

147 The Hindu, 'Cauvery Stir Intensifies in Mandya' (3 October 2012) <http://www.thehindu.com/news/national/cauvery-stir-intensifies-in-karnataka/article3961704.ece>.

148 Leadership Group on Water Security in Asia, 'Asia's Next Challenge: Securing the Region's Water Future' at 21.

149 Ibid.

and 3,000 minor ones on the Narmada River and its tributaries. Given the fact that an estimated 1 million people had to be relocated, it – like most large-scale infrastructure projects – faced strong opposition and protests from local communities.[150] However, it is not only the government which is the target of criticism. The involvement of the World Bank in this and various other water projects in India has also caused grievances, as it supposedly failed to alleviate poverty and step up environmental protection in the process.[151]

By far the most ambitious plan of the Indian government is to add more freshwater storage capacity and convey water across the vast country through the gigantic River Linking Project (see Figure 6.5).

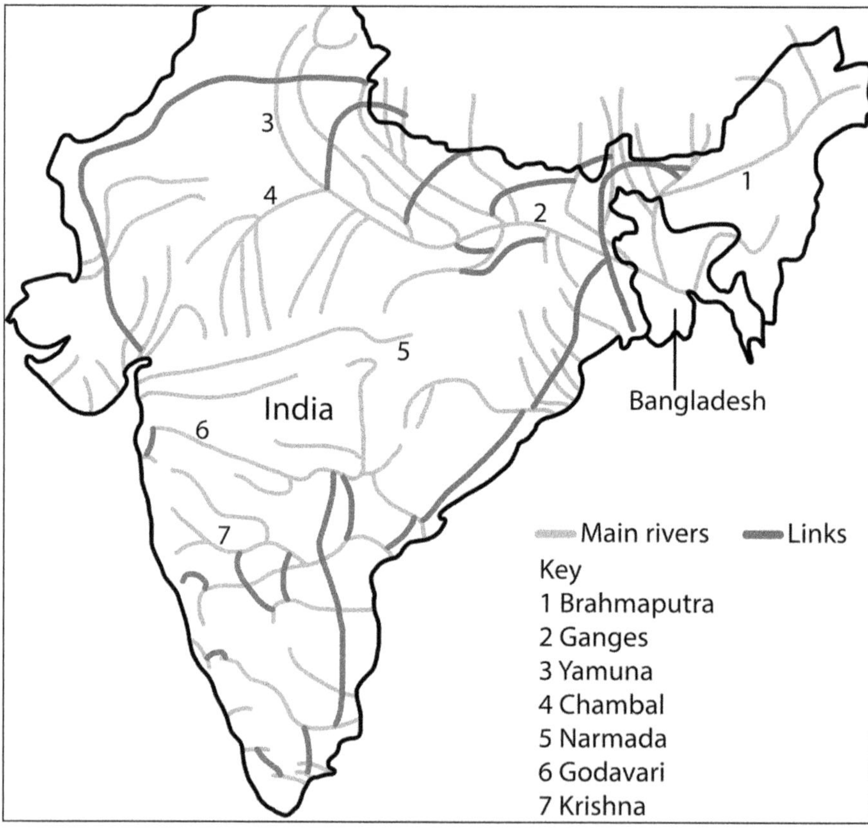

Figure 6.5 India's River Linking Project. Sources: *The Guardian*; International Water Management Institute (IWMI)

150 V Shiva, 'Water Wars in India' in Brauch HG and others (eds), *Facing Global Environmental Change: Environmental, Human, Energy, Food, Health and Water Security Concepts* (Springer 2009) at 590.

151 S Mori, 'Institutionalization of NGO Involvement in Policy Functions for Global Environmental Governance' in Kanie N and Haas PM (eds), *Emerging Forces in Environmental Governance* (United Nations University Press 2004) at 169; K O'Neill, *The Environment and International Relations* (Cambridge University Press 2009) at 56.

This gigantic US$200 billion scheme, again partly supported by the World Bank, will eventually interlink 37 major rivers in order to divert their flow to rather dry south and south-west India, and is thus seen as key to India's future path of development.[152] The sheer size of the projects becomes apparent when realising that even the lowest estimated cost equals around one-quarter of India's annual GDP and US$12 billion more than its total outstanding external debt.[153]

While the project was announced by former Prime Minister Vajpayee in 2002, it was not implemented until India's Supreme Court ordered the government to finally do so, since the delay was causing costs to increase steadily.[154] Recently, the National Water Development Agency has started its surveying work for a section of the scheme – the diversion of water from the Brahmaputra through a 457-km long canal to the Ganges.[155] The problem with large water infrastructure in India is fourfold: (1) little energy is being invested in the assessment of whether existing storage capacity can be used more effectively in order to provide the services desired; (2) only limited effort is being made to stop the deterioration of existing storage capacity – mainly caused by siltation; (3) there is minimal interstate coordination and cooperation regarding interstate river basins, which is vital should the storage facilities produce the maximum benefits, and (4) in cases where additional storage capacity is none the less needed, options of providing decentralised surface and underground capacities or increasing the soil's capacity to better hold moisture are rarely explored.[156]

This is why, in addition to the large-scale infrastructure projects, India is also constantly working to improve its water policies and regulations. In 1987, the government formulated a comprehensive National Water Policy (NWP), which was revised in 2002.[157] The legal framework for managing freshwater in India is considered as complex, overlapping and often contradictory. It includes the Constitution, federal and state laws, common law, human rights principles which have been recognised by courts and various unwritten local customary rules.[158] While the federal government controls the development and

152 ARM Khalid, 'The Interlinking of Rivers Project in India and International Water Law: An Overview' (2004) *Chinese Journal of International Law*, 3, 553 at 553.

153 Shiva, 'Water Wars in India' at 591.

154 B Walton for Circle of Blue, 'India Supreme Court Again Pushes National River Linking Project to Proceed' (1 March 2012) <http://www.circleofblue.org/waternews/2012/world/india-supreme-court-again-pushes-national-river-linking-project-to-proceed/>.

155 Times of India, 'Brahmaputra Diversion Survey Work Begins' (21 March 2012) <http://timesofindia.indiatimes.com/city/guwahati/Brahmaputra-diversion-survey-work-begins/articleshow/12350954.cms>.

156 H Thakkar, *Water Sector Options for India in a Changing Climate* (South Asia Network on Dams, Rivers & People 2012) at 44.

157 Indian Ministry of Water Resources, *National Water Policy* (2002) available at <http://wrmin.nic.in/writereaddata/linkimages/nwp20025617515534.pdf>.

158 Taenzler and others, *Water, Crisis and Climate Change in India: A Policy Brief* at 10.

regulation of interstate rivers, state governments control all remaining water sources and infrastructure – including irrigation and drainage systems, canals, freshwater storage and hydropower.[159] In 2012, a new NWP was drafted and put forward for discussion, which aims to change the overall direction of the policy towards decreasing the involvement of the government while giving the market more space to operate.[160] This draft was heavily criticised due to the absence of a commitment towards the right to water, even though India voted in favour of the 2010 UN General Assemby resolution on the human right to water and sanitation,[161] and for failing to recognise that the growing inequity in access to water is the main driving force behind the current water crisis, rather than absolute water scarcity. Thus, in order to better tackle India's water crisis, the government needs to address these issue of fragmentation, which seems to make things worse, as the rights to make use of water resources are unclear and vary in each state. Additionally, the agreement must tackle the fundamental challenge of breaking with the existing practice of determining access to water based on gender or belonging to a certain class or caste.[162]

6.2.3 Will transboundary impacts turn water into Asia's new 'battleground'?

Regardless of whether China's and India's emphasis on technological solutions is the most sensible option for their own socio-economic and environmental future, it already has a huge impact on states downstream within their shared river basins. The governments' ambitious plans to step up hydropower capacity and realise inter-basin water transfers will certainly increase the geopolitical risks of international freshwater cooperation in Himalayan Asia, since the actions of the two hegemons either directly or indirectly affect the whole region.

China has made its stance on exploiting the Brahmaputra (Yarlung Tsangpo in China) clear by saying it will definitely utilise its water resources. China's plans to build three hydropower plants on the middle reaches of the river in order to fulfil its 12th 5YP caused concern in both downstream countries, India and Bangladesh. China's foreign ministry spokesman, Hong Lei, was quoted saying that 'the Chinese side always takes a responsible attitude towards the exploitation of cross-border rivers and every new project will be planned and reasoned in a scientific way before being started'.[163] Given the

159 For an in depth discussion about water law in India, see P Cullet, 'Water Law in India: Overview of Existing Framework and Proposed Reforms' (2007) IELRC Working Paper 1.

160 Indian Ministry of Water Resources, *Draft National Water Policy* (2012) available at <http://mowr.gov.in/writereaddata/linkimages/DraftNWP2012_English9353289094.pdf>.

161 UN General Assembly Resolution A/RES/64/292, 'The Human Right to Water and Sanitation' (28 July 2010) available at <http://www.un.org/ga/search/view_doc.asp?symbol=A/RES/64/292>.

162 UNICEF, FAO and SaciWATERs, *Water in India: Situation and Prospects* at 49.

163 China Daily, 'China justifies YarlungZangbo River exploitation' (30 January 2013) <http://www.chinadaily.com.cn/china/2013-01/30/content_16188877.htm>.

lack of information on the planned projects, this lip service did little to calm fears downstream. This, however, makes the recent developments regarding the hydro-diplomacy on the Brahmaputra even more interesting. In 2010, Bangladesh and China signed a Memorandum of Understanding (MoU) on the management of freshwater resources of the river.[164] The MoU stated that both parties would cooperate with each other on three topics: (1) to carry out sustainable cooperation on hydrological data sharing and flood control of the Brahmaputra river in view of its necessity to the disaster reduction in Bangladesh; (2) to strengthen cooperation on water resources management, hydrological data sharing, disaster reduction, based on the exchange of letters between the two ministries of water resources of the two countries in 2005, and (3) to provide assistance for dredging of riverbeds and capacity building through training personnel. While the Chinese adhered to their obligation by providing hydrological data, which is supposed to help in flood and drought forecasting, Bangladesh has, so far, not taken any steps regarding the implementation of the MoU. The main reason why Bangladesh might forfeit the chance for closer cooperation with China is actually the second hegemon in the region – India. The current Bangladeshi government fears that working more closely with China on transboundary water issues could be interpreted negatively by India, which, being midstream on the Brahmaputra, also has a strong interest in the water resources of the river.[165]

The Teesta, a tributary of the Brahmaputra, also caused diplomatic tensions between Bangladesh and India recently, when Bangladeshi Prime Minister Sheikh Hasina urged the Indian government to accelerate the process of reaching a deal on water sharing. In 2011, Indian Prime Minister Manmohan Singh surprised many by backing out of signing the treaty at the last minute during his visit to Dhaka.[166] This delay has caused several politicians in Bangladesh to call for halting all trade negotiations with India and denying India transit permission through Bangladesh if the Indian government does not agree to allow Bangladesh its fair share of Teesta's water resources.[167] While India and Bangladesh share 54 transboundary rivers, the two states have only entered into one agreement for the Ganges.[168]

India's River Linking Project will certainly affect its neighbours' water security.[169] The recent beginning of actual work to implement the grand scheme has raised serious concerns downstream in Bangladesh, which is heavily dependent

164 The News Today, 'Dhaka-Beijing MoU on Brahmaputra on Hold' (4 April 2012) <http://www.newstoday.com.bd/index.php?option=details&news_id=57888&date=2012-04-04>.

165 Ibid.

166 OOSKAnews, 'Bangladesh Presses India to Resolve Teesta Treaty Issue' (28 March 2012) <http://www.ooskanews.com/international-water-weekly/bangladesh-presses-india-resolve-teesta-treaty-issue_21826>.

167 Ibid.

168 JC Keetelaar, 'Transboundary Water Issues in South Asia' Erasmus University Rotterdam, 2007) at 23.

169 NS Khadka for BBC News, 'Concerns over India Rivers Order' (30 March 2012) <http://www.bbc.co.uk/news/science-environment-17555918>.

on the Brahmaputra, arguing that 'India seems to be quite indifferent to the havoc the project will wreak on agriculture, environment, and ecology of the neighbouring countries, especially Bangladesh.'[170] There is a high probability that the negative transboundary social and environmental impacts the scheme carries will trigger intra- and interstate unrest, as the resulting movements of internally displaced persons (IDPs) in Bangladesh may eventually spill over into India.[171] This is why the management of the Ganges-Brahmaputra simply must be considered of common concern to both nations.[172]

Another large-scale project which causes serious objections is the US$3.6 billion Myitsone Dam on the Irrawaddy River in Burma, which is being planned and financed by the China Power Investment Corporation. The area in which the dam is supposed to be built is home to a strong separatist movement, and thus experiences frequent armed clashes between Burmese military and the Kachin Independence Army.[173] Myitsone is religiously highly significant for the Kachin, who worship the area as the birthplace of their culture. This is why, in the case that the dam will actually be built, it will be perceived as a symbol of 'China's lack of cultural sensibilities and disregard for local minority groups'.[174] The fact that the environmental issues surrounding the Myitsone Dam are not at all straightforward and that water security issues are closely linked to energy security becomes evident when realising that after the government officially ordered that work should be halted on the hydropower project, owing to environmental concerns, investment immediately picked up on various other hydropower and coal-powered plants, as well as on oil and gas exploration in the country.[175] Furthermore, recently leaked documents show that the controversial dam was never in fact halted, as background preparations were ongoing and Chinese Power Investment is 'planning to restart' the project shortly.[176] Furthermore, the future of the Mekong River will also clearly depend upon the actions of China, since its dam projects on the river could

170 Times of India, 'Brahmaputra Diversion Survey Work Begins' (21 March 2012) <http://www.readability.com/articles/accvz7hv>.

171 ANM Muniruzzaman, 'Bangladesh (Part I)' in Ziemke-Dickens C and Droogan J (eds), *Asian Transnational Security Challenges: Emerging Trends, Regional Visions* (The Council for Asian Transnational Threat Research (CATR) 2010) at 61.

172 HS Sen, 'The Drying up of River Ganga: An Issue of Common Concern to Both India and Bangladesh' (2010) *Current Science*, 99, 725.

173 J Motlagh for Pulitzer Center, 'Myanmar's Minorities: Caught in the Middle' (12 July 2012) <http://pulitzercenter.org/reporting/myanmar-burma-kachin-myitsone-independence-army-china-conflict>; Kachin News, '2 Burma Army Soldiers Dead after Myitsone Dam Clash' (14 May 2012) <http://www.kachinnews.com/news/war/2295-2-burma-army-soldiers-dead-after-myitsone-dam-clash.html>.

174 S Johnson-Reiser, 'China's Hydropower Miscalculation' (2012) *China Brief*, 12, 8 at 11.

175 Asian Development Bank, 'Asian Development Outlook 2012: Confronting Rising Inequality in Asia' at 207.

176 Kachin News, 'Leaked Document Says CPI 'Planning to Restart' Myitsone Dam Project' (4 April 2012) <http://www.kachinnews.com/news/2267-leaked-document-says-cpi-planning-to-restart-myitsone-dam-project.html>.

substantially affect Cambodia, Laos, Thailand and Vietnam – while the most prominent water dispute in the region is between India and Pakistan over the Indus. Those two basins, however, will be discussed in more depth later.

This selection of projects affecting transboundary watercourses in Himalayan Asia has shown that water is already a matter high on the agenda of international relations in the region. The unilateral development of these contested projects without involving the respective riparian countries in some form will most certainly impair the already tense relations over water sharing.[177] Given the sheer size of the modifications of rivers in China and India, it is apparent that they will have impacts on neighbouring countries – which are also experiencing difficult water management challenges.[178] The distinction between national and transboundary waters becomes more and more obsolete when realising that bad national water management often has a direct impact on international (water) relations. It has become obvious that transboundary freshwater management in Himalayan Asia will face testing times in the near future. While it is expected that by 2025 around 50 per cent of the world's population will live in water-scarce countries, the majority of them will be in China and India.[179] It is also becoming more and more clear that other cross-cutting national issues – such as the race for energy security in the examples of China and India – often have a transboundary or even regional impact within and beyond the water box. The recent assessment conducted by US intelligence agencies claims (with high confidence) that in Asia, 'water in shared basins will increasingly be used as [political] leverage; the use of water as a weapon or to further terrorist objectives also will become more likely' in the near future.[180] As water scarcity and quality issues intensify, the peaceful management of the river basins in Himalayan Asia is becoming increasingly critical, with ramifications affecting the natural environment, social stability and economic development of the whole region. More tragically, nationalism and narrow-minded technical approaches to these complex management challenges aggravate the situation.[181] In terms of impact on international relations, the Asian water crisis can be compared with the melting of the Arctic – which is set to redraw the global geopolitical map[182] – but the former poses a much more imminent threat to people's livelihoods and various other national and international securities. The bleak prospects for peaceful and sustainable

177 Brennan, 'The China-India-Pakistan Water Crisis: Prospects for Interstate Conflict' at 31.

178 Leadership Group on Water Security in Asia, 'Asia's Next Challenge: Securing the Region's Water Future' at 15.

179 WJ Cosgrove and FR Rijsberman, *World Water Vision : Making Water Everybody's Business* (Earthscan 2000) at xxi.

180 National Intelligence Council, *Global Water Security : Intelligence Community Assessment* (Office of the Director of National Intelligence 2012) at 3.

181 N Langton and S Prasai, 'Will Conflicts over Water Scarcity Shape South Asia's Future' (2012) 2 CSIS Issue Perspective 1.

182 P Apps for Reuters, 'Melting Arctic May Redraw Global Geopolitical Map' (3 April 2012) <http://www.reuters.com/article/2012/04/03/us-arctic-resources-idUSBRE8320DR20120403>.

transboundary freshwater interaction caused by the multifarious issues directly or indirectly linked to water resources management seems to play into the hands of security hawks and the media, who increasingly talk about 'water wars' in Asia.[183]

Indeed, there seems to be much reason for despair, given the division between the two states determining regional politics – China and India. The intensity of the constant struggle for economic and political supremacy in Himalayan Asia is evident in several recent developments. The frictions surrounding China's refusal to approve an Asian Development Bank's loan of US$2.9 billion for India is a rather mild example.[184] Far more worrying was the recent stand-off between military patrols in the disputed border areas between China and India – an issue over which the two states fought a war in 1962.[185] While it is true that the region is a highly critical one regarding global politics, the two hegemons, China and India, have more in common than what divides them. One could witness the ability of both countries to join forces and present a coordinated position between the two during recent climate change negotiations, when both were persistent in refusing legal obligations to curb their emissions of GHGs.[186] It is not in the least suggested that China's and India's common position in the global climate change negotiations is positive for global cooperative efforts to tackle climate change. However, it shows that both regional powers share a great deal of interests. While this circumstance has already been exploited to their (apparent) advantages in some areas of international relations, it has yet to be utilised in their regional water interactions.

The problem here is that neither country seems to realise that the time for a joint approach to freshwater management in Himalayan Asia is ripe. While it is highly unlikely that war will be fought over water, the short-term benefits of unilateral development of watercourses is being weighted higher than the long-term benefits of a regional approach. The management of freshwater resources in Himalayan Asia will certainly be one of the decisive factors in foreign policy and shape the region's international relations and security in the future. The question is whether China and India want to continue on the path of short-sighted and self-centred water development, or whether they are finally willing to accept that water security is of common concern in Himalayan Asia. This is why even small steps towards more meaningful cooperation over the Brahmaputra have to be appreciated. The recent signing of a MoU between the two countries is

183 See, e.g., Chellaney, *Water: Asia's New Battleground*.

184 R Minder, J Anderlini and J Lamont for the Financial Times, 'China Withholds Approval for ADB's India Loan' (11 April 2009) <http://www.ft.com/cms/s/0/aec31a92-2630-11de-be57-00144feabdc0.html>.

185 G Harris and E Wong for The New York Times, 'Where China Meets India in a High-Altitude Desert, Push Comes to Shove' (2 May 2013) <http://www.nytimes.com/2013/05/03/world/asia/where-china-meets-india-push-comes-to-shove.html?_r=0>.

186 J Lamont, J Chaffin and F Harvey for the Financial Times 'India Widens Climate Rift with West' (24 July 2009) <http://www.ft.com/cms/s/0/c2896b88-77bd-11de-9713-00144feabdc0.html>.

definitely a positive sign for the future outlook of the basin – even though it merely focuses on the exchange of hydrological data.[187] Due to the complexity of transboundary water interaction in the region, a peaceful management of the resource can only be guaranteed if the frameworks governing water resources fully support the contemporary notion of common water security.

6.3 International water law and Himalayan water security

Interesting conclusions on how countries in Himalayan Asia perceive international water law can be drawn by looking at the negotiation and ratification process of the UN Watercourses Convention. One of this region's countries – China – voted against the adoption of the Convention; five of them – Afghanistan, Bhutan, Burma, India and Pakistan – abstained or were absent, and six of them – Bangladesh, Cambodia, Laos, Nepal, Thailand and Vietnam – voted in favour. However, only one of the latter states – Vietnam – has so far ratified the Convention. Of particular interest here is China's statement on the Convention:

> The Chinese Government appreciates the efforts made by the International Law Commission over the years to draft the articles on the non-navigational uses of international watercourses, and it believes that the draft articles have laid a fairly good foundation for the formulation of an international convention. However, there are obvious drawbacks to some major clauses of the draft Convention, which was hastily adopted by the Working Group of the Whole in April 1997. First, the draft Convention fails to represent or reflect general agreement by all countries. Quite a number of countries have reservations on its major clauses . . . Secondly, territorial sovereignty is a basic principle of international law. A watercourse State enjoys indisputable territorial sovereignty over those parts of international watercourses that flow through its territory. It is incomprehensible and regrettable that the draft Convention does not affirm this principle . . . Fourthly, Article 33 of the United Nations Charter lays down that States may seek a peaceful solution to a dispute by means of their own choice. The compulsory fact-finding dictated by the draft Convention goes against the provisions of the Charter. The Chinese Government favours the settlement of all disputes by peaceful means, through consultations . . . On the basis of those considerations, the Chinese delegation will be obliged to vote against the draft resolution . . . The Chinese Government reserves the right to address the question of the non-navigational uses of international watercourses with its neighbours in a fair and reasonable manner and in accordance with relevant international practice and with bilateral watercourse agreements.[188]

187 W Hussain for Eurasia Review, 'India, China and the MoU on Brahmaputra – Analysis' (5 July 2014) <http://www.eurasiareview.com/05072014-india-china-mou-brahmaputra-analysis/>.

188 United Nations General Assembly, Fifty-first Session, 99th Plenary Meeting (21 May 1997) UN Doc A/51/PV.99; available at <http://www.un.org/ga/search/view_doc.asp?symbol=A/51/PV.99>.

Reading these statements, one wonders how the legal regimes in the region address water security, when we recall the definition of water security proposed in this book, that

> [a] community is water secure when it has sustainable access to freshwater of sufficient quantity and quality, or to the benefits derived therefrom; and the ability to minimise water-related risk and its various repercussions to an acceptable level – without compromising the supporting ecosystems.[189]

The following section investigates whether international water law in Himalayan Asia is reflecting, at least to some extent, this contemporary understanding of water security which is based on the concept of regional common concern (see Chapter 5). While certainly all river systems originating in the Himalayas have their particular challenges, it is beyond the scope of this book to consider them all. Thus, the following analysis of whether the legal frameworks in Himalayan Asia are catering for a contemporary understanding of common water security will focus on two of the major rivers – the Mekong and the Indus– which both provide for the required institutional and legal frameworks in order to be able to utilise the 4A water security methodology for analysis and study the regional water security from an international law perspective.

6.3.1 The Mekong River

The Mekong River basin is the largest in Himalayan Asia and is shared by six countries – Burma, Cambodia, China, Laos, Thailand and Vietnam (see Figure 6.6). Growing demand for its water has led to more intense use of freshwater resources, leading to political stress among the riparians. The resulting regional security implications of dam construction – mainly for the production of hydropower – have been considered to be a point of contestation between all six basin states.[190] One of the major security threats of the river is flooding, affecting up to 8 million people and causing damages of US$100–400 million every year.[191] Interestingly, in addition to providing socio-economic benefits, infrastructure for flood mitigation and hydropower production also has a strong political impact, as it helps authorities to gain or maintain their political legitimacy.[192] Of particular importance in the basin, for social-economic development and the environment, is the Tonle Sap Great

189 See Chapter 2.

190 Barnett, 'Environmental Security in the Asia-Pacific Region: Contrasting Problems, Places, and Prospects' at 945.

191 B Affeltranger, 'Sustainability of Environmental Regimes: The Mekong River Commission' in Brauch HG and others (eds), *Facing Global Environmental Change: Environmental, Human, Energy, Food, Health and Water Security Concepts* (Springer 2009) at 594.

192 Ibid.

Figure 6.6 The Mekong River basin. Source: OSU Transboundary Freshwater Dispute Database.

Lake system in Cambodia. Here, the annual floods cause the Tonle Sap River to reverse the direction of its flow and fill the Great Lake – which swells from 1.5 billion cubic metres to 70 billion cubic metres during the wet season.[193] This yearly occurrence underpins one of the world's most productive aquatic ecosystems.

The Mekong River Commission (MRC) is the pre-eminent organisation entrusted with transboundary management of water in the basin. Its creation

193 H Brühl and M Waters, 'Transboundary Cooperation in Action for Integrated Water Resources Management and Development in the Lower Mekong Basin' in Lenton R and Muller M (eds), *Integrated Water Resources Management in Practice: Better Water Management for Development* (Earthscan 2009) at 192.

can be seen as the pinnacle of the continuous attempt to manage the basin's water resources more cooperatively – a process which already started in 1957 when the UN founded the Mekong Committee.[194] The MRC finds its legal basis in the 1995 Mekong Agreement, which, in the Preamble, sets the goal to

> cooperate and promote in a constructive and mutually beneficial manner in the sustainable development, utilisation, conservation and management of the Mekong River Basin water and related resources for navigational and non-navigational purposes, for social and economic development and the well-being of all riparian States.[195]

However, its membership does not include China, which controls the upper reaches of the catchments, or Burma, which only contributes 2 per cent to the annual flow of the river.[196]

The question now is whether the legal framework can successfully defuse the increasingly tense relationship between the Mekong basin states? The Mekong is increasingly coming under pressure, since the combination of multiple dams in the upper basin and several dam proposals in the lower Mekong basin will most likely bring about dramatic change to the ecosystems and human livelihoods.[197] The new momentum for this development is being enabled by the major drivers (demographics, economic development and climate change) and new dam financiers (which involves a move away from the World Bank towards China).

6.3.1.1 Availability

The Mekong Agreement contains several provisions which deal with issues of freshwater quantity and quality – its availability. The maintenance of flows on the mainstream, for example, is addressed in Article 6, which states that the parties agree to 'cooperate in the maintenance of the flows on the mainstream from diversions, storage releases, or other actions of a permanent nature; except in the cases of historically severe droughts and/or floods'.[198] Furthermore, situations in the event of substantial damage to one or more riparians caused by

194 G Browder, 'An Analysis of the Negotiations for the 1995 Mekong Agreement' (2000) *International Negotiation*, 5, 237 at 237.

195 Preamble of the Agreement on the Cooperation for the Sustainable Development of the Mekong River Basin (5 April 1995) reprinted in 34 ILM 864 (1995) [hereinafter Mekong Agreement]; available at <http://www.mrcmekong.org/assets/Publications/agreements/agreement-Apr95.pdf>.

196 MS Babel and SM Wahid, *Freshwater under Threat: South East Asia : Vulnerability Assessment of Freshwater Resources to Environmental Change: Mekong River Basin* (United Nations Environment Programme 2009) at 11.

197 RE Grumbine, J Dore and J Xu, 'Mekong Hydropower: Drivers of Change and Governance Challenges' (2012) *Frontiers in Ecology and the Environment*, 10, 91 at 91.

198 Art 6 of the Mekong Agreement.

harmful effects from the use of and/or discharge to waters of the Mekong River by any riparian State,[199] or in the event of emergency that requires an immediate response,[200] are also being addressed. Interestingly, the obligation

> [t]o make every effort to avoid, minimize and mitigate harmful effects that might occur to the environment, especially the water quantity and quality, the aquatic (eco-system) conditions, and ecological balance of the river system from the development and use of the Mekong River Basin water resources or discharge of wastes and return flows[201]

does not explicitly mention that the resulting harmful effects have to be transboundary.[202] Rather, the general obligation to protect the environment is supported by Article 3 of the Mekong Agreement, which stipulates that the parties agree to 'protect the environment, natural resources, aquatic life and conditions, and ecological balance of the Mekong River Basin from pollution or other harmful effects resulting from any development plans and uses of water and related resources in the Basin'.[203] This points towards comprehensive regulations for the protection of the environment; and thus water quality and quantity. However, environmental impact assessments, for example, often solely focus on the country that carries them out, thus neglecting upstream and downstream impacts as well as ecological and social factors.[204]

6.3.1.2 Access

Regarding the access to freshwater in the basin, i.e., issues revolving around the (re)allocation of the resource, the Mekong Agreement applies the customary rule of equitable and reasonable utilisation, as the parties agreed 'to utilize the waters of the Mekong River system in a reasonable and equitable manner . . . pursuant to all relevant factors and circumstances'.[205] Article 5(A)(B), deals with intra-basin uses and inter-basin diversion on tributaries and the mainstream of the Mekong. Mechanisms for dispute settlement have also been included in the Mekong Agreement. Articles 34 and 35 provide that disputes (or differences) are to be resolved, first by the Mekong River Commission,[206]

199 Art 8 of the Mekong Agreement.

200 Art 10 of the Mekong Agreement.

201 Art 7 of the Mekong Agreement.

202 A Rieu-Clarke and G Gooch, 'Governing the Tributaries of the Mekong : The Contribution of International Law and Institutions to Enhancing Equitable Cooperation over the Sesan' (2010) *Pacific McGeorge Global Business & Development Law Journal*, 22, 193 at 214.

203 Art 3 of the Mekong Agreement.

204 Grumbine, Dore and Xu, 'Mekong Hydropower: Drivers of Change and Governance Challenges' at 91.

205 Art 5 of the Mekong Agreement.

206 Under Chapter IV of the Mekong Agreement, the Mekong River Commission is comprised of three permanent bodies: Council, Joint Committee, and Secretariat. The Council is composed of one member 'from each participating riparian State' at the ministerial and cabinet level, empowered to make policy decisions on behalf of his/her government. The Joint Committee is composed of one member from each participating riparian state at no less than Head of Department level.

failing which the matter is referred to the governments for negotiation, possible mediation, or eventual settlement 'according to the principles of international law'.[207] It is noteworthy, however, that the agreement contains no reference to any form of compulsory third-party participation in the resolution of disputes.

6.3.1.3 Adaptability

The Mekong basin faces huge challenges of adaptability, since it is affected by climatic changes and the development of large infrastructure projects. The capacity of the MRC to quickly adapt to new circumstances is strengthened by several institutional design factors. For instance, it benefits from being a multi-issue river basin organisation, since it allows for including all relevant issues in the basin and opens the door for new issues which may emerge over time.[208] Furthermore, the MRC does have a well-developed data and information-sharing mechanism in place; even though there certainly is still room for improvement regarding the quality of data being shared.[209] With regard to climate change adaptation, the MRC is developing an adaptation planning process through projects under the Climate Change Adaptation Initiative to assess climate change impacts and to improve planning and implementation within the Mekong basin.[210] Yet, the biggest impediment to improve the adaptability of the MRC is the lack of strong linkages to national and regional governance levels.[211]

6.3.1.4 Ambit

In terms of the ambit of the Mekong Agreement, several challenging issues manifest themselves. The fact that China is not a party to the legal regime is being seen as one of the treaty's major shortcomings.[212] Its approach of unilateral development of large-scale infrastructure on the Mekong has created tensions between and among China and its lower riparians; causing serious environmental degradation, compromising food security and even endangering regional stability.[213] Yet, even if one could leave aside the challenge of including China in the legal framework governing the Mekong, the controversies

207 Art 35 of the Mekong Agreement.

208 S Schmeier, *Resilience to Climate Change-Induced Challenges in the Mekong River Basin: The Role of the MRC* (World Bank 2011) at 49.

209 Art 24(c) of the Mekong Agreement.

210 Mekong River Commission, 'Climate Change and Adaptation Initiative' (2012) <http://www.mrcmekong.org/about-the-mrc/programmes/climate-change-and-adaptation-initiative/>.

211 Schmeier, *Resilience to Climate Change-Induced Challenges in the Mekong River Basin: The Role of the MRC* at 48.

212 In 1986, China was the first country in the basin to construct a dam on the mainstream of the Mekong – the Manwan Dam – as part of a cascade of 8 hydropower projects. Wirsing, Stoll and Jasparro, *International Conflict over Water Resources in Himalayan Asia* at 106.

213 See RP Cronin, China and the Geopolitics of the Mekong River Basin: Part I (World Politics Review 2012).

among the lower riparians would be enough to mire the sustainable and peaceful management of the river basin. One example which shows this quite vividly is the US$3.5 billion Xayaburi Dam, one of twelve hydropower projects planned on the Mekong mainstream. 95 per cent of the 1,285 MW produced by the hydropower plant will be exported to Thailand.[214]

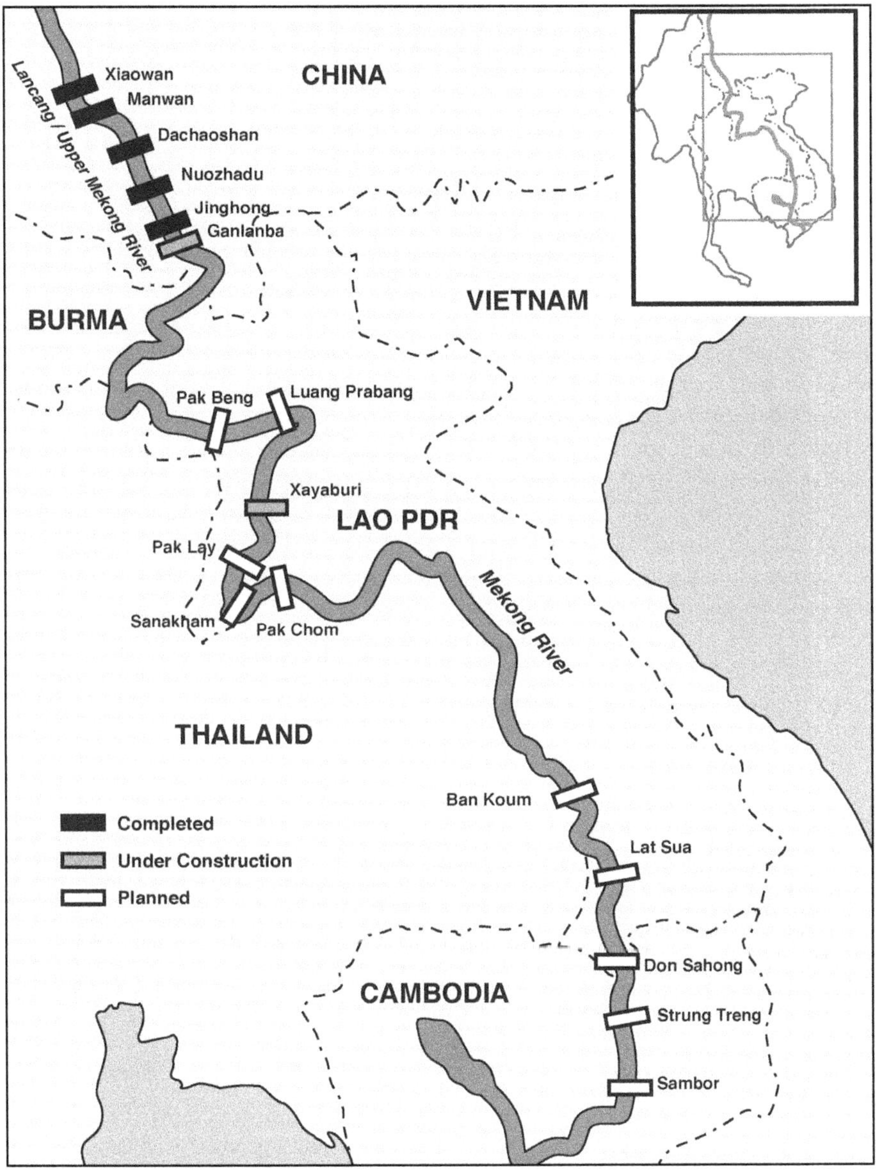

Figure 6.7 Dams in the lower Mekong River basin. Courtesy of International Rivers

214 International Rivers, 'Xayaburi Dam' (2012) <http://www.internationalrivers.org/campaigns/xayaburi-dam>.

The impacts of dams on the mainstream are understood to be far more severe than infrastructure projects on the tributaries, since they will directly affect millions of people who rely on migratory fish as a source of nutrition and income; although cumulative impacts from dams on smaller tributaries can also have a significant impact.[215] The MRC Procedures for Notification, Prior Consultation and Agreement demand that countries planning to build dams on the mainstream of the Mekong must first conduct detailed impact studies to evaluate the potential transboundary impact of such a project.[216] The EIA which had been conducted in the case at hand, however, has been criticised as being flawed, as it only studied the potential impacts within a rather limited area (the actual site of the dam, the area to be flooded by the reservoir and 10 kilometres downstream of the dam) and did not comprise a proper process of prior consultation.[217]

Nevertheless, preparations for the dam began in April 2011, when the Thai developer (CH Karnchang) started with preparatory earthworks. Immediately, Vietnam, which will benefit least from the dam, called for a ten-year moratorium on mainstream hydropower development. Interestingly, Thai officials have also failed to endorse Xayaburi, requesting that further research be carried out on the expected environmental impacts.[218] This led to the decision of the Lao government to delay the project in July 2012 – pending further impact studies.[219] A consensus among MRC member states on the future of the Xayaburi Dam seems elusive, as current developments are rather obscure. While work on the Xayaburi Dam itself had indeed been suspended, construction on the dam's access road and camp for workers was still going ahead at a rapid pace.[220] On 7 November 2012, Laos held an official ground-breaking ceremony after claiming that Cambodia and Vietnam now support the construction of the Xayaburi Dam.[221] During a recent MRC Council meeting, however, Cambodia, Vietnam and the MRC's donor governments continued to raise their concerns about the dam and the

215 G Vaidyanathan, 'Remaking the Mekong' (2011) *Nature*, 478, 305 at 305.

216 See Mekong River Commission, *Procedures for Notification, Prior Consultation and Agreement* (2003) available at <http://www.mrcmekong.org/assets/Publications/policies/Procedures-Notification-Prior-Consultation-Agreement.pdf>. For more detailed information about the process in the case of the Xayaburi Dam, see MRC, 'Xayaburi Hydropower Project Prior Consultation Process'(22 April 2011) <http://www.mrcmekong.org/news-and-events/consultations/xayaburi-hydropower-project-prior-consultation-process/>.

217 P Hirsch for International Rivers, 'Review of Xayaburi Dam EIA Incorporation into Regional Consultation on Impacts' (2011) <http://www.internationalrivers.org/files/attached-files/hirsch_xayabouri_dam_esia_consultation_process.pdf>.

218 SWD Pearse-Smith, '"Water War" in the Mekong Basin?' (2012) *Asia Pacific Viewpoint*, 53, 147 at 154.

219 PC Thul for Reuters, 'Laos Confirms has Suspended Controversial Xayaburi Dam' (13 July 2012) <http://www.reuters.com/article/2012/07/13/us-laos-dam-idUSBRE86C0GI20120713>.

220 See photos of the construction site as of July 2012 at <http://www.flickr.com/photos/internationalrivers/sets/72157627208507467/>.

221 A Chenaphun for Reuters, 'Laos holds Groundbreaking Ceremony for Contentious Mekong Dam' (7 November 2012) <http://www.reuters.com/article/2012/11/07/us-laos-dam-idUSBRE8A618I20121107>.

prior consultation procedures.[222] Hence, the highly sensitive issue remains unresolved at present. This highlights the fact that even if procedural rules are in place (such as conducting EIAs), it will not lead to stronger regional water cooperation if there is no common understanding of how to perceive regional water security.

It becomes obvious that the MRC is still struggling to be accepted as an institutional framework for assessing and managing the freshwater resources, and as a political forum for deciding on water-related issues.[223] The most likely reason for this is the reluctance of the member states to fully delegate certain powers to the MRC – in fear of cutting back their own national sovereignty. Hence, the MRC can formulate policies and recommendations, but their implementation still lies in the hands of the national governments.[224] As the controversies surrounding the Xayaburi Dam show, hydropolitics in the Mekong basin are heavily influenced by the hydro-hegemon, China, sidelining the Mekong Agreement. The problem here is the lack of concepts and methodologies to fully understand why transboundary water management in the Mekong basin is working the way it is, as the main focus of analysis is always the 1995 treaty – while many important decisions are actually being made outside of it by actors not involved in hard law negotiations. This underlines the importance of socio-legal research on the basin.[225] The shortcomings regarding the ambit of the current framework cause the future of the Mekong River to be primarily dependent upon the outcomes of two interlinked power struggles – (1) between China and the countries downstream, and (2) among the member states of the MRC themselves.

A positive development can be witnessed in the Greater Mekong Subregion (GMS), which has been set up between all six basin states and involves the implementation of wide-ranging series of regional projects covering transport, energy, telecommunications, environmental management, tourism and agriculture.[226] It has been acknowledged that GMS 'enhanced cross-border trade

222 Cambodia called for 'a more effective framework;' MRC, 'Statement by H.E. Mr. Sin Niny – 19th Meeting of the MRC Council' (17 January 2013) <http://www.mrcmekong.org/news-and-events/speeches/statement-by-h-emr-sin-niny-19th-meeting-of-the-mrc-council>. Thailand recognised the need to 'strengthen the MRC;' MRC, 'Statement by Mr. Chaiporn Siripornpibul – 19th Meeting of the MRC Council' (17 January 2013) <http://www.mrcmekong.org/news-and-events/speeches/statementby-mr-chaiporn-siripornpibul-19th-meeting-of-the-mrc-council>. MRC partners asked the Mekong basin states to strengthen the notification and consultation procedures; MRC, 'Joint Development Partner Statement – 19th Meeting of the MRC Council' (17 January 2013) <http://www.mrcmekong.org/news-and-events/speeches/jointdevelopment-partner-statement-19th-mrc-council-meeting-17-january-2013>.

223 Affeltranger, 'Sustainability of Environmental Regimes: The Mekong River Commission' at 593.

224 Rieu-Clarke and Gooch, 'Governing the Tributaries of the Mekong: The Contribution of International Law and Institutions to Enhancing Equitable Cooperation over the Sesan' at 217.

225 See FE Johns and others, 'Law and the Mekong River Basin: A Social-Legal Research Agenda on the Role of Hard and Soft Law in Regulating Transboundary Water Resources' (2010) *Melbourne Journal of International Law*, 11, 154.

226 For more information, see Asian Development Bank, 'Greater Mekong Subregion' (2013) <http://www.adb.org/countries/gms/main>.

while reducing poverty levels and creating shared interests in economic stability and peace'.[227] This is a prime example for the creation of a strong regional bond between nations which are bound together by a watercourse while also allowing for discussions of various non-water-related issues – even though the focus of the GMS still mainly lies on economic development.

6.3.2 The Indus River

India, as a riparian country of the river basins of Brahmaputra, Ganges and Indus has been in disagreement over freshwater sharing with several of its neighbours recently.[228] The most prominent dispute, however, is between India and Pakistan over the Indus, which is the bloodstream of Pakistan's economic (i.e., the textile industry) and food security (see Figure 6.8).[229]

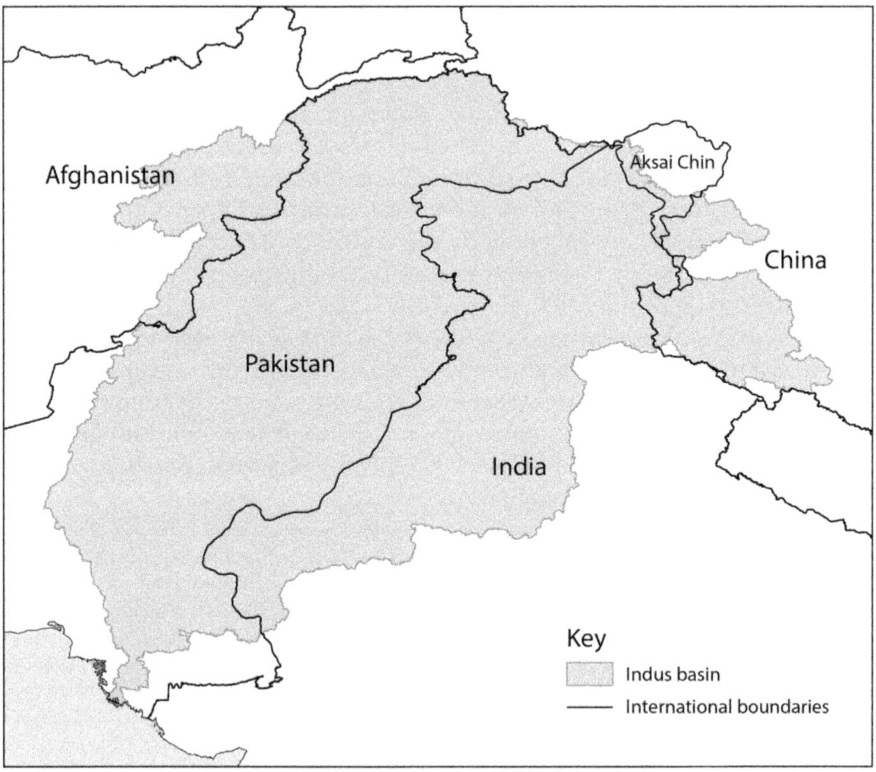

Figure 6.8 The Indus River basin. Source: OSU Transboundary Freshwater Dispute Database

227 World Bank, World Development Report 2011 : Conflict, Security, and Development (World Bank 2011) at 43.

228 Taenzler and others, *Water, Crisis and Climate Change in India: A Policy Brief* at 12.

229 W Wheeler for the National Geographic, 'India and Pakistan at Odds Over Shrinking Indus River' (12 October 2011) <http://news.nationalgeographic.com/news/2011/10/111012-india-pakistan-indus-river-water/>.

Relations between the two neighbours have always been highly tense. So it might not come as a surprise to hear even more of the 'water wars' propaganda here.[230] What makes a potential military conflict between the two states even more frightening is the fact that both India and Pakistan are nuclear nations.[231] It has been argued that the general perception that India is threatening the survival of Pakistan simply by 'cutting off' the waters of the Indus raises the potential of Pakistan using nuclear weapons as a last resort.[232] Yet, scholars often celebrate the longstanding 1960 Indus Waters Treaty[233] as a success, since it survived three wars (1965, 1971 and 1999) between the two hostile neighbours.[234] Throughout the times of military conflict, the water kept flowing. The conflict over the water resources of the Indus became international with the partition of British India, as the newly formed states were in disagreement over how to share and manage the previously unitary network of irrigation infrastructure. While the Indus River basin is shared between Pakistan (47 per cent), India (39 per cent), China (8 per cent) and Afghanistan (6 per cent), the treaty does not involve the latter two nations.[235] It is the power asymmetry between the two contracting parties which has been identified as the main reason for the delayed completion of the agreement.[236] Here, the involvement of a third party, the World Bank, played a key role in continuously pushing negotiations forward.[237] The next section will analyse whether the Indus Treaty is indeed successful in strengthening transboundary freshwater cooperation in the basin – based on the understanding of common water security.

6.3.2.1 Availability

In terms of availability, the Indus Waters Treaty does not contain effective binding provisions addressing water quality or pollution. From the beginning of the negotiation process, the whole framework was focused on issues

230 See, e.g., the Guardian, 'War over Water : It Could Happen With India and Pakistan' (3 June 2002) <http://www.guardian.co.uk/world/2002/jun/03/kashmir.india1>; N Mandhanda for Time Magazine, 'Water Wars: Why India and Pakistan Are Squaring Off Over Their Rivers' (16 April 2012) <http://www.time.com/time/world/article/0,8599,2111601,00.html>.

231 J Daly for OilPrice, 'Pakistani Editorial Says Nuclear War with India 'Inevitable' as Water Dispute Continues' (9 December 2011) <http://oilprice.com/Geopolitics/International/Pakistani-Editorial-Says-Nuclear-War-with-India-Inevitable-as-Water-Dispute-Continues.html>.

232 Brennan, 'The China-India-Pakistan Water Crisis: Prospects for Interstate Conflict' at 40.

233 Treaty between India and Pakistan Regarding the Use of the Waters of the Indus (19 September 1960; entered into force 1 April 1960) 419 UNTS 125 (1960) [hereinafter Indus Waters Treaty].

234 See, e.g., Khalid, 'The Interlinking of Rivers Project in India and International Water Law: An Overview' at 557.

235 AQUASTAT of FAO, 'Indus River Basin' (2011) <http://www.fao.org/nr/water/aquastat/basins/indus/index.stm>.

236 Center for Policy and Human Development, *Afghanistan Human Development Report 2011. The Forgotten Front: Water Security and the Crisis in the Sanitation* at 65.

237 See AK Biswas, 'Indus Water Treaty: The Negotiating Process' (1992) *Water International*, 17, 201.

of quantity, apportioning the tributaries among the two nations. India's plan was to hold sway over all of the Eastern rivers and 7 per cent of the Western rivers; while Pakistan demanded 70 per cent of the Eastern rivers and all of the Western rivers.[238] Ultimately, the parties agreed to allocate the tributaries, with India receiving three tributaries – Sutlej, Beas and Ravi (Eastern rivers) – while Pakistan received the main Indus, Jhelum and Chenab (Western rivers).[239] However, the Indus Waters Treaty also allows India to tap the hydropower potential of the Jhelum and Chenab rivers before they enter Pakistan.[240]

6.3.2.2 Access

The approach to resolving issues of access to water found in the Indus Waters Treaty is rather complex. Here, the principal institutional mechanism of the agreement, the permanent Indus Commission, plays a significant role in the settlement of disputes, serving 'as the regular channel of communication on all matters relating to the implementation of the Treaty'.[241] Under the agreement, issues that cannot be resolved by the Commission will be deemed 'differences', which may, depending upon their classification, be heard by a 'neutral expert' ('qualified engineer') at the request of either commissioner.[242] The difference will be considered to be a 'dispute' if the matter falls outside those issues listed in Annex F. Disputes are to be resolved through negotiation and, failing any successful outcome, are subject to arbitration. This mechanism has been triggered for the first time in the 45-year history of the treaty with a neutral expert providing a determination of the difference regarding the Baglihar hydropower plant in February 2007.[243] While some rightly argue that the differences were handled in a 'transparent and fair manner' and acknowledge that the decision was accepted by the two parties,[244] the process did not manage to completely calm freshwater interactions between India and Pakistan, nor did it give it a

238 Ibid. at 206.
239 Arts II & III of the Indus Waters Treaty.
240 Art III(2) of the Indus Waters Treaty.
241 Art VIII of the Indus Waters Treaty, 'Permanent Indus Commission.'
242 Art IX of the Indus Waters Treaty.
243 In 2005, Pakistan contacted the World Bank stating that a 'difference' has arisen with India under the Indus Water Treaty, relating to the Baglihar hydropower plant, being constructed by India on the Chenab River in breach of the provisions under paragraph 8 of Annex D to the treaty. The bank appointed a neutral expert, who rendered a decision in February 2007, which was accepted by the two parties. See 'Expert Determination on Points of Difference Referred by the Government of Pakistan under the Provisions of the Indus Water Treaty, Executive Summary' (12 February 2007) available at <http://siteresources.worldbank.org/SOUTHASIAEXT/Resources/223546-1171996340255/BagliharSummary.pdf>; see also SMA Salman, 'The Baglihar Difference and Its Resolution Process : A Triumph for the Indus Waters Treaty?' (2008) *Water Policy*, 10, 105.
244 Ibid.

far-sighted direction.[245] This becomes obvious when analysing the outcome of the most recent legal dispute – the Kishenganga Arbitration (see Figure 6.9).[246] Following a Request for Arbitration by Pakistan in 2010, a dispute was (for the first time in the history of the Indus Waters Treaty) referred to a Court of Arbitration concerning India's construction of the Kishenganga Hydro-Electric Project (KHEP). The design of the project is intended to divert waters from a dam site on the Kishenganga/Neelum River in the Jammu and Kashmir region to the Jhelum River– another tributary of the Indus. Pakistan identified two questions: (1) whether India's proposed diversion of the Kishenganga River for the run-of-the-river hydroelectric project into another tributary breaches India's legal obligations under Article III(2) of the Indus Waters Treaty, and (2) whether the agreement allowed India to deplete or bring the reservoir level of a run-of-river storage plant below the 'Dead Storage Level' in circumstances other than unforeseen emergencies.[247]

In September 2011, the Court issued an Order on Interim Measures, prohibiting India from constructing any permanent works on or above the Kishenganga/Neelum riverbed at the dam site that may inhibit the restoration

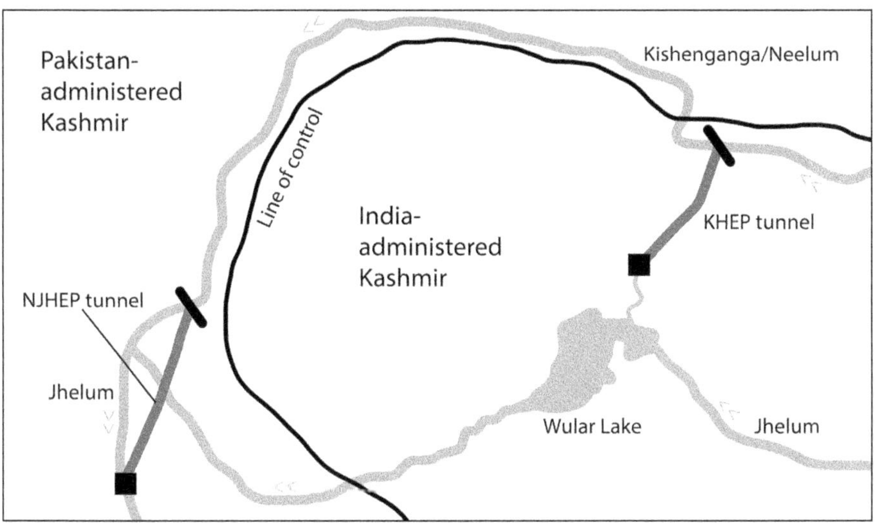

Figure 6.9 The Kishenganga Arbitration. Source: Permanent Court of Arbitration

245 See also, UK Sinha, 'Water a Pre-Eminent Political Issue between India and Pakistan' (2010) *Strategic Analysis*, 34, 482 at 485.

246 For a detailed analysis of the steps taken by the parties in accordance with the dispute settlement provisions of the treaty, see A Rieu-Clarke, R Moynihan and B-O Magsig, *UN Watercourses Convention: User's Guide* (IHP-HELP Centre for Water Law, Policy and Science 2012) at 247.

247 Ibid.

of the full flow of the river to its natural channel.[248] In February 2013, the Court issued a Partial Award, finding that India was permitted under the Treaty to divert water for the generation of electricity by the KHEP, arguing that Pakistan's water uses – of relevance here, the Neelum-Jhelum Hydro-Electric Project (NJHEP) – were preceded by the KHEP.[249] Hence, the NJHEP was not considered an 'existing use' under the Indus Waters Treaty, which India was required to take into account at the time of planning its KHEP. The Court did, however, make clear that India's right to divert the waters of the Kishenganga/Neelum was not absolute, since relevant principles of customary international law, including principles of international environmental law, have to be taken into account. Accordingly, the award allows India to proceed with the construction of the KHEP, subject to ensuring a minimum downstream flow to be determined in the Final Award. Further, it prohibits India from using drawdown flushing for sediment control at the Kishenganga project and any future run-of-river plant on the Western rivers. On 20 December 2013, the Permanent Court of Arbitration rendered its Final Award,[250] stating that in deciding the rate of minimum flow, it was necessary to 'mitigate adverse effects to Pakistan's agricultural and hydro-electric uses throughout the operation of the KHEP, while preserving India's right to operate the KHEP and maintaining the priority it acquired from having crystallized prior to the NJHEP', and to give due regard to 'the customary international law requirements of avoiding or mitigating trans-boundary harm and of reconciling economic development with the protection of the environment'.[251]

While the decision 'serves as a useful reminder of the potential of pacific dispute settlement in resolving complex disputes in tense settings',[252] it contradicts the outcome of the Baglihar difference. While the Baglihar judgment allowed India to draw down water below the dead storage level under certain conditions and apply a technique called 'drawdown flushing' in order to protect the hydropower plan from siltation, the Permanent Court of Arbitration, of course, did not treat the Baglihar findings and outcome as a precedent.[253] To the contrary, it

248 Permanent Court of Arbitration, Order on Interim Measures in the Matter of the Indus Waters Kishenganga Arbitration (Pakistan v. India)(23 September 2011) <http://www.pca-cpa.org/showfile.asp?fil_id=1726>.

249 Permanent Court of Arbitration, Partial Award in the Matter of the Indus Waters Kishenganga Arbitration (Pakistan v. India)(18 February 2013) <http://www.pca-cpa.org/showfile.asp?fil_id=2101>.

250 Permanent Court of Arbitration, Final Award in the Matter of the Indus Waters Kishenganga Arbitration (Pakistan v. India)(20 December 2013) <http://www.pca-cpa.org/showfile.asp?fil_id=2471>.

251 Ibid., para 87.

252 S Kumar, 'The Indus Waters Kishenganga Arbitration (Pakistan v. India)' (2013) *ASIL Insights*, 17, 1 at 5.

253 See also AK Biswas for The Indian Express, 'Straining at the Floodgates' (4 March 2013) <http://www.indianexpress.com/news/straining-at-the-floodgates/1082529/0#sthash.vNtsJJYC.dpuf>.

decided that from now on, this technique shall be prohibited. Interestingly, the Court's use of customary international law in the Kishenganga Arbitration was limited by Paragraph 29 of Annexure G to the Indus Waters Treaty.[254] While in its Partial Award it emphasised that it was 'incumbent upon [it] to interpret and apply this 1960 Treaty in light of the customary international principles for the protection of the environment in force today', in the Final Award the Court qualified this duty by arguing that 'if customary international law were applied not to circumscribe, but to negate rights expressly granted in the Treaty, this would no longer be "interpretation or application" of the Treaty but the substitution of customary law in place of the Treaty.'[255] Thus, it seems illusive to expect an end of disputes revolving around the same issues, as a clear far-sighted direction of how to manage the Indus basin is missing.

6.3.2.3 Adaptability

Due to climatic changes and pressures of population growth, the Indus basin faces huge challenges in terms of the adaptability of the regime. The whole Treaty resembles more of a divorce settlement, rather than a future-proof agreement for the sustainable management of a river basin. Since the Indus Waters Treaty fails to accommodate flexible mechanisms, other than the customary rules of interpretation, it has been argued that the Treaty should be amended to better cope with climate change uncertainty.[256]

6.3.2.4 Ambit

While the majority of scholars still view the Indus Waters Treaty as a success,[257] when looking at the actual ambit of the agreement, this author agrees with the minority view that on the whole it can only be perceived as a failure. The reason for the dramatically diverging views on the quality of the Treaty might originate from asking a completely different question. While most commentators seem to be satisfied with the 'survival' of the Treaty during times of war, should one not be able to demand more from a treaty governing a shared watercourse, such a vital resource for both countries? Is it too bold to ask why the Indus Waters Treaty did not *prevent* three wars? In claiming that 'The Indus

254 T Meshel for Kluwer Arbitration Blog, 'The Indus Waters Kishenganga Arbitration – Reviving the Indus Waters Treaty and Arbitration of Interstate Water Disputes' (21 January 2014) <http://kluwerarbitrationblog.com/blog/2014/01/21/the-indus-waters-kishenganga-arbitration-reviving-the-indus-waters-treaty-and-arbitration-of-interstate-water-disputes/>.

255 Permanent Court of Arbitration, Final Award in the Matter of the Indus Waters Kishenganga Arbitration (Pakistan v. India)(20 December 2013), para 112.

256 P Bagla, 'Along the Indus River, Saber Rattling over Water Security' (2010) *Science*, 328, 1226 at 1227.

257 DC McKinney, *Transboundary Water Challenges: Case Studies* (Center for Research in Water Resources, University of Texas 2011) at 97. Calling the Indus Waters Treaty 'one of the most successful settlements of a transboundary water basin conflict.'

Waters Treaty, which is the most successful India-Pakistan agreement to date, has held up for 46 years largely because the Treaty does not require daily interaction and joint decision making by those two estranged governments',[258] do we imply that we consider treaties which do not require adequate cooperation to be a success? International legal scholarship would certainly damage itself if it followed such an absurd understanding of international law.

Following a contemporary understanding of common water security, ethically based on the notion of hydrosolidarity, a freshwater treaty should not merely be able to muddle through difficult bilateral times. It should provide an impetus for riparian countries to develop relations outside the water box – and ultimately lead to more peaceful relations. In this regard, as well as concerning the vital issues of water quality and adaptability, the Indus Waters Treaty has missed an important opportunity. While it has been argued before that renegotiations are inevitable;[259] the examination through the contemporary security lens has made it even more obvious that the agreement between India and Pakistan in its current form has no future, as it does not contribute to the water security of the region.

6.4 A regional legal framework for water security?

Given the fact that neither the Mekong Agreement nor the Indus Waters Treaty support the understanding of water security which is necessary for regional peace and security, the question now arises: how can international law help avoiding water conflicts in Himalayan Asia? Or more precisely: are there any signs which can be interpreted as potential pathways towards a new approach based on regional common concern? While the previous sections have shown that both the Indus Waters Treaty and the Mekong Agreement have their respective weaknesses, one should not underestimate the impact these legal frameworks have on the transboundary water interaction in the region. The negotiation of treaties, their signatures and, ultimately, the implementation of their obligations depend to a large extent on issues outside the actual water box. Often, the right timing is perceived as more important than the actual legal content, as, arguably, a non-perfect treaty might still be better than none.[260] If the time is ripe for a regional framework in Himalayan Asia, how could it emerge and develop in a climate where the political willingness among the various riparian countries might not be strong enough to actually change course? The following section highlights some of the potential

258 TC Schaffer, 'Putting the Kashmiris into the Kashmir Issue' (2007) *Asia Policy*, 3, 192 at 195.

259 See, e.g., The Atlantic Council, 'Leaders Call for Modernizing Indus Water Treaty' (3 April 2013) <http://www.acus.org/press/leaders-call-modernizing-indus-water-treaty>; M Bhatnagar, 'Reconsidering the Indus Waters Treaty' (2009) *Tulane Environmental Law Journal*, 22, 271; UK Sinha, '50 Years of the Indus Water Treaty: An Evaluation' (2010) *Strategic Analysis*, 34, 667 at 670.

260 This underlines the importance of including flexible mechanisms within legal frameworks governing freshwater resources.

pathways – including hard and soft law and policy pathways – the actors in the region should pursue in order to generate the political will needed in order to arrive at a point where the challenges of freshwater management are being seen as of regional common concern.

While there has been some research on cross-border governance in Asia,[261] only a few scholars have looked into the development of a regional regime.[262] In terms of governance of transboundary freshwater resources in Asia, there is only one comprehensive study which proposes a regional framework. The work of the Strategic Foresight Group provides an in-depth analysis of the manifold challenges connected to the water crisis of four countries in Himalayan Asia (Bangladesh, China, India and Nepal), before it looks at best-practice case studies from around the world regarding integrated water resources management.[263] Regrettably, the authors spend only the last few pages elaborating on how they envision a sub-regional regime governing the river systems of the Ganges and Brahmaputra.[264] However, some of their ideas are none the less thought provoking. The organisational set-up proposed here is a series of multi-layered 'mini-commissions', each with a specific focus area (glaciers, agriculture, desertification, economic activities and emergency responses), under the umbrella of an overarching legally constituted Himalayan Rivers Commission (HRC) with some binding authority.[265] The HRC also serves as a framework in which the two river basin organisations of the Brahmaputra and the Ganges operate on more basin specific issues.[266] A rather novel approach is being proposed when it comes to incorporating the two Chinese national basins originating in the Himalayas – the Yangtze and Yellow – under the umbrella of the HRC. While the authors rightly argue that an inclusion of national watercourses will benefit all parties due to the increased knowledge exchange between the various basins facing similar challenges, the claim that such a set-up would also increase the incentive for China to be involved in the HRC is rather doubtful.[267] The most important feature of the suggested framework, however, is the inherent flexibility through its modular structure and the frequent meetings on various levels of water governance. This type of governance framework would seem to include a range of hard and soft legal and policy instruments.

Whether such a framework in its entirety will ever be agreed on among the four countries, let alone all states in Himalayan Asia, is highly unlikely. However, a more gradual development towards closer regional cooperation

261 See, e.g., GS Cheema, CA McNally and V Popovski (eds), *Cross-Border Governance in Asia: Regional Issues and Mechanisms* (United Nations University Press 2011).

262 One of the few exceptions is looking at biodiversity in the Himalayas; AM Bhattarai, *Protection of Himalayan Biodiversity: International Environmental Law and a Regional Legal Framework* (SAGE 2010).

263 Strategic Foresight Group, The Himalayan Challenge: Water Security in Emerging Asia.

264 Ibid. at 131.

265 Ibid. at 133.

266 Ibid.

267 Ibid.

on freshwater issues is by no means impossible. In order to avoid regional water security to deteriorate, international water law has to provide a framework which is capable in accommodating the much-needed changes in transboundary water interaction while respecting the regional particularities – both hydrological and political. While such a regional framework for water security seems highly ambitious and proceeds well beyond previous proposals to tackle Himalayan Asia's water crisis, the severity of the situation has also shown that the time is ripe for a fundamental change in how the region is managing its transboundary watercourses; several initiatives in the region are already working towards this.[268] If politicians in Himalayan Asia can be convinced that a 'best fit' strategy which accommodates their specific needs in the regional contexts is actually possible, the whole venture becomes more feasible.

What this region desperately needs in order to move towards a truly regional approach to water security is engendering deeper trust between the conflicting parties. This is particularly relevant for the rather tense relationship between India and Pakistan, which is hampered by a sense of negative engagement and a media which misuses bilateral dialogues around water for sensationalism, feeding mistrust between the two nations.[269] This can be achieved by encouraging communication, sharing data and conducting joint research projects. Such tools to increase cooperation could be created utilising a mix of policy, soft and hard legal instruments. Here, the new initiative between India and China to cooperate over Himalayan glaciers seems promising. In order to better understand the state of the glaciers, research bodies on both sides of the mountain range are sharing information.[270] Furthermore, research networks are another promising tool for fostering cooperation, as they strengthen existing collaborative efforts and bring in new programmes. Recently released research on this topic by the British Council found that for many Asian universities, this is nothing unusual. Across the disciplines, the international research collaboration rates are already high.[271] Here new impetus has to be given for joint research on issues related to freshwater management.

Another tool for improving transboundary relations in the Himalayas could be setting up peace parks along the contested borders between China, India and Pakistan. The idea of turning these areas into connected parks which enjoy

268 See, e.g., the International Centre for Integrated Mountain Development (ICIMOD) which 'aims to assist mountain people [in the Hindu Kush Himalayas] to understand these changes, adapt to them, and make the most of new opportunities, while addressing upstream-downstream issues.' More information available at <http://www.icimod.org/>.

269 H Brock, *Competition over Resources: Drivers of Insecurity and the Global South* (Oxford Research Group 2011) at 15.

270 J Lamont for the Financial Times, 'India and China Co-operate over Himalayan Glaciers' (2 August 2009) <http://www.ft.com/cms/s/0/5e729abe-7fa8-11de-85dc-00144feabdc0.html >.

271 See also, a promising programme which is trying to push the already existing initiatives forward and help establishing new ones: British Council, 'Global Education Dialogues: The Asia Series' (2012) <http://ihe.britishcouncil.org/sites/default/files/GED_brochure.pdf>.

environmental protection would have a direct impact on the management of the watercourses originating there, while opening new doors for negotiating other water-related issues among the parties.[272] While it is unrealistic to expect India and Pakistan to make peace based on a commitment to shared conservation alone, it becomes much more likely if a peace park agreement is being tied on a greater plan to manage the freshwaters rising from the Himalayas jointly.[273] The recent tragedies on the Siachen glaciers brought the idea of the use of peace parks as a way to demilitarise the contentious border between India and Pakistan back to the table.[274] While China and India are also in disagreement over their shared border,[275] recent efforts to calm down the politically charged issue might eventually open up the possibility of a Sino-Indian peace park.[276]

While these examples are all valid steps towards a more regional approach to freshwater interaction, they need to be tied into one institutional mechanism in order to be of long-term value. Here, regional organisations can play an important role, since they allow for gradual strengthening and deepening of relations on a whole range of different topics.[277] This is of particular importance, given that both China and India have a long history in committing to address conflicts through bilateral talks, rather than allowing third-party states to interfere, or even supporting a regional solution.[278] In order to be able to arrive at a framework which overcomes this prejudice towards regional approaches, one has to find a starting point which already provides at least some of the necessary features. In this regard, it might be worth taking a closer look at the Association of Southeast Asian Nations (ASEAN) (see Figure 6.10).

This geopolitical and economic organisation was founded in 1967 by Indonesia, Malaysia, the Philippines, Singapore and Thailand and now includes Brunei, Burma, Cambodia, Laos and Vietnam. Among its main goals are

272 See A Ali, 'A Siachen Peace Park: The Solution to a Half-Century of International Conflict?' (2002) 22 Mountain Research and Development 316; NA Kemkar, 'Environmental Peacemaking: Ending Conflict between India and Pakistan on the Siachen Glacier through the Creation of a Transboundary Peace Park' (2006) *Stanford Environmental Law Journal*, 25, 67.

273 IUCN and WCPA, *Protected Areas: Benefits Beyond Boundaries* (IUCN 2000) at 15.

274 Bhagwandas for Dawn, 'Plea to Turn Siachen into Peace Park' (8 April 2012) <http://dawn.com/2012/04/09/plea-to-turn-siachen-into-peace-park/>.

275 G Harris and E Wong for The New York Times, 'Where China Meets India in a High-Altitude Desert, Push Comes to Shove' (2 May 2013) <http://www.nytimes.com/2013/05/03/world/asia/where-china-meets-india-push-comes-to-shove.html?_r=0>.

276 BBC News, 'Premier Li Keqiang's Visit: India and China in Border Row Pledge' (20 Mai 2013) <http://www.bbc.co.uk/news/world-asia-india-22592770>; BBC News, 'Why China Seeks Better Relations With India' (7 May 2013) <http://www.bbc.co.uk/news/world-asia-india-22430301>.

277 R Moynihan and B-O Magsig, 'The Rising Role of Regional Approaches in International Water Law: Lessons from the UNECE Water Regime and Himalayan Asia for Strengthening Transboundary Water Cooperation' (2014) *Review of European Community & International Environmental Law*, 23, 43.

278 See, e.g., People's Daily Online, 'China Rejects Philippines' Arbitral Request: FM' (19 February 2013) <http://english.peopledaily.com.cn/90883/8135272.html>.

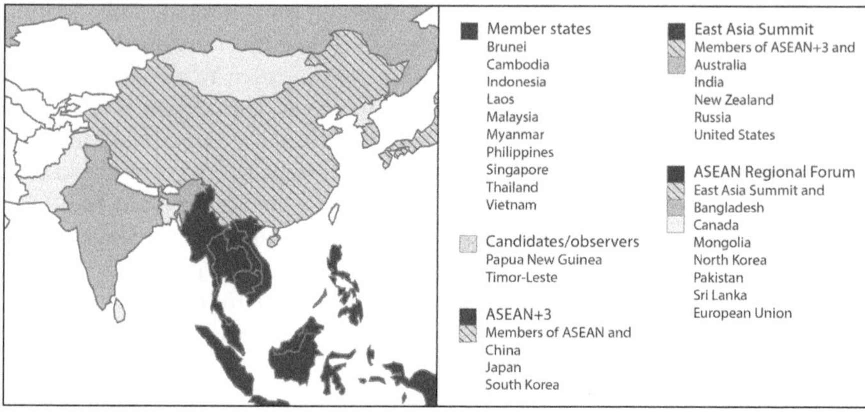

Figure 6.10 Member states of ASEAN

> to accelerate the economic growth, social progress and cultural development in the region . . . to promote regional peace and stability through abiding respect for justice and the rule of law in the relationship among countries of the region and adherence to the principles of the United Nations Charter . . . to promote active collaboration and mutual assistance on matters of common interest in the economic, social, cultural, technical, scientific and administrative fields . . . to maintain close and beneficial cooperation with existing international and regional organizations with similar aims and purposes, and explore all avenues for even closer cooperation among themselves.[279]

The reason for choosing the framework of ASEAN as a potential avenue for promoting the concept of water security as being one of common concern to all states of Himalayan Asia is that it possesses the necessary political clout to involve both China and India – and thus become the core of Asian efforts towards regionalism.[280] While neither of the two hydro-hegemons of Himalayan Asia are members of ASEAN, they are none the less actively involved; mainly through the ASEAN+3 (China, Japan, and South Korea) and the East Asia Summit (ASEAN+3 together with Australia, India, New Zealand, Russia and the US), initiatives which have been established to create an integrated market in the Asia-Pacific region.[281] The cooperation amongst ASEAN countries has continually broadened and deepened to also include subjects other than economics.

279 The ASEAN Declaration (Bangkok, 8 August 1967) available at <http://www.asean.org/news/item/the-asean-declaration-bangkok-declaration>.

280 EZ Bower for CSIS, 'ASEAN's Opportunity to Become the Core of Asian Regionalism' (2 April 2010) <http://csis.org/publication/aseans-opportunity-become-core-asian-regionalism>.

281 The Jakarta Post, 'ASEAN+6 start regional FTA Talks' (10 Mai 2013) <http://www.thejakartapost.com/news/2013/05/10/asean6-start-regional-fta-talks.html>.

In 1976, the Treaty of Amity and Cooperation in Southeast Asia, a peace treaty among South East Asian countries, was signed by the founding members of ASEAN and adopted fundamental principles of their relations with one another, which have been coined 'the ASEAN way': (1) mutual respect for the independence, sovereignty, equality, territorial integrity, and national identity of all nations; (2) the right of every state to lead its national existence free from external interference, subversion or coercion; (3) non-interference in internal affairs; (4) settlement of differences or disputes in a peaceful manner; (5) renunciation of the threat or use of force and (6) effective regional cooperation.[282] Interestingly, China and India were the first nations outside ASEAN to sign the Treaty in 2003. While some would argue that the 'ASEAN way' – the region's method of multilateralism – might constitute a stumbling block for overcoming the prevailing focus on national interests and arriving at a truly regional understanding of water security, there are several initiatives within the framework of ASEAN which paint a more hopeful picture.

For instance, the ASEAN Ministerial Meeting on Environment (AMME) was established in 1981 with the aim to discuss environmental issues affecting the group of states. In 2002, AMME agreed to further synergise regional environmental cooperation by focusing on ten areas – freshwater resources being one of them.[283] In 1983, the ASEAN Group on Nature Conservation proposed a set of principles and objectives for the selection, establishment and management of protected areas in the ASEAN region and ultimately issued the Declaration on Heritage Parks and Reserves which established the first group of heritage sites. The establishment of such parks stresses the fact that the member states share a common natural heritage – and thus should cooperate in their efforts to protect the biodiversity which supports the lives of their own citizens, as well as those living beyond their borders. According to the ASEAN Declaration on Heritage Parks of 2003, member states agreed that 'common cooperation is necessary to conserve and manage the ASEAN Heritage Parks for the development and implementation of regional conservation and management action plans as well as regional mechanisms complementary to and supportive of national efforts to implement conservation measures'.[284] In 1985,

282 Treaty of Amity and Cooperation in Southeast Asia, as amended by the First Protocol amending the Treaty of Amity and Cooperation in Southeast Asia, 1987, the Second Protocol amending the Treaty of Amity and Cooperation in Southeast Asia, 1998 and the Third Protocol amending the Treaty of Amity and Cooperation in Southeast Asia, 2010 (24 February 1976) available at <http://www.official-documents.gov.uk/document/cm84/8472/8472.pdf>.

283 'The Ministers also noted that the newly established ASEAN Working Group on Water Resources Management to be chaired by Thailand would further strengthen cooperation among member countries in research, conservation and information exchange on integrated water resources management;' see ASEAN, 'Press Release: 7th Informal ASEAN Ministerial Meeting on the Environment' (21 November 2002) <http://haze.asean.org/news/1038197275/back=media/1038197275/PRESS+RELEASE%3A+7th+Informal+ASEAN+Ministerial+Meeting+on+the+Environment>.

284 2003 ASEAN Declaration on Heritage Parks (18 December 2003) available at <http://cil.nus.edu.sg/rp/pdf/2003%20ASEAN%20Declaration%20on%20Heritage%20Parks-pdf.pdf>.

several member states signed the ASEAN Agreement on the Conservation of Nature and Natural Resources.[285] For example, it stipulates that

> Contracting Parties shall especially co-operate together and, where appropriate, shall endeavour to co-operate with other Contracting Parties, with a view to: (a) the conservation and management of (1) border or contiguous protected areas; (2) shared habitats of species listed in Appendix 1; (3) shared habitats of any other species of common concern . . .].[286]

While the Treaty text might suggest close cooperation between ASEAN countries in the area of nature conservation, it has not entered into force, since only three of the six signatory member states (Indonesia, the Philippines and Thailand) have ratified it so far. Other agreements and initiatives on environmental cooperation under the umbrella of ASEAN include the 1995 Cooperation Plan on Transboundary Pollution,[287] the 2002 Agreement on Transboundary Haze Pollution,[288] the ASEAN Wildlife Enforcement Network launched in 2005[289] and the 2007 ASEAN Declaration on Environmental Sustainability.[290]

Since 2005, the East Asian Summit (EAS) has been held annually just after the ASEAN leaders' meetings. With regard to regional security, the summit in 2007 was of particular importance, as it brought forth the Cebu Declaration on East Asian Energy Security, in which the states agreed to promote energy security and find energy alternatives to conventional fuels with the aim to provide 'reliable, adequate and affordable energy supplies'.[291] It was signed by the ten ASEAN members (Brunei, Burma, Cambodia, Indonesia, Laos, Malaysia, the Philippines, Singapore, Thailand and Vietnam), as well as Australia, China, India, Japan, New Zealand and South Korea. This was followed by the Singapore Declaration on Climate Change, Energy and the Environment at the third EAS in 2008.[292] With regard to freshwater resources,

285 1985 ASEAN Agreement on the Conservation of Nature and Natural Resources (9 July 1985; not entered into force) available at <http://www.jus.uio.no/english/services/library/treaties/06/6-01/asean-conservation-nature.xml>.

286 Art 19(3)(a) of the ASEAN Agreement on the Conservation of Nature and Natural Resources.

287 1995 ASEAN Cooperation Plan on Transboundary Pollution; reprinted in 12 ASEAN Economic Bulletin 89.

288 2002 ASEAN Agreement on Transboundary Haze Pollution; available at <http://haze.asean.org/docs/1128506236/ASEANAgreementonTransboundaryHazePollution.pdf/view>.

289 For more information, see <http://asean-wen.org/>.

290 ASEAN Declaration on Environmental Sustainability (20 November 2007) available at <http://environment.asean.org/index.php?page=agreements:aseandeclarationenvsus>.

291 2007 Cebu Declaration on East Asian Energy Security (15 January 2007) available at <http://www.enecho.meti.go.jp/policy/international-affairs/data/CEBU%20DECLARATION.pdf>.

292 2007 Singapore Declaration on Climate Change, Energy and the Environment (21 November 2007) available at <http://www.asean.org/asean/external-relations/east-asia-summit-eas/item/singapore-declaration-on-climate-change-energy-and-the-environment>.

the environmental ministers of ASEAN adopted the 2003 ASEAN Strategic Plan on Water Resources Management, which is aimed at promoting the vision for water in South East Asia by 2050: 'The attainment of sustainability of water resources to ensure sufficient water quantity of acceptable quality to meet the needs of the people of Southeast Asia in terms of health, food security, economy and environment.'[293] In the most recent meeting of AMME, the ministers agreed to 'enhance existing transboundary water cooperation within ASEAN which aims to reduce poverty, protect natural resources, prevent crisis and resolve conflicts between countries'.[294] However, these initiatives to strengthen cooperation have not been implemented yet, as the current struggles for the region's freshwater resources show.

Hence, when it comes to transboundary freshwater management in Himalayan Asia, selective partnerships are still the norm. The reasons for this are twofold: (1) at the international level, states still see transboundary water interaction as a zero-sum game, as it is the limiting factor of their respective economic growth; (2) at the various national levels, the power interplay is preventing a joint approach, due to the prevailing fragmentation caused by bureaucratic competition.[295] Within the sub-region of the Lower Mekong, for instance, this competition and resulting fragmentation can be witnessed in the way each state's department of irrigation is, of course, interested in utilising infrastructure such as dams to regulate the freshwater flow for agriculture; while the energy sector's main goal, obviously, is generating hydropower, and the agencies responsible for fisheries perceive these structures as impediments to fish migration.[296] There is, however, a shimmer of hope for a more coherent and regional stance on freshwater management. The recently held 2nd Asia-Pacific Water Summit on the topic of 'Water Security and Water-related Disaster Challenges: Leadership and Commitment' was organised by the Royal Thai Government in collaboration with the Asia-Pacific Water Forum and supporting international and regional NGOs.[297] While Thailand's Prime Minister, Yingluck Shinawatra, believes that 'there could be a fight over resources' unless countries enter into water sharing agreements, she stressed the importance of regional forums to resolve water conflicts peacefully, since 'No

293 ASEAN Strategic Plan on Water Resources Management (18 December 2003) available at <http://cil.nus.edu.sg/rp/pdf/2003%20ASEAN%20Strategic%20Plan%20on%20Water%20Resource%20Management-pdf.pdf>.

294 Bangkok Resolution on ASEAN Environmental Cooperation (26 September 2012) available at <http://www.asean.org/images/2012/news/documents/Agenda%2016%20-%20ADOPTED%20Bangkok_Resolution_12AMME%20-%2026Sep.pdf>.

295 D Suhardiman, M Giordano and F Molle, 'Scalar Disconnect: The Logic of Transboundary Water Governance in the Mekong' (2012) *Society & Natural Resources*, 25, 572 at 573.

296 Ibid.

297 International Institute for Sustainable Development, 'Second Asia-Pacific Water Summit' (23 May 2013) <http://www.iisd.ca/water/apws/2013/html/crsvol211num1e.html>.

country in this region can handle these challenges alone.'[298] In the outcome document of the summit, the Chiang Mai Declaration, the heads of state and government declared, among other things, to 'enhance regional and international cooperation on sharing, exchange and dissemination of scientific and technical knowledge, as well as best practices, related to integrated water resources management'.[299] It further invites the Asia-Pacific Water Forum to mobilise initiatives to support the recommendations and to consider establishing an Asian Water Information System.[300]

Yet it seems that the potential for states dependent on the rivers rising in the Himalayas agreeing on a truly regional framework for governing their transboundary water resources seems rather elusive at present. While there already are various promising initiatives in place which promote a more regional approach to environmental issues in the region through a mix of hard and soft law and policy instruments, the task now is to build on those and strengthen them. Given China's and India's growing responsibility in the international arena, there might be a chance for making the case for a moral obligation of the two hydro-hegemons to move into the direction of regional common concern. Are China and India responsible international players who can promote the concept of water security in Himalayan Asia as a regional common concern? No doubt, the two regional hydro-hegemons are the rising powers in world politics – but do they also accept new responsibilities? So far, China's participation in global governance has been rather disappointing, and there is 'little evidence that it will seek international leadership'.[301] With regard to his foreign policy, the new leader of the Chinese Communist Party, Xi Jinping, has made it clear that his nation will continue to 'never compromise its core interests' or swallow the 'bitter fruit' of accepting harm to its sovereignty, security and development.[302] India's strategy to claim its status as a 'great power' seems even less clear, as its hands are tied by domestic constraints.[303]

The contemporary concept of water security, as it has been developed in this study, attempts to persuade states that a regional approach to water security not only serves the region as a whole, but ultimately also constitutes the best option for the respective national security interests when taking a long-term view. More research is needed with regard to how Chinese and Indian positions on

298 AFP, 'Asia-Pacific Leaders Warn of Water Conflict Threat' (20 May 2013) <http://www.asiaone.com/News/AsiaOne+News/Asia/Story/A1Story20130520-424064.html>.

299 The Second Asia-Pacific Water Summit, Chiang Mai Declaration (20 May 2013) available at <http://apws2013.files.wordpress.com/2013/05/chiang-mai-declaration.pdf>.

300 Ibid.

301 H Wang and E French, 'China's Participation in Global Governance from a Comparative Perspective' (2013) *Asia Policy*, 15, 89 at 89.

302 Economist Intelligence Unit, 'China: New Leader Hints at Tough Foreign Policy' (2013) <http://country.eiu.com.proxy1.athensams.net/article.aspx?articleid=60102990&Country=China&topic=Politics&subtopic=Forecast&subsubtopic=International+relations&u=1&pid=1510105735&oid=1510105735&uid=1>.

303 A Narlikar, 'India Rising: Responsible to Whom?' (2013) *International Affairs*, 89, 595 at 613.

international challenges evolve as they gain more influence in the international arena. While both nations seem to prefer a stable Himalayan Asia which will allow them to sustain their economic growth, they still perceive threats to their security differently, and thus employ different strategies.[304] Although it is of tremendous importance that the water security strategy for Himalayan Asia is being developed from within, the role of external powers in the process should not be underestimated. Not only do international NGOs already influence the transboundary water interaction in the region; freshwater is also high on the foreign policy agenda of the EU and US – both having a deep interest in the social stability of the region. However, the international community as a whole is not only part of the solution; it also carries a huge responsibility:[305] avoiding 'environmental colonialism' at all cost and not to play off one state against the other(s).[306] The concept of 'regional common concern' can only unfold properly if understood at a regional level by all relevant stakeholders. The international community, then, has to encourage and enable both China and India to play a more prominent role in providing water security in Himalayan Asia.

This chapter has outlined the water crisis in Himalayan Asia and analysed two of the important legal frameworks governing transboundary watercourses. While there is evidence that the current approach towards common water security is rather weak, the last section tried to give an outlook into the future as to how the two hydro-hegemons might work towards a more common understanding of the crisis. The reason for selecting Himalayan Asia, as well as the Indus and Mekong River basins, as test cases was not to show that applying the concept of water security developed in this book will immediately provide a fertile ground for deepening cooperation on transboundary water issues. The chapter did, however, point towards the particular challenges of the concept of water security in general, as well as the specific political obstacles in Himalayan Asia. Given the embryonic stage of 'water security', the lessons learned here might inform the further development of the concept.

304 See AJ Tellis and S Mirski (eds), *Crux of Asia: China, India, and the Emerging Global Order* (Carnegie Endowment for International Peace 2013).

305 A positive development is the joint announcement on emission-cutting goals by the United States and China, the two biggest GHG polluters, during the 2014 Asia-Pacific Economic Cooperation (APEC) forum in Beijing. While the actual impact of the announcement on emission levels can only be determined over the next years, the deal none the less marked a step-change in diplomacy in the run-up to negotiating a legally binding global climate agreement in 2015. See M Levi for Council on Foreign Relations, 'What the Big U.S.-China Climate Announcement Means' (12 November 2014) <http://blogs.cfr.org/asia/2014/11/12/michael-levi-what-the-big-u-s-china-climate-announcement-means/>.

306 See, e.g., A Agarwal and S Narain, *Global Warming in an Unequal World: A Case of Environmental Colonialism* (Centre for Science and Environment 1991).

7 Conclusion

7.1 The contribution of the 4A operational methodology

The availability of, and access to, freshwater resources is one of the most challenging global security concerns of the twenty-first century. Only a small number of issues have the potential to create as much friction between states as the management of freshwater resources which cross international boundaries. Water, the gossamer linking various other security concerns – environment, food and energy – has gradually acquired an independent status within the security discourse.[1] However, this recently gained prominence has done little in strengthening the concept's substance and actual impact on transboundary freshwater management. The reason for the gap between apparent omnipresence and actual influence lies in the fact that water security has different dimensions – individual, local, national, regional and global – and is being debated in the realms of various disciplines – political science, international relations, economics and law – which are influenced by countless players trying to shape the discussion for the benefit of their own agenda. This makes the concept of water security hard to grasp and utilise for triggering the desperately needed change in how we manage our freshwater resources. For that reason, the international legal scholarship has included water security thinking only hesitantly in its research. The few scholars who have taken this step have done so in an incomplete manner which has often lacked the rigorous theoretical depth and analysis required to fully establish the way international law needs to be refined in order to better address water security.[2] The prevalent approach of squeezing the complex notion of water security into the rigid frames of established and familiar tools and concepts, however, has prevented an understanding of

1 See the emerging literature on the topic, e.g., J Briscoe, 'Water Security: Why It Matters and What to Do About It' (2009) *Innovations: Technology, Governance, Globalization*, 4, 3; C Cook and K Bakker, 'Water Security: Debating an Emerging Paradigm' (2012) *Global Environmental Change*, 22, 94; UK Sinha, 'The Why and What of Water Security' (2009) *Strategic Analysis*, 33, 470; S Thapliyal, 'Water Security or Security of Water? A Conceptual Analysis' (2011) *India Quarterly: A Journal of International Affairs*, 67, 19.

2 See, e.g., P Wouters, 'Water Security: What Role for International Water Law?' in Doddle F (ed.), *Human and Environmental Security: An Agenda for Change* (Earthscan 2005).

water security which reflects current international developments; and thus, it has prohibited the shaping of new ideas which could help the evolution of the notion in the international legal sphere. This is why the need to dramatically re-think the framework of water security, where the 'contribution of [water] law is more dynamically considered and integrated', has been acknowledged.[3]

In order to move this debate forward, water security has been conceptualised in Chapter 2 by reviewing existing perspectives and viewpoints from a range of disciplines on the concept. The definition of water security has been developed with the improvement of the accessibility of the concept within international legal scholarship in mind:

> A community is water secure when it has sustainable access to freshwater of sufficient quantity and quality, or to the benefits derived therefrom; and the ability to minimise water-related risk and its various repercussions to an acceptable level – without compromising the supporting ecosystems.

In drawing from the widening and deepening process of the general security debate and acknowledging the complexity of the water crisis, the definition has several advantages over previous ones which are constrained by orthodox thinking. Its scalability ensures that it can address water security at the local, national, international, or even global level, while it does justice to the fact that several of these levels overlap in practice. In addition, by including the benefits derived from the access to water and the repercussions of water-related risks, the true complexity of the water crisis comes into play. The (re)allocation is rarely an end in itself, since the opportunities and issues linked (directly or indirectly) to it are the actual crunch points. This opens the door for discussions of concepts and challenges such as virtual water, water footprint, land grabs, rapid urbanisation or changing migration patterns. Furthermore, the definition also offers the needed flexibility through its undetermined parameters of 'sufficient quantity and quality of freshwater' and 'acceptable level of water-related risk and repercussions'. This is needed to accommodate the specific requirements depending on the hydrological, political and social background of the respective community – which is subjected to constant change.[4] This renders water security as a concept which is not set in stone. Rather, it should be understood as a platform for debating the constantly evolving challenges.

Following a contemporary path of security, rather than applying the orthodox state-centred and military-focused approach is the only way to overcome the concerns about securitising water. Since it is no longer perceived as necessary for there to be a violent conflict over resources to affect the security and development of nations, the perception of the concept has changed

3 D Tarlock and P Wouters, 'Reframing the Water Security Dialogue' (2009) *Journal of Water Law*, 20, 53 at 60.

4 D Grey and CW Sadoff, *Water Resources, Growth and Development: A Working Paper for Discussion* (The World Bank 2005) at 7.

dramatically as well.[5] However, in order to function, this new perception has to be supported by a system of values which leads societies. Here, international law has to play a central role in supporting those values, establishing the substantive and procedural 'rules of the game' and thus, fulfilling one of its core functions: the promotion of peaceful relations between states.[6] Only through international law can water security move beyond its status as political rhetoric and obtain normative impact.

The calls of opponents to 'de-securitise' water, due to fears that discussions of water security allow freshwater interaction to be detached from any legal process trying to level the playing field, can be counteracted, as this study has shown. International law, pushed by the securitisation process, can be developed further in order to fully comprehend the advanced perception of common security. It has been recognised that

> the integrated and interdependent nature of the new challenges and issues contrasts sharply with the nature of the institutions that exist today. These institutions tend to be independent, fragmented, and working to relatively narrow mandates with closed decision processes . . . The real world of interlocked economic and ecological systems will not change; the policies and institutions concerned must.[7]

While some states are reluctant to change their stance and keep defining water security as a national security issue, international law can counter this mulish behaviour. In order to do so, however, international law has to appropriately address water security's four core elements: (1) availability, (2) access, (3) adaptability and (4) ambit.[8] 'Availability' relates to issues of water quantity and quality, and deals with the actual management (including its control and protection) of the resource as such. 'Access' describes the right to actually make use of the shared resource. The element of 'adaptability' does justice to the fact that in many cases, the most important variable to the successful sharing of freshwater resources is the resilience of the legal and policy frameworks (including institutions) that govern water management, rather than absolute water scarcity.[9] Thus, a future-proof framework for transboundary watercourses has

5 HG Brauch, 'Introduction: Globalization and Environmental Challenges: Reconceptualizing Security in the 21st Century' in Brauch HG and others (eds), *Globalization and Environmental Challenges: Reconceptualizing Security in the 21st Century* (Springer 2008) at 27; RH Ullman, 'Redefining Security' (1983) *International Security*, 8, 129 at 129.

6 WJ Cosgrove, *Water Security and Peace: A Synthesis of Studies Prepared under the PCCP Water for Peace Process* (UNESCO 2003) at 25.

7 World Commission on Environment and Development, *Our Common Future* (Oxford University Press 1987) at 310.

8 See Chapter 3.

9 G Eckstein, 'Water Scarcity, Conflict, and Security in a Climate Change World: Challenges and Opportunities for International Law and Policy' (2009) *Wisconsin International Law Journal*, 27, 409; AT Wolf, 'Troubled Waters: Conflict and Cooperation over Shared Rivers' (2009) World Politics Review 3 at 5.

to include a fair amount of flexibility. Finally, 'ambit' delimits the scope of water security – i.e., the sphere of influence of the notion.[10] In addition to the orthodox concept of scope,[11] the approach here is to better echo the common character of the global water crisis by linking the diverse influencing factors in an encompassing fashion. Only with the support of an underlying framework which can bring about a more equitable way of transboundary water resources management, can the concept of water security play the important role of the long-yearned-for change agent.

The newly developed operational methodology for identifying the four core elements of water security which have to be addressed by international law revealed the challenges and shortcomings of the current legal framework governing transboundary freshwater resources. The first challenge is the (legal) tension between the task to provide for 'security of expectations' (status quo) and the innovation needed to meet fluctuating demands and supplies, i.e., the ability to respond to change. The second challenge is the (environmental/political) tension between the ecological unity of the water resource and the diverging sovereign interests of states. This in turn leads to friction between the aims of maximising the overall benefit of sustainable aquatic ecosystems and maximising the relative benefit of states. While the analysis has shown that international water law does – at least to some extent – provide guidance on the elements of availability, access, adaptability and ambit, it lacks the ability to overcome state-centrism and truly level the playing field of transboundary water interaction. Hydropolitics based on power still determine the rules of the game in many basins around the world. Furthermore, the intertwinement of water security issues with other crises (i.e. food, energy and environment) is changing the dynamics of international relations on a global scale at a pace which international law seems to be unable to keep up with. The reason for this lies in the perceived threat of losing national sovereignty, which increases the political costs of implementing flexible mechanisms.[12] The prevailing focus on short-term gains has to be addressed by raising the awareness of policy makers that freshwater agreements have to be seen as a long-term process of involving stakeholders in water resources management, rather than an ultimate outcome.[13] This in turn would also help moving from the dominant 'react-and-correct' approach of international water law to the much more adequate one of 'foresee-and-prevent'.[14] Furthermore, such a new take would fully comprehend the concept of 'common' water security, which is inherently preventative compared to the

10 B-O Magsig, 'Introducing an Analytical Framework for Water Security: A Platform for the Refinement of International Water Law' (2009) *Journal of Water Law*, 20, 61 at 67.

11 See P Wouters and others, *Sharing Transboundary Waters: An Integrated Assessment of Equitable Entitlement: The Legal Assessment Model* (UNESCO 2005) at 19.

12 I Fischhendler, 'Legal and Institutional Adaptation to Climate Uncertainty: A Study of International Rivers' (2004) *Water Policy*, 6, 281 at 298.

13 Ibid.

14 AS Timoshenko, 'Ecological Security: Response to Global Challenges' in Weiss EB (ed.), *Environmental Change and International Law: New Challenges and Dimensions* (United Nations University Press 1992).

conservative understanding of security as a reactive control paradigm. Hence, international water law has to be developed further based on a more common and regional normative basis – and water security serves as a perfect concept to study the progressive development of the legal framework.

The birth of the concept of water security did not come unexpectedly, but has to be seen as the confluence of already existing streams of thought – whose roots still shape the debate around it. The 4A operational methodology, then, works like a lens giving those subsisting schools of thought the necessary force to initiate and influence the global and regional negotiations on transboundary freshwater management. Ultimately, if it is being followed through properly, it puts international water law on a new track – one which strengthens regionalism and fosters cooperation; and thus gives the principle of equitable and reasonable utilisation more weight. Hence, a newly proposed conceptualisation of water security with a deeper connection to international water law can open up new pathways towards closer regional cooperation.

7.2 Water security and the future of international law

The important questions, however, are: what should this path look like – and how does it have to be prepared in order to effectively implement the novel water security thinking in international law? In any case, it has to challenge the orthodox understanding of water security as being solely of national concern. While this will most likely be an arduous path to take, it is without alternative if transboundary water cooperation is to be prevented from failing. In case the debate on water security does not trigger any transformative reforms of international law, it will produce nothing more than old wine in new bottles. In order to prevent such a standstill and to achieve truly joint management of transboundary waters, a legal framework is needed which is fundamentally different to current approaches of international water law.[15] The future direction of the legal regime, however, will not change by merely developing procedural rules further. Certainly, the continuous proceduralisation of international water law is already contributing towards the same goal;[16] but the revealed shortcomings of the legal framework are too grave to be potently counteracted by an incremental change which often only scratches the surface of international law. While some scholars have long realised that

> In international law it is today of both theoretical and practical importance to distinguish between the international law of 'coexistence,' governing essentially diplomatic inter-state relations, and the law of co-operation, expressed in the growing structure of international organization and the pursuit of common human interests . . . [17]

15 See analysis of the current legal framework governing transboundary watercourses in Chapter 3.

16 See O McIntyre, 'The Proceduralisation and Growing Maturity of International Water Law' (2010) *Journal of Environmental Law*, 22, 475.

17 W Friedmann, *The Changing Structure of International Law* (Columbia University Press 1964) at xiii.

little has been done to actually level the playing field of international freshwater interaction and ensure a more cooperative legal framework.[18]

The concept of solidarity has already been integrated into various norms of international law – such as development law, international humanitarian law and refugee law.[19] Some argue that since the principle of solidarity is operating across several fields of international law and strives to protect fundamental values of the international community by penetrating both primary and secondary rules, it can even be claimed to have reached 'constitutional status';[20] however, even without going so far, its influence on various fields of law cannot be denied. In the realm of international environmental law, it is the concept of common but differentiated responsibilities which has tried to prove itself as a powerful tool towards the clarification and future development of the principle of solidarity. Yet, as the analysis in Chapter 4 has shown, it falls short on various grounds. With regard to international water law, it has been proposed to base transboundary freshwater management on the concept of hydrosolidarity. The main goal of the notion is to inject a common understanding, based on the ideas of collective action, shared responsibility, interdependence and ethics, into international water cooperation.[21] Ultimately, following an approach of solidarity in this sphere implies that reconciliation of conflicts over water have to be based on the solidarity among all water users – doing justice to the ambit of water security, as it would bring together a community of states and ensure a truly joint management of shared water resources. This desperately needed ethical underpinning for water security can help in framing the negotiations between riparians of a transboundary watercourse and challenge inequity in the form of abusive hydro-hegemony. Yet, if hydroegoism continues to define hydropolitics in a particular region, the idea of hydrosolidarity might be a noble one – but one without any meaningful effect. The moral principle of (hydro)solidarity can only facilitate the required change, and thus challenge the self-interests of states, by allowing international law to play a more prominent role. As Chapter 4 has shown, several examples in international law exist where solidarity already influences actions of states pursuant to a common interest. Thus, international law is able to induce the orderly change that international society needs to address the world water crisis more effectively – and ultimately sustain peace and security.

This, however, infers that in order to do so, international water law itself needs to undergo a process of refinement, as addressing the core characteristics of water security – availability, access, adaptability and ambit – requires

18 See Chapter 3.

19 See Chapter 4.

20 K Wellens, 'Revisiting Solidarity as a (Re-)Emerging Constitutional Principle: Some Further Reflections' in Wolfrum R and Kojima C (eds), *Solidarity: A Structural Principle of International Law* (Springer 2010) at 5.

21 A Gerlak, R Varady and A Haverland, 'Hydrosolidarity and International Water Governance' (2009) *International Negotiation*, 14, 311 at 312.

reviewing established paradigms in order to find a way out of the environment-sovereignty conundrum. Up to now, orthodox interpretations of international water law have not managed to provide such a transition. Chapter 5 did elaborate on the legal foundation needed to support the concept of hydrosolidarity, since the conceptualisation of water security, which inevitably has a normative dimension, raises questions about international law in general. It became obvious that in order to be able to implement hydrosolidarity for the benefit of common water security, one of the most fundamental tenets of international law – state sovereignty – has to be reinterpreted in a light which truly reflects the realities of the global water crisis. Considering the main shortcoming of the current legal regime – the state-centred approach to the water crisis based on an orthodox understanding of sovereignty – the question arises: how can we arrive at an understanding of 'cooperative sovereignty' which supports attaining common water security?

Here, the concept of considering water security as a matter of 'regional common concern' was introduced as a promising way forward in striving for true regional water management – and thus, for allowing international law to play a more prominent role in addressing the challenges of global water insecurity. It attempts to do this without abandoning acknowledged principles of international water law – such as equitable and reasonable utilisation – but rather by providing the necessary space for developing novel interpretations of tenets of international law. While the approaches of 'common area' and 'common heritage' are limited to a certain geographical area and its resources, and the concept of 'community of interest' seems to be too sovereignty-intrusive, the notion of 'common concern' appears to be more promising for the progressive development of international law and a renewed understanding of cooperative sovereignty. In agreeing that a particular challenge is being perceived as a matter of common concern results in the appreciation that it can no longer be considered as mere national issue. It also triggers a shift from the orthodox reciprocity and material benefit sharing we often find in treaties to joint action in the long-term interest of community.[22] However, is it politically feasible to consider water security as a common concern of humankind? Given the sheer scope and impact of the global water crisis, as discussed in Chapter 2, it might be possible to construct an analogous mindset to the loss of biodiversity or global climate change for transboundary freshwater management. Even so, it is still difficult to sufficiently prove international consensus on whether water security is indeed of common concern.[23] Yet, scaling one level down by looking at the regional layer could be a fruitful middle road which can

22 IUCN Commission on Environmental Law and International Council of Environmental Law, *Draft International Covenant on Environment and Development* (4th edn, IUCN 2010) at 40.

23 On the idea of a global water law, see JW Dellapenna and J Gupta, 'The Evolution of Global Water Law' in Dellapenna JW and Gupta J (eds), *The Evolution of the Law and Politics of Water* (Springer 2009).

sufficiently accommodate the national interests within the global challenge.[24] Hence, applying the 4A operational methodology for the analysis of the key issues related to water security can serve as a point of departure for the refinement of international (water) law. While the notion of common water security is still in its infancy, it none the less provides a promising novel mindset – one which may, if backed by the normative concept of 'regional common concern', ultimately be capable of overcoming state-centrism. However, this idea could also face the same destiny as other concepts before it, if it does not manage to bridge the gap between interesting theory and practice. Therefore, it is important to know what the chances of this notion have to actually influence real hydropolitics on the ground.

This is the debate on which Chapter 6 is built – by analysing how likely a change of transboundary water interaction is in Himalayan Asia. Are there signs which can be interpreted as potential pathways towards a new approach based on regional common concern? While neither of the two regimes examined, the Mekong Agreement and the Indus Waters Treaty, fully support the understanding of water security which is necessary for regional peace and security, there is none the less evidence which allows for hope regarding a change in attitude from bilateralism to regionalism. A few delicate tendrils exist, which indicate the potential for a move away from the state-centred approach towards closer cooperation between India and China on a regional basis. They do, however, need constant support from all actors involved – for instance, regional organisations such as ASEAN, international legal scholars and hydro-diplomats – in order to truly overcome the still prevailing nationalism in Himalayan Asian hydropolitics.

Throughout this study, it has become clear that international water law does not merely constitute a niche product of the international system. Due to the unique characteristics of the global water crisis and the conglomerate challenges they pose to the international community, international water law can – and should – affect the very substance of general international law.[25] Its status as a relatively young field of international law allows it to introduce new methods and new ways of thinking into the wider sphere of legal research – like common water security. Here, one intrinsic feature of the notion, the process of securitisation, can be hugely beneficial, since it considers the time for 'politics as usual' as being over. As Wolfrum rightly stated: 'The development of general concepts like the freedom of the high seas or the common heritage principle reflects the spirit of a given historic period (Zeitgeist).'[26] Growing global water insecurity brings about a new 'Zeitgeist' which demands from the

24 See J Brunnée and SJ Toope, 'Environmental Security and Freshwater Resources: A Case for International Ecosystem Law' (1994) *Yearbook of International Environmental Law*, 5, 41 at 74.

25 For a discussion on how global environmental concerns affect international law see DA French, 'A Reappraisal of Sovereignty in the Light of Global Environmental Concerns' (2001) *Legal Studies*, 21, 376 at 377.

26 R Wolfrum, 'The Principle of the Common Heritage of Mankind' (1983) *Zeitschrift für ausländisches öffentliches Recht und Völkerrecht*, 43, 312 at 312.

international legal framework nothing less than a self-reinvention.[27] If it attains success in doing so by regarding water security as being of regional common concern, it will not only help to address the global water crisis, it will also avert a further demise of international law in the domain of transboundary freshwater interaction – and potentially in other areas as well.[28]

7.3 A research agenda for international water security

The lack of water security will be a defining reality for international relations and global policy in the decades to come. By looking at the concept of water security through a legal lens, a forum has been created which can serve as a foundation for future scholarship on the role of international law in matters of security. In order to allow this notion to mature, new tracks for further research have to push this school of thought further. Here, several catalytic paths are useful for better understanding and influencing transboundary freshwater interaction to that effect.

It has been argued that studies on the global political and legal governance framework 'remain preoccupied either with sovereign states that are presumed to be isolated from other states or with modern individual subjects caught between desires for autonomy and desires for collectivity'.[29] Thus, it seems like today's international system is still locked up in a conceptual prison. In order to break out of gaol, more research is needed in areas which have traditionally been neglected by the international legal scholarship. We desperately need to introduce 'our moral responsibility to the legal dimension. A pure interstate approach in our thinking is consciously or unconsciously deemed insufficient to resolve the problems we are facing today.'[30] This humanisation process of international law – in principle, the establishment of international law to ensure the very survival of mankind[31] – prompts questions of the role of ethics in international law.[32] These questions get even more complex when realising the interlacing of water security with other securities (e.g., environmental,

27 See K Mickelson, 'Between Crisis and Complacency: Seeking Commitment in International Environmental Law' (2014) *Netherlands Yearbook of International Law*, 44, 139.

28 On the role of international law in addressing other global crises, see C Kaufmann, 'International Law in Recession? The Role of International Law When Crisis Hits: Food, Finance, and Climate Change' in Fastenrath U and others (eds), *From Bilateralism to Community Interest : Essays in Honour of Bruno Simma* (Oxford University Press 2011) at 1189.

29 RBJ Walker, *After the Globe, before the World* (Routledge 2010) at 10.

30 See the discussion following the presentation by L Boisson de Chazournes, 'Responsibility to Protect: Reflecting Solidarity?' in Wolfrum R and Kojima C (eds), *Solidarity: A Structural Principle of International Law* (Springer 2010) at 119.

31 See C Tomuschat, 'International Law: Ensuring the Survival of Mankind on the Eve of a New Century : General Course on Public International Law' in Hague Academy of International Law (ed.), *Collected Courses of the Hague Academy of International Law 281*, vol. 281 (Martinus Nijhoff Publishers 2001) at 9.

32 A Gillespie, *International Environmental Law, Policy and Ethics* (Oxford University Press 2000); R Higgins, 'Ethics and International Law' (2010) *Leiden Journal of International Law*, 23, 277; M Koskenniemi, *The Turn to Ethics in International Law* (2002); AP Rubin, *Ethics and Authority in International Law* (Cambridge University Press 1997).

food, or energy) at the various levels of governance.[33] Do countries have moral obligations towards their riparians – or even nations beyond the basin – to manage their national water resources more effectively? International legal scholars have often shown deep interest in other disciplines – for instance, international relations, economics, or even history. The field of ethics, as vast as it is, does not have to represent any greater challenge.[34]

Since future international water law will have to be more dynamic – as it has to keep up with, and control, the complex fluxes of the global water cycle it tries to help manage peacefully – the questions arise: how do international norms change over time, and are there ways to speed up this complex process? How did it come about that practices which were perceived as normal (e.g., slavery) are now prohibited by international law? While international lawyers and international relations scholars acknowledge norm change, we do not fully understand how and why international rules develop in the ways and with the speed they do.[35] Here, two developments are of particular interest: (1) the role of non-state actors in international law, and (2) the value of soft law in the process of norm formation. Neither has been studied with the necessary rigour or breadth as to its effect on the refinement and implementation of international water law. How can NGOs or epistemic communities influence transboundary freshwater interaction without negatively affecting the legitimacy of the legal framework?[36] International law has to break new ground if it wants to go beyond symbolism – such as proclaiming 2013 the UN International Year of Water Cooperation[37] – and trigger real change.

The above-mentioned strands of research can support the novel approach in international law which has been portrayed in this study in putting hydrodiplomacy on a new track towards hydrosolidarity. Due to the particularities and complexities of the crisis, freshwater is the medium which can actually bring about change to some of the tenets of international law. Hence, by changing the way we address transboundary water issues – through the water security lens – we might even change general international law, as it demands for the further development of public international law with the cross-cutting challenges in mind. In doing so, we not only ensure a more peaceful management of shared freshwater resources; we can also demonstrate how other insecurities (e.g., food, environment and energy) can be mitigated. By inventing new concepts, we reconstruct the ways of our thinking – and ultimately,

33 E Lopez-Gunn, L De Stefano and MR Llamas, 'The Role of Ethics in Water and Food Security: Balancing Utilitarian and Intangible Values' (2012) *Water Policy*, 14, 89.

34 S Ratner, 'Ethics and International Law: Integrating the Global Justice Project(S)' (2013) *International Theory*, 5, 1 at 34.

35 W Sandholtz and KW Stiles, *International Norms and Cycles of Change* (Oxford University Press 2008).

36 See PF Diehl and C Ku, *The Dynamics of International Law* (Cambridge University Press 2010) at 108.

37 See UN Water, '2013: United Nations International Year of Water Cooperation'(2013) <http://www.unwater.org/watercooperation2013.html>.

we reconstruct our world as such.[38] This is because fact and value become interwoven in the process; only by adding value – legal implications – to it, will this process take a positive course. The changing expectations of the international community produce a demand for additional functions of international law – beyond the rules of conduct in international diplomacy.[39] In order to design future-proof international legal frameworks, the question of how the international issues we see today, and the ones we have not yet identified as international, will develop, needs to be addressed.[40] Those future challenges will then trigger different requirements – both normative and structural – for international cooperation. With the help of international law, the notion of water security can create a space which transcends national boundaries – real and imaginary. However, in order to be able to do so, international law has to accept the challenge posed by the concept of common water security. Here, the momentum created by the securitisation of water is vital for driving international legal research forward. By considering securitisation as a reflexive rule-altering process, it can even provide relevant insights into the transformation and development of international law.[41] Securitisation of water kick-starts a process which otherwise would not exist – one looking beyond water and beyond nation states.

38 See the discussion following the presentation by Boisson de Chazournes, 'Responsibility to Protect: Reflecting Solidarity?' at 119.

39 Friedmann, *The Changing Structure of International Law* at 5.

40 JP Trachtman, *The Future of International Law: Global Government* (Cambridge University Press 2013) at 4.

41 See also MC Kettemann, 'The Conceptual Debate on Human Security and Its Relevance for the Development of International Law' (2006) *Human Security Perspectives*, 1, 39.

Index

For Product Safety Concerns and Information please contact our EU representative GPSR@taylorandfrancis.com
Taylor & Francis Verlag GmbH, Kaufingerstraße 24, 80331 München, Germany

www.ingramcontent.com/pod-product-compliance
Ingram Content Group UK Ltd.
Pitfield, Milton Keynes, MK11 3LW, UK
UKHW022129190926
475702UK00013B/1716
9780815378921